HANDBOOK
OF
GERIATRIC
ASSESSMENT

Second Edition

Contributors

John R. Delfs, MD
Director, Deaconess Center for ElderCare
Chief, Section of Geriatric Medicine
Department of Medicine
New England Deaconess Hospital
Assistant Professor of Medicine
Harvard Medical School
Boston, Massachusetts

David J. Doukas, MD
Assistant Professor
Department of Family Practice
University of Michigan Medical School
Ann Arbor, Michigan

Laurence B. McCullough, PhD
Professor of Medicine, Community Medicine, and Medical Ethics
Center for Ethics, Medicine, and Public Issues
Baylor College of Medicine
Houston, Texas

Laura Stanley, MS, RN,C
Gerontological Nurse Practitioner
Deaconess ElderCare
New England Deaconess Hospital
Boston, Massachusetts

Joan Yesner, MSW, LICSW
Senior Social Work Gerontologist/Administrator
Deaconess ElderCare
New England Deaconess Hospital
Boston, Massachusetts

HANDBOOK
OF
GERIATRIC
ASSESSMENT

Second Edition

Joseph J. Gallo, MD, MPH
Assistant Professor
Department of Mental Hygiene
The Johns Hopkins University
School of Hygiene and Public Health
Baltimore, Maryland

William Reichel, MD
Clinical Professor of Community Health
Tufts University School of Medicine
Boston, Massachusetts
Adjunct Professor of Family Medicine
Brown University School of Medicine
Providence, Rhode Island

Lillian M. Andersen, RN, EdD
Consultant in Gerontology
Arlington, Virginia

An Aspen Publication®
Aspen Publishers, Inc.
Gaithersburg, Maryland
1995

Library of Congress Cataloging-in-Publication Data

Gallo, Joseph J.
Handbook of geriatric assessment / Joseph J. Gallo, William
Reichel, Lillian M. Andersen. — 2nd ed.
p.   cm.
Includes bibliographical references and index.
ISBN 0-8342-0566-1
1. Aged—Diseases—Diagnosis—Handbooks, manuals, etc.   2. Aged—
Psychological testing—Handbooks, manuals, etc.   3. Aged—Care—Handbooks,
manuals, etc.   4. Aged—Long-term care—Handbooks, manuals, etc.
I. Reichel, William 1937–   .   II. Andersen, Lillian.   III. Title.
[DNLM: 1. Geriatric Assessment.   WT 30 G172h 1995]
RC953.G34   1995
618.97′075—dc20
DNLM/DLC
for Library of Congress
94-49603
CIP

Editorial Resources: Donald L. Delauter

Library of Congress Catalog Card Number: 94-49603
ISBN: 0-8342-0566-1

Printed in the United States of America

1   2   3   4   5

Contents

Preface

The concept for a book about multidimensional assessment in primary care geriatrics arose from the experience of working with the assessment program of the Baltimore County Department of Health of Baltimore County, Maryland, from 1970 until 1988 (William Reichel), and from the experience of establishing a geriatric assessment program at Franklin Square Hospital Center in Baltimore, Maryland, in 1985–1986 (Joseph J. Gallo and William Reichel). The authors have also gained new insights since the first edition of the *Handbook of Geriatric Assessment* through collaboration with colleagues at The Johns Hopkins University School of Hygiene and Public Health, The Johns Hopkins University School of Medicine, the Georgetown University School of Medicine, the Georgetown University School of Nursing, the Uniformed Services School of Medicine, the Tufts University School of Medicine, the Brown University School of Medicine, and the Harvard Divinity School.

Families, social workers, visiting nurses, and physicians refer patients to a geriatric assessment unit for a variety of reasons, including crisis management, placement, evaluation of confusion or multiple medical problems, or provision of help for caregivers in coping with an ailing elder. Since the first edition, there has been heightened interest in the use of standard instruments and questionnaires to evaluate, in clinical settings and in the patient's home, significant aspects of an elderly person's life. The literature of geriatric assessment confirms what wise professionals who deal with the elderly have known all along: In the clinical evaluation of an older person, the mental, functional, social, value, and economic spheres cannot be neglected. The intent of the second edition, like that of the first edition, is to foster a comprehensive approach in assessing older persons.

The *Handbook of Geriatric Assessment* again emphasizes material that has practical application in primary care settings in order to encourage a multidimensional approach. The goal is to discuss the assessment of domains that have a significant bearing on the life of elderly patients. We hope that physicians, nurses, social workers, and others will find this material useful in their encounters with older persons. We also hope that gathering this information on assessment in one convenient place will foster better understanding of the multiple facets affecting all of our lives.

Joseph J. Gallo
William Reichel
Lillian M. Andersen

1

Caring for the Elderly

A s the 21st century approaches, there are more older persons alive on the
earth than have reached old age in all of history.[1] From 1900 to 1984,
the population of persons aged 65 years and older in the United States
grew from about 3 million to 28 million, from 4% of the population to about 12%.[2]
Each month, of the 1.2 million people around the world who reach later life, 1
million live in developing countries; thus, population aging is a worldwide
phenomenon.[3]

The aged population is itself aging and changing in composition. The oldest old,
persons over the age of 85 years, constitute the fastest-growing segment of the
aged population; 3.5 million people in the United States are over the age of 85
years.[4,5] The ethnic composition of the aged population is changing as well; the
African American older population is growing at a faster rate than other older pop-
ulations.[6] Aging members of minority groups face special challenges. The age,
ethnic, and cultural diversity of the older population affects all the domains of
geriatric assessment.

Caring for older patients can be a challenging task for clinicians. A clinician is
frequently called on to assist older patients and their families in decisions that can
have a direct effect on quality of life. Small changes in the ability of an older person to perform daily activities or in the ability of a caregiver to provide support
can have an impact on major life decisions. Older persons are vulnerable to reversible problems that contribute to disability, but therein lies the clinician's

1

strength, since even small improvements in functional status can have significant positive implications. Therefore, caring for an elderly person requires that the clinician assess functional, social, and other aspects of the patient's condition.

The domains of multidimensional assessment include mental health, physical health, function, and social situation. The breadth of assessment required sets the field of geriatrics apart from other fields of medicine. Performing a multidimensional assessment in clinical practice can be a daunting task. The purpose of this book is to assist health care professionals who work with the elderly. We are mindful of the primary care practitioner whose time with each patient is limited, and we hope that professionals will find assessment instruments that are useful in everyday practice.

Geriatric assessment is mandatory prior to admission to a nursing home or a specialized care unit.[7,8] Not all older persons who could benefit from multidisciplinary assessment will have access to a team, but practicing physicians and other health care professionals can utilize community expertise and standardized instruments.[9] Instruments such as the Folstein Mini-Mental State Examination[10] or the five-item Instrumental Activities of Daily Living Screen[11] can be incorporated into the evaluation of elderly persons.[12]

THE CONTEXT OF GERIATRIC CARE

The role of the elderly in other societies has often been more clearly defined than in our own. In preindustrial society, older persons frequently had considerable accumulation of wealth and power, which they passed on to the younger members of the group at the appropriate time. Often some special functions were performed by the elders, who knew about family histories and sacred rituals and how to mediate with ancestors. In addition, the elders may have provided some services to the community, such as serving as judges or as experts in childrearing. Today's elderly are unfortunately not often as highly esteemed by the society at large, and their wealth of experience and first-hand knowledge of history frequently go unheeded.[13]

Even in a technological society, the elderly can be a valuable resource. Without exposure to older persons, the young (middle-aged persons as well as children) lose their sense of history, of belonging to a community larger than their immediate experience in space and time. The universal aging process becomes something to be feared, even a taboo topic. After all, the values of society place great emphasis on youth. It can seem as if growing older were something to be ashamed of, as if old age means nothing but static existence or, worse, decline and deterioration.

On the contrary, the elderly have significant developmental work to do. Persons who are successfully aging have made remarkable adaptations and show considerable resiliency. Erikson explains this developmental work in terms of the dichotomy of ego integrity versus ego despair: despair, when one looks back on life with regret, not having accomplished what was wanted, and integrity, when one looks back on life and is able to accept it as a unique life in history, a life that had to be.[14]

Erikson's first "age of man" relates to the infant's development of "basic trust versus basic mistrust" in the world. The life cycle comes full circle in the relation of ego integrity and basic trust because "healthy children will not fear life if their elders have integrity enough not to fear death."[14] The elderly also integrate, in "age-appropriate" ways, the psychosocial themes from previous stages, reflecting back over the entire life cycle. For example, "intimacy and isolation" in young adulthood refers to the development of the ability to be intimate with another versus a failure to develop such relationships. Older adults also face this issue, since they must deal with the restructuring of relationships.[15]

The considerable developmental and adaptive tasks of the elderly include dealing with the loss of family and friends through death or relocation, adjusting to changes in living arrangements, adjusting to retirement, managing with less income, dealing with changed social roles, making good use of increased leisure time, adjusting to changes in sexual and physical functioning, and accepting the inevitability of one's own death. The gracefully aging elder who is able to perform all these tasks successfully has a great deal to teach younger persons about life.

Although the changes that occur in the body with age are frequently associated with physical and physiological decline, health care professionals who treat the elderly must avoid the temptation to accept them as immune to treatment. Much of what is ascribed to aging may actually be related to disuse or disease.[16]

Old age is a time of significant growth for many persons. One model of successful aging is based on "selective optimization with compensation."[17] "Selection" refers to prioritization of activities in order of importance or pleasurableness and to the adjustment of expectations; "optimization" refers to maximization of the chosen behaviors through practice and by accommodating conditions to the ability of the elder; "compensation" refers to use of strategies that compensate for age-related losses. Baltes notes strategies used by the pianist Artur Rubenstein as an illustration of selective optimization with compensation. Rubenstein selects a smaller number of pieces to play, rehearses more often, and slows down before allegro movements to give the listener the impression of speed.[17] Perhaps the strategies of successful aging can be taught.[18]

In the future, the role of the elderly in society may undergo further development. Toffler has called the latest technological revolution, including the proliferation of computers, the third wave.[19] Contrary to expectations engendered by Orwell's *1984,* this revolution could lead to increased freedom and leisure time. During the first wave (preindustrial society), each household formed an economic unit. The home or the field was the focus of work, and families labored together. Home life and work were intimately related. The second wave was marked by the industrial revolution. Work now took place in the factory. Behavior became dictated by schedules and the division of labor. There was consequently less need for the elderly as repositories of history and culture. The third wave is marked by the advent of the "electronic cottage." The average size of work units will decrease, and many people will work at home. Work again will become less centralized, as it was in the agricultural society of the first wave. Because employees will have the ability to work at home, centralized places of work may become a thing of the past. The result will be that children will once again be near their working parents, a situation that has not been prevalent since the agricultural age. Family roles may then undergo transformation.

Persons may have more than one career over the course of a lifetime. The experience gained by the elderly would be invaluable in helping younger workers apply theory to practical problems. Technological change will also demand that education continue throughout the life span. It may not be unusual for persons to move in and out of formal educational situations at different ages. Older persons may again be seen as mentors to the young.[20]

The instruments of geriatric assessment in use today could conceivably need to be modified in response to coming changes. Older adults in the future are likely to be better educated than the elderly of today, who frequently were immigrants or grew up at a time when they were virtually forced by circumstances to work. Today's older adults grew up during the Depression and were teenagers during World War II, times of great social and economic upheaval. Work was often thrust on children during the Depression, and the roles of men and women underwent substantial change during World War II. The fads, values, dreams, aspirations, expectations, and perspectives on life and politics with which these elders grew up will not be the same as those for future cohorts of older adults.

Expectations about medical care will likely be different as well. For example, the elderly in the future may have other ideas about the role of the family in caring for an impaired adult. In a mobile society, informal social networks may be strained. Expectations about retirement may be different and a low standard of living or poor health might not be tolerated. Better educated elders, especially those educated about health matters, might be more questioning of their physicians than today's elderly and perhaps would want to participate to a greater degree in health care decisions, seeing themselves as more responsible for the quality of their own health. Such changes as these, if they in fact occur, will affect the provision of care to the elderly.

MULTIDIMENSIONAL ASSESSMENT

Implementing multidimensional assessment in primary care settings could make an important contribution to the care of older persons.[21] A number of strategies can be employed to bring the facets of geriatric assessment into geriatric care despite the time and reimbursement barriers that confront the primary care physician and others who care for the elderly.[22] Professionals working individually can arrive at the same recommendations as a multidisciplinary team.[23,24] At the same time, practitioners should develop a relationship with a special geriatric assessment program or unit (such as that described in Chapter 9) for evaluation and advisement regarding elderly patients whose cases are especially complicated. The use of instruments and questionnaires like the ones described in this book can improve the recognition and management of functional and medical problems.[23-27]

Mental Status

Although much can be gleaned from observation of the speech and mannerisms of a patient, formal evaluation with school-like tests of cognitive status can yield valuable information that is accessible to all who use the chart. In the office, use of standardized questions to assess mental function may be particularly important for older patients who are experiencing difficulty in performing certain daily tasks, such as using the telephone or handling money.[28] Mental status testing at the time of admission to the hospital or nursing home serves to establish a baseline and helps identify persons at risk for delirium. The effects of depression, substance use, prescribed medications, and medical conditions on a patient's mental state should also be considered. We will discuss specific sets of questions that the practitioner can use to assess mental status.

Functional Status

Functional assessment includes evaluation of the ability of the patient to perform various tasks of daily life, such as dressing and housework. Driving, sexuality, and nutrition are other aspects of function that contribute to the quality of life of older adults. Aside from specific medical diagnoses, functional status is associated with the care the patient needs, the risk of institutionalization, and mortality. Several methods for assessing functional status will be presented.

Social Support

An older person often presents with problems of living and requires the physician to adopt a comprehensive outlook, one that includes the family. In some cases, the health of a caregiver may be of great importance to the patient's well-being. Most long-term care is provided by familial caregivers, who often need physical and emotional support in order to maintain an elder at home. Caregivers are often women, especially daughters and daughters-in-law. In contrast to the common myth that families "dump" the elderly in institutions, our experience shows that families tend to go "above and beyond the call of duty" in providing care for their elderly members. Evaluation of an elderly person is not complete without some assessment of the social milieu.[29,30]

Values Assessment

Older adults are encouraged to "plan for uncertainty" with regard to their medical care, but few do.[31] Advance directives are legally binding documents that allow individuals to project their wishes about medical treatment into a future period of incapacity. The Patient Self-Determination Act of 1990 requires all hospitals, nursing facilities, and home health agencies in the United States to inform patients about their right to create advance directives. A later chapter contains a method for addressing values assessment in a systematic way. A discussion of advance directive options between the well patient and the doctor may someday become an ordinary part of office practice in the care of the elderly, with informed patients having the opportunity to state wishes, preferences, and values that are relevant to their future medical care.

Economic Status

Finances may have an impact on health, nutrition, and residence. Although a clinician need not engage in a detailed inquiry into an older patient's economic situation, the possibility that an older person may fail to take prescribed medication or alter the dosage schedule because of lack of funds should be kept in mind. Although the economic situation of older Americans has generally improved in recent decades, many, especially those who have faced lifelong discrimination, are still impoverished.

Physical Examination

The history and physical examination should be tailored to the older patient, with the focus on the discovery of remediable problems. The presenting complaint may involve the most vulnerable organ system rather than the organ system expected, so that infection presents as delirium. Medical diagnoses should be considered from the point of view of each dimension of geriatric assessment.[21] Hearing and vision impairment, restricted mobility, and slowed response time must be considered in the physical examination. We will describe these and other differences in the physical examination of older versus younger adults.

Health Promotion and Disability Prevention

The domains of multidimensional geriatric assessment highlight "prevention" from the geriatric perspective. In addition to standard prevention (approaches to cancer, cardiovascular disease, cerebrovascular disease, and the infections preventable through immunization), geriatric prevention focuses on problems that may not easily fit into a disease model of illness or that touch on functional, social, or values issues.[32] An individualized plan for health promotion and disability prevention is imperative and can be informed by multidimensional assessment.

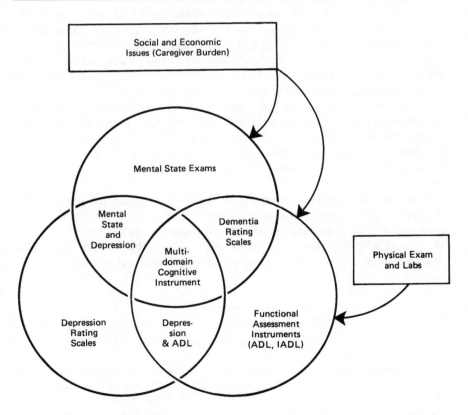

Figure 1–1 Domains of multidimensional assessment: instruments. Mental state exams, functional assessment instruments, and depression rating scales may be combined in various ways or to various degrees. Their use is intended to uncover social, economic, and physical difficulties.

CONCLUSION

In the following chapters, the descriptions of the domains of geriatric multi-dimensional assessment are accompanied by instruments that have been found useful. Some assessment instruments overlap several domains; for example, the dementia rating scales include items on ability to function in the environment as well as mental status items. Some scales attempt to cover several domains, such as the Cambridge Mental Disorders of the Elderly Examination, which screens for dementia, depression, and other mental disorders, provides data on functioning in activities of daily living, and quantifies the severity of dementia when present.[33]

The interrelationships of assessment domains and instruments in this book are illustrated in Figure 1–1: (1) mental status examinations, (2) depression rating scales, (3) depression and measurement of mental status, (4) functional assessment (activities of daily living [ADLs] and more complex tasks, the instrumental activities of daily living [IADLs]), (5) dementia rating scales and other instruments that overlap several domains, (6) social issues and assessment (including caregiver burden), (7) economic issues, and (8) physical examination.

To be useful, assessment findings must be linked to treatment. Values and circumstances vary from individual to individual and from family to family, precluding the use of set recommendations for particular findings from geriatric assessment. Although linking assessment findings to treatment requires clinical training and experience, a systematic approach to assessment helps the clinician cover the important issues.

Somehow all these concerns must be united in a coordinated whole by the practitioner for the proper assessment of the older patient, whether in the office, the hospital, or the long-term care facility. The authors hope that practitioners will glean from this book assessment instruments and ideas useful in the routine assessment of elderly patients, leading to more effective and systematic care of older persons.

REFERENCES

1. Dychtwald K, Flower J. *Age Wave: The Challenges and Opportunities of an Aging America.* Los Angeles, Calif: Jeremy P Tarcher, 1989.

2. *Developments in Aging.* Vol. 1. Washington, DC: US Senate Special Committee on Aging, 1988.

3. Macfadyen D. International demographic trends. In: Kane RL, Evans JG, Macfadyen D, eds. *Improving the Health of Older People: A World View.* New York, NY: Oxford University Press, 1990:19–29.

4. Suzman RM, Willis DP, Manton KG, eds. *The Oldest Old.* New York, NY: Oxford University Press, 1992.

5. Campion EW. The oldest old. *N Engl J Med.* 1994;330:1819–1820.

6. Jackson JS, ed. *The Black American Elderly: Research on Physical and Psychosocial Health.* New York, NY: Springer Publishing Co, 1988.

7. Coons DH, ed. *Specialized Dementia Care Units.* Baltimore, Md: Johns Hopkins University Press, 1991.

8. Levenson SA, ed. *Medical Direction in Long-Term Care.* 2nd ed. Durham, NC: Carolina Academic Press, 1993.

9. AGS Public Policy Committee. Comprehensive geriatric assessment. *J Am Geriatr Soc.* 1989;37:473–474.

10. Folstein MF, Folstein SE, McHugh PR. "Mini-Mental State": a practical method for grading the cognitive state of patients for the clinician. *J Psychiatr Res.* 1975;12:189–198.

11. Fillenbaum G. Screening the elderly: a brief instrumental activities of daily living measure. *J Am Geriatr Soc.* 1985;33:698–706.

12. Applegate WB, Blass JP, Williams TF. Instruments for the functional assessment of older patients. *N Engl J Med.* 1990;322:1207–1214.

13. de Beauvoir S. *The Coming of Age.* New York, NY: Warner, 1973.

14. Erikson EH. *Childhood and Society.* New York, NY: WW Norton and Co, 1963.

15. Erikson EH, Erikson JM, Kivnick HQ. *Vital Involvement in Old Age: The Experience of Old Age in Our Time.* New York, NY: WW Norton and Co, 1986.

16. Bortz WM. Redefining human aging. *J Am Geriatr Soc.* 1989;37:1092–1096.

17. Baltes PB. The many faces of human ageing: toward a psychological culture of old age. *Psychol Med.* 1991;21:837–854.

18. Baltes PB, Baltes MM, eds. *Successful Aging: Perspectives from the Behavioral Sciences.* New York, NY: Cambridge University Press, 1990.

19. Toffler A. *The Third Wave.* New York, NY: Bantam Books, 1980.

20. Toffler A. *Future Shock.* New York, NY: Bantam Books, 1970.

21. Gallo JJ, Stanley L, Zack N, Reichel W. Multidimensional assessment of the older patient. In: Reichel W, ed. *Clinical Aspects of Aging.* 4th ed. Baltimore, Md: Williams & Wilkins, 1995:15–30.

22. Beck JC, Freedman ML, Warshaw GA. Geriatric assessment: focus on function. *Primary Care.* February 28, 1994;28:10–32.

23. Robinson BE, Lund CA, Keller D, et al. Validation of the Functional Assessment Inventory against a multidisciplinary home care team. *J Am Geriatr Soc.* 1986;34:851–854.

24. Pinholt EM, Kroenke K, Hanley JF, et al. Functional assessment of the elderly: a comparison of standard instruments with clinical judgement. *Arch Intern Med.* 1987;147:484–488.

25. Miller DK, Morley JE, Rubenstein LZ, Pietruszka FM, Strome LS. Formal geriatric assessment instruments and the care of older general medical outpatients. *J Am Geriatr Soc.* 1990;38:645–651.

26. Lachs MS, Feinstein AR, Cooney LM, et al. A simple procedure for general screening for functional disability in elderly persons. *Ann Intern Med.* 1990;112:699–706.

27. Siu AL, Beers MH, Morgenstern H. The geriatric "medical and public health" imperative revisited. *J Am Geriatr Soc.* 1993;41:78–84.

28. Barberger-Gateau P, Commenges D, Gagnon M, Letenneur L, Sauvel C, Dartigues JF. Instrumental activities of daily living as a screening tool for cognitive impairment and dementia in elderly community dwellers. *J Am Geriatr Soc.* 1992;40:1129–1134.

29. Gallo JJ. The effect of social support on depression in caregivers of the elderly. *J Fam Pract.* 1990;30:430–436.

30. Gallo JJ, Franch MS, Reichel W. Dementing illness: the patient, caregiver, and community. *Am Fam Physician.* 1991;43:1669–1675.

31. Doukas D, Reichel W. *Planning for Uncertainty: A Guide to Living Wills and Other Advance Directives for Health Care.* Baltimore, Md: Johns Hopkins University Press, 1993.

32. Stults BM. Preventive health care for the elderly. *West J Med.* 1984;141:832–845.

33. Roth M, Tym E, Mountjoy CQ, et al. CAMDEX: a standardised instrument for the diagnosis of mental disorder in the elderly with special reference to the early detection of dementia. *Br J Psychiatry.* 1986;149:698–709.

2

Mental Status Assessment

Many studies since Dr. Michael Shepherd's seminal work *Psychiatric Illness in General Practice,*[1] published almost 30 years ago, reveal that mental disorders are common in the primary care setting but that individuals with these disorders frequently go unrecognized, with adverse consequences for the patients, their families, and the health care system. In the United States, Regier and colleagues have called attention to the de facto mental health services system composed of the general medical services and have highlighted the need to understand how to integrate general medical care and mental health care.[2-4] The literature dealing with mental health care in primary care settings has been extensively reviewed elsewhere.[5-7]

Mental state assessment is pivotal in evaluating the health of older persons. The accuracy of the medical and social history obtained from an older person will depend on adequate mental and affective functioning. For example, cognitive impairment predicts poor agreement between self-reported and observer-rated measures of functioning.[8] In this chapter, the psychological aspects of mental life, as well as the cognitive aspects that usually are emphasized in tests of mental status, are discussed. Most practitioners who deal with elderly patients have had the experience of treating an elder who is able to carry on a reasonably coherent casual conversation but is shown by mental status testing to suffer from significant difficulties. The elder may be able to perform well in a job that has been held for many years as long as the routine is not interrupted, but the extent of the deficit may become painfully evident to family or coworkers in novel situations. Perhaps the family is not even aware that behavioral changes are secondary to subtle intellectual deterioration.

Ample evidence reveals that cognitive impairment and psychiatric disorders are often not recognized by health care professionals. Fully one third of elderly patients admitted to a medical floor in one study of cognitive status in the elderly had significant mental impairment.[9] Other investigators demonstrated that only 14 of 65 patients (21%) with cognitive deficits detected on the screening examination had documentation by the patient's physician that such deficits had been recognized. In only two cases was a mental status examination a part of the patient's record.[10] Other studies have documented the failure of physicians to routinely perform mental status testing on elderly patients. Thirty-seven percent to 80% of demented elders were not diagnosed by their physicians yet were identified by a brief mental status screening examination as impaired.[11,12] Among patients evaluated by a psychiatrist prior to discharge from medical or surgical wards, only 27% of patients with mental impairment were diagnosed prior to discharge; most were believed to have moderate to severe impairment. In outpatient practice, few patients with cognitive impairment are recognized without screening.[13-15] Lack of recognition also extends to depression, alcohol abuse, and drug misuse.[7,16]

The recognition of mental impairment is of more than just academic importance. Patients with an abnormal score on the mental status examination had a greater chance of having episodes of confusion during the hospitalization,[10] after discharge,[17] and postoperatively.[18] Cognitive-impaired hospitalized patients are less stable, and have increased morbidity and mortality,[19,20] risk of loss of independence,[17,20] postoperative complications,[18] and behavioral difficulties.[21]

The discovery of cognitive impairment should prompt a search for an etiology. The best hope of finding a reversible process may hinge on early recognition by the clinician. Vision and hearing loss may mimic cognitive impairment and should be considered. Behavioral or personality changes may be placed in context when mental impairment is found to be present. Drugs that impair cognition should be avoided if at all possible. Specific pharmacologic therapy may mandate early detection of dementia.[22] For these reasons, it seems compelling to insist that mental status testing be included in the assessment of older patients, particularly at the time of nursing home or hospital admission,[10,15,23] if behavior changes occur, or in the face of functional impairment.

The failure of many physicians to perform mental status testing on elderly patients is unfortunate. Frequently it is the patient's personal physician who is best able to judge the patient's competence, not a consultant, who does not have an ongoing relationship with the patient. A periodic assessment of mental status in the chart can be valuable in these circumstances, particularly when legal questions arise.[24] Mental status testing of asymptomatic older adults must be balanced by concerns about falsely labeling a patient as demented.

In this chapter, the definition of "mental status testing" includes instruments for depression. Indeed, cognitive and psychologic status are closely related, and it is probably inappropriate to neglect one in discussing the other. Inventories to screen for depression cannot establish a diagnosis, but their use at least keeps the affective disorders in the forefront and imparts to the patient a sense that feelings are important to the clinician and appropriate for discussion and consideration. Depression is associated with diminished functional capacity in its own right.[25-29] Treatment of depression is effective in older persons, so a case can be made for careful consideration of the symptoms of depression underlying somatic complaints or functional decline.[30,31P]

THE MENTAL STATUS EXAMINATION

The mental status examination samples behavior and mental capability over a range of intellectual functions (Table 2–1). The shorter standardized examinations to detect cognitive impairment that are discussed later in this chapter attempt to crystallize the examination so a range of intellectual functions can be tested by one or two questions in each area. When the screening instrument detects impairment, further examination is warranted. In clinical settings, this usually means more detailed mental status testing to localize and define the problem. When further char-

---

Table 2–1 Components of the Mental Status Examination

Level of consciousness
Attention

Language
  Fluency
  Comprehension
  Repetition

Memory
  Short-term memory
  Remote memory

Proverb interpretation
Similarities
Calculations
Writing
Constructional ability

Source: Adapted from *The Mental Status Examination in Neurology* (pp 163–172) by RL Strub and FW Black with permission of FA Davis Company, © 1980.

acterization of cognitive functioning is required, neuropsychologic testing may be in order. Such testing becomes particularly salient when the patient's cognitive strengths and weaknesses must be delineated to make decisions about supervision and rehabilitative services, in the differential diagnosis of dementia and depression, or after stroke.[32]

For some health care professionals, the mental status examination consists solely of a few questions about orientation; perhaps the ability to calculate and the ability to remember three items are tested. In some situations, however, a thorough assessment can be crucial for establishing an appropriate diagnosis and aiding management. The classic example is a patient with an intracranial hemorrhage who is not making any sense and is mistakenly thought to be psychotic or confused because a specific language disturbance is not recognized. Granted, not every patient needs to be examined in precisely the way described here, but the standard mental status instruments discussed later in this chapter are short enough to be used in their entirety to assist in identifying cognitive impairment.

The complete mental status examination encompasses an assessment of the level of consciousness, attention, language skills, memory, proverb interpretation, ability to identify similarities (e.g., "How are an apple and an orange alike?"), calculating and writing skills, and constructional ability (copying complex figures). A detailed overview of the mental status examination is provided by Strub and Black in *The Mental Status Examination in Neurology*.[33]

Higher Cognitive Functions

The interview should start with questions of significance to the patient. Beginning this way helps the interviewer gauge the patient's memory and may help allay anxiety. Introductory questions that express interest in the patient as a person, such as questions about occupation, children, grandchildren, and hobbies, often provoke responses that indicate the patient's current and previous level of mental and social functioning. General appearance and grooming, posture, behavior, speech, and word choice can speak volumes to the careful observer.[34] The examiner should always be aware of the possibility of hearing and visual deficits that may mimic cognitive impairment.

An elderly patient meeting a physician or nurse for the first time may be anxious about the encounter. The patient may be coming to the interview reluctantly or may even have been coerced by family or neighbors. The patient may worry that the physician or nurse will be trying to determine if he or she is "crazy." Even in a nonthreatening environment, the interview can cause anxiety, resulting in apparent confusion, inaccurate or incomplete reporting of information, and poor performance on testing. There is fear of error, and the patient may become hesitant to perform requested tasks. Disturbances of memory and intelligence exhibited during the examination may be a reflection of psychic stress and depression rather than dementia. It is wise to intersperse questions that are stressful or that focus on disability with others that are not and to end interviews on a positive note.[35]

The higher cognitive functions that may be specifically tested include the patient's fund of information and ability to reason abstractly and perform calculations (Table 2–2). Once some preliminary questions about the patient's personal history are discussed, the patient may be asked questions regarding current events ("Who is the president now?") or commonly known historical events ("When did World War II end?") to assess the patient's fund of information. In evaluating the patient's responses, it is critical to know how much education the patient has had and whether English is the patient's first language.

Assessment of insight and judgment has important implications for the assessment of driving skills and independence. Accidents and burns may be more common among cognitive-impaired persons with poor insight and judgment. Observe the patient's responses to mental status testing and conversation to note whether statements belie lack of insight into deficits.[36]

Proverb testing and similarities shed light on the patient's reasoning ability, intelligence, and judgment. The examiner needs to be careful that the patient is not repeating the meaning of a proverb from memory rather than reasoning what an abstract interpretation might be. The Cognitive Capacity Screen[9] and the Kokmen Short Test of Mental Status,[37] discussed below, are examples of screening instruments that include a test of identification of similarities, a task requiring the subject to think in abstract categories to discover how two concepts are alike (e.g., "How are a poem and a novel alike?"). It has been suggested that the use of simi-

Table 2–2 Higher Cognitive Functions

Location	Assessment
Frontal lobes	Points finger each time the examiner makes a fist and makes a fist when the examiner points
Temporal lobes	*Dominant:* standard aphasia testing (spontaneous speech, repetition, comprehension, writing, and naming)
	Nondominant: interprets affect (names affects shown in photos of faces or conveyed in examiner's voice)
Parietal lobes	*Dominant:* names fingers, knows left and right, performs calculations on paper, reading
	Nondominant: constructs copy of matchstick figure made by the examiner
Occipital lobes	Matches colors and objects if unable to name them

Source: Adapted with permission from American Geriatrics Society, "Memory Function and the Clinical Differentiation of Dementing Disorders" by EC Shuttleworth, *Journal of the American Geriatrics Society* (1982;30:365–366).

larity testing is better than the use of proverb testing for the assessment of abstraction ability.[38]

The ability to do calculations may be tested using serial 7s ("Take 7 away from 100 and keep subtracting 7 from the answer all the way down"), serial 3s ("Take 3 away from 20 and keep subtracting 3 from the answer all the way down"), or simple math problems. Corrected mistakes should not be counted as errors. Calculation ability also requires substantial memory and concentration ability. Occasionally, patients who have difficulty with serial 7s will handle the subtractions flawlessly if the problem is expressed in dollar terms ("If you had $100 and took away $7, how much would you have left?").

Memory

Of all the components of the mental status examination, memory assessment most commonly engenders anxiety, and understandably so. It sometimes puts the patient at ease if the examiner prefaces the examination, particularly if it is a standard questionnaire, with a statement such as the following: "I'm going to ask you some school-type questions. Some are easy. Some may be hard. Please don't be offended, because it's a routine I use for everyone." Give positive reinforcement during the examination with expressions such as "That's OK" or "That's fine."

Memory can be thought of as comprising three components. First and most fleeting is immediate recall. This can be assessed using digit repetition. Older adults in excellent health can correctly recall five to seven digits.[39,40] The second component of memory is short-term memory, ranging over a period of minutes to days. This is usually tested by asking the patient to remember three or four objects or abstract terms and then requesting their recall 5–10 minutes later, following intervening conversation or other testing. Examples of words used are "apple, table, penny"[41] and "brown, honesty, tulip, eyedropper."[33] The memory of aphasic patients may be tested by asking them to recall where items have been hidden in the room. It has been suggested that older persons do not use mnemonics when given a memory task and that this in part accounts for their failure to recall items.[40] Also, there is some evidence for increased processing time in elderly persons, and this may interfere with learning.[42] A third component of memory is remote or long-term memory. In one study, older adults were able to recall 80% of a catechism that had been learned some 36 years before.[43]

In general, elderly persons' self-report of memory difficulty correlates poorly with objective measures of memory function. Not uncommonly, patients who complain fervently of memory loss are depressed. Patient's with Alzheimer's disease may be oblivious to profound memory deficit, but early in the course of the disease, they may complain of memory loss.[44] Middle-aged or older persons without dementia may also complain of memory difficulties; their memory symptoms fit what has been called benign senescent forgetfulness or, more recently, age-associated memory impairment[45,46] or aging-associated cognitive decline.[47,48] These patients may be aware of a problem and apologize. They may not recall details of an experience even though they remember the experience itself. The forgetfulness fluctuates so that details not recalled at one time may be remembered at another.

Patients with more significant memory loss often have accompanying intellectual deficits. Kral referred to this as "malignant" memory loss because the patients in his original series with this type of memory decline had greater mortality than a group who did not.[46] Patients with malignant memory loss not only forget details of an event but may not recall the experience itself or may confabulate details.[39,46]

New nomenclature is emerging to describe the memory decline that is associated with normal aging and to replace the term "benign senescent forgetfulness." Some middle-aged and elderly persons exhibit memory dysfunction due to age in the routine tasks of daily life (e.g., they have trouble remembering items on a shopping list or telephone numbers). To fulfill the criteria for age-associated memory impairment, the patient must demonstrate impairment on a memory function test, such as the Wechsler Associate Learning Subtest, but must also lack dementia (the diagnosis of which would imply a more global intellectual impairment), as evidenced by the Folstein Mini-Mental State Examination.[45,49] Subjects with a family history of Alzheimer's dementia who met criteria for age-associated memory impairment did not have evidence of altered brain glucose metabolism.[50] Criteria for aging-associated cognitive decline will stimulate further developments regarding subthreshold dementia.[50,51] The fourth edition of the *Diagnostic and Statistical Manual of Mental Disorders (DSM-IV)* includes research criteria for "mild neurocognitive disorder," which is characterized by memory and other cognitive impairment that is due to a general medical condition but does not meet the full criteria for dementia.[52]

Attention and Level of Consciousness

Before an examiner can test and comment on the higher intellectual functions of the brain, including memory, some assessment (even if informal) must be made of the patient's level of consciousness. Obviously, functions such as orientation and memory cannot be tested in a comatose patient.

Orientation to surroundings is a fundamental beginning to mental status testing, but unfortunately, in routine clinical situations, the mental status evaluation often ends there. Questions regarding orientation to time, place, person, and situation are basic. Most of us continually orient ourselves by means of our daily routine, clocks and watches, calendars, news media, and social activities. Older persons, on the other hand, particularly those living alone or in nursing homes, may not experience these activities and as a result may have poor orientation to time and events.[35,53]

Once it is determined by observation that the patient is alert enough for mental status testing to proceed, the attentiveness of the patient is assessed. Assessing attentiveness is important because a patient who is easily distracted and unable to attend to the examiner will have poor performance on mental status testing solely because of inattention. Special note must be taken of the patient who is inappropriately distracted by environmental noise or talking in the hallway. In such a case, specific examination for attention deficit indicative of delirium may be warranted. Tests of attention sometimes used include digit repetition and the *A* test of vigilance. The length of a string of digits able to be repeated immediately after presentation tends to remain stable with age. A 90-year-old in good health should be able to repeat four digits, perhaps even seven or eight, after the examiner.[39] In the *A* test, the patient is asked to tap the table when the letter *A* is heard while the examiner presents random letters at a rate of one letter per second. The examiner observes for errors of commission and omission.

Neglect is a form of inattention in which the patient does not attend stimuli presented from a particular side. It occurs most commonly with nondominant hemisphere lesions (usually in the right hemisphere). The examiner needs to avoid interviewing a patient with this condition from the neglected side if communication is to be effective.

Language

Language should be observed and tested in a comprehensive mental status examination.[54] Spontaneous speech is observed during the initial interview. Does the patient make errors in words or grammatical construction? Patients with dysarthria, who have difficulty in the mechanical production of language, use normal grammar. Do spoken words flow smoothly? Fluency is one of the features that is used to differentiate the aphasias.

A simplified approach to aphasia divides the spoken language functions to be tested into three categories: comprehension, fluency, and repetition. Comprehension can be tested by asking the patient questions that can be answered by yes or no. If there is doubt about the responses, the patient may be asked to point to objects in the room. The task may be made more difficult by having the patient try to point to objects in a particular sequence or after the examiner has provided a description of the item rather than the item's name.

Fluency is tested by focusing on the rate and rhythm of speech production and the ease in initiating speech. Patients may be asked to name objects and their parts, such as a wristwatch and its band, buckle, and face. Repetition is tested starting with easy expressions ("ball" or "airplane") and progressing to more difficult ones ("Methodist Episcopal" or "Around the rock the rugged rascal ran").

The aphasias can be organized around the three characteristics of comprehension, fluency, and repetition (Figure 2–1). The patient in whom the entire language neural substrate is destroyed (e.g., due to infarction and edema after a stroke) has a global aphasia and indeed may be mute. All three language parameters are impaired in the patient with a global aphasia. After a period of recovery, some language function may return.

Wernicke's aphasia is characterized by impaired comprehension and repetition. Speech is fluent but marked by paraphasia (words or sounds that are replaced by other sounds, such as "wife" or "car" for "knife") and neologisms (nonsense words). Patients with this type of aphasia have severe difficulty with comprehension and may not even be aware that their own speech output is incoherent, which can be a considerable obstacle in rehabilitation. The patient with Wernicke's apha-

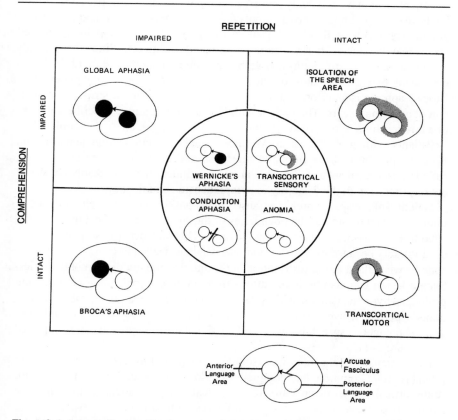

Figure 2–1 Aphasia diagram: The three components of language function to be tested are comprehension, fluency, and repetition. Aphasias depicted within the central circle are the fluent aphasias.

sia may describe a picture of a boy reaching into a cookie jar this way: "It's a barl, a boil, oh, you know, getting the thing, the thing, it's just the top, boy, you know."

Patients with Wernicke's aphasia may improve significantly in their comprehension but continue to exhibit fluent speech with paraphasia. This condition is called conduction aphasia. The neurologic lesion in conduction aphasia may involve the arcuate fasciculus, the connection between the anterior (motor) and posterior (sensory) language areas. Patients with conduction aphasia usually do not have the amount of verbal output noted in patients with Wernicke's aphasia. They may be able to read well for comprehension but cannot read aloud.

Patients with an initial Wernicke's aphasia may continue to improve beyond a conduction type of aphasia (better comprehension) and ultimately be left with an anomic aphasia. Patients with anomic aphasia have word-finding difficulty but are capable of fluent speech, good repetition, and good comprehension.

Patients who have relatively preserved comprehension and impaired repetition but have severely limited verbal output consisting of mostly nouns and verbs (telegraphic speech) have Broca's aphasia. Although repetition is impaired, repeated words may be clearer than the patient's spontaneous speech. Since the patient's speech contains mostly nouns and verbs, the patient may have difficulty with an expression like "No ifs, ands, or buts." The lesion in the brain of the patient with Broca's aphasia is anterior, and if it involves the nearby motor strip, a concomitant hemiplegia occurs. The patient with Broca's aphasia may describe a picture of a boy reaching into a cookie jar this way: "Boy . . . yes, ah . . . jar, cookie."

Patients with global aphasia, Wernicke's aphasia, conduction aphasia, and Broca's aphasia all have impaired repetition ability. There are rarer aphasias, called transcortical aphasias, in which repetition function is remarkably preserved out of proportion to the disability in comprehension and fluency.

Isolation of the speech area is a transcortical aphasia that occurs when a zone of infarction extends around the boundaries of the speech areas so that they are isolated from the associative regions of the brain. This may occur in so-called watershed infarcts because of hypotension and resultant ischemia in the "watershed" zone between the areas of distribution of the anterior and middle cerebral arteries. Such a lesion can also be found after carbon monoxide poisoning or following prolonged hypoxia. Patients with isolation of the speech area can repeat words and phrases perfectly, even words from foreign languages they have never heard. Their spontaneous speech is sparse and nonfluent and comprehension is impaired (see Figure 2–1).

Partial transcortical syndromes, isolating only part of the speech apparatus, are probably more common than complete isolation of the speech area. The anterior (transcortical motor) or posterior (transcortical sensory) language areas may be isolated from the associative cortices of the rest of the brain.

Comprehension is relatively preserved in a patient with transcortical motor aphasia. The speech of such a patient is similar to that of a patient with Broca's aphasia, which is an aphasia that also involves anterior portions of the cortex. Patients with transcortical sensory aphasia have fluent speech and impaired comprehension, similar to patients with Wernicke's aphasia. Both transcortical sensory aphasia and Wernicke's aphasia involve posterior portions of the cortex. The spontaneous speech of the patient with transcortical sensory aphasia is filled with paraphasic errors (word substitutions), but repetition is preserved. Sorting out aphasia is easier when the three domains of fluency, comprehension, and repetition are kept in mind. Other language syndromes include reading difficulty only (alexia), alexia with writing difficulty (agraphia), and Gerstmann's syndrome (acalculia, agraphia, right/left disorientation, and finger agnosia, or inability to name the fingers).

Writing and Construction Ability

The components of the mental status examination discussed to this point can smoothly follow the history interview, since they are primarily oral in nature. At this point in the examination, the patient may be presented with a blank sheet of paper for subsequent tests.

The patient is asked to write his or her name at the top of the page. Although the signature is usually overlearned and the ability to write it can be intact even if the patient experiences writing difficulty in the case of more complex tasks, asking for the signature acclimates the patient to the idea that he or she is going to be asked to do some writing and is a nonthreatening way to begin. Below the signature the patient is asked to write a complete sentence, perhaps about the weather. While the patient has pen in hand, construction ability may be tested by asking the patient to reproduce line drawings made by the examiner. This can be a very sensitive test of parietal lobe damage, and lack of construction ability is an early abnormality in dementia. Trouble with construction is not something most patients will complain of specifically, but testing constructional ability can be revealing. The testing begins with simple figures such as a triangle or square, and progresses to more complex drawings such as a cube, house, or flowerpot. Lack of ability to copy figures is not specific to dementia and may reflect motor incoordination or apraxia.[38]

Getting the patient to attempt to draw a clock showing the numerals and time (e.g., "ten minutes past eleven o'clock") can act as a single-item screen for cognitive impairment. The examiner draws a large circle on a blank sheet of paper and asks the patient to fill in the numbers as on a clock. This task is thought to be a sensitive test of parietal lobe dysfunction. Patients with primarily right or nondominant hemisphere dysfunction write the numbers correctly but plan poorly. Patients with primarily left or dominant hemisphere dysfunction have trouble writing the numbers but get the general plan of the clock correct, perhaps placing lines where the numbers should be. Clock drawing has been used to screen for cognitive impairment[55] as well as to follow progression of diagnosed Alzheimer's disease.[56] Several scoring methods for the clock-drawing task are available.[55–59] The assessment of higher cognitive functions is summarized in Table 2–2.[60]

DIFFERENTIAL DIAGNOSIS OF DEMENTIA

In diagnosing cognitive impairment, the clinician must distinguish between dementia, delirium, depression, and specific neurologic deficits (such as aphasia or amnesia).

Dementia is a syndrome characterized by loss of intellectual capacity involving not only memory but also cognition, language, visuospatial skills, and personality. All five components need not be impaired, but they frequently are to varying degrees. Dementia entails intellectual impairment in *clear consciousness,* and it may be progressive, stable, or remitting. The term "organic mental disorder" has been dropped in the *DSM-IV.*[52] Criteria for several subtypes of dementia are delineated in the *DSM-IV:* dementia of the Alzheimer's type, vascular dementia, dementia due to human immunodeficiency virus, dementia due to head trauma, dementia due to Pick's disease, dementia due to Creutzfeldt-Jakob disease, dementia due to other medical general conditions, substance-induced persisting dementia, and dementia due to multiple etiologies.

Delirium is marked by clouding of consciousness, usually of acute onset (hours or days). Patients who are delirious may be agitated or lethargic, and levels of activity may vary throughout the day. Agitated delirium calls attention to the patient, while the delirium of quietly delirious patients may go unrecognized and unattended. It cannot be overemphasized, however, that delirium is a syndrome, not a diagnosis. The recognition of delirium, like fever, requires further investigation.[61] Standardized schedules to detect delirium have been published,[62,62a] but short instruments that assess cognitive function may serve the purpose of detection, as discussed later in this chapter.

Once the clinician determines that global intellectual impairment is present and consistent with dementia, a consideration of the specific etiology is in order. Although the chance of finding a remedial condition seems remote, the list of diagnostic possibilities is so large and the scope of the problem in our aging society is so great that dementia and any concurrent conditions need to be assessed thoroughly.

The notion of searching for a "reversible" dementia (implying that nothing can be done to help the patient with an "irreversible" dementia) is only helpful in so far as it prompts a consideration of the myriad causes of intellectual decline. In a study of 107 demented elderly patients, 16 improved 6 months after their initial assessment.[63] Eleven were patients with reversible dementia, but they showed a deteriorating course typical of Alzheimer's disease on further follow-up. The 5 remaining patients with irreversible dementia who improved did so after concurrent conditions (congestive heart failure, depression, anemia, and other medical conditions) were addressed. Classifying dementia as reversible (treatable) or irreversible (not treatable) may unnecessarily compromise patient management. Instead, all demented patients must be considered to be at increased risk for secondary treatable conditions.[63,64]

One helpful scheme (Table 2–3) for organizing the differential diagnosis of dementia and aiding the clinician's memory was suggested by Cummings and Benson.[65] By considering a hierarchy of clinical features, the dementias can be systematically reviewed.

First, are the features consistent with a cortical dementia such as Alzheimer's or Pick's disease? Alzheimer's disease is characterized by an insidious onset with a progressive deteriorating course. Typically memory is affected early on. Clinical criteria for the clinical diagnosis of Alzheimer's disease reported by

---

Table 2–3 Differential Diagnosis of Dementia: Systematic Approach

Cortical Features
  Alzheimer's disease
  Pick's disease

Subcortical Features
  Multiple ischemic episodes
    Vascular dementia
  Movement disorder
    Parkinson's disease
    Progressive supranuclear palsy
    Huntington's disease
    Wilson's disease
  Affective disorder
    Dementia syndrome of depression
  Classic triad of hydrocephalus
    Normal pressure hydrocephalus
  Chronic confusional state
    Toxin or drug reaction
    Metabolic abnormality
    Endocrine disorder
    Nutritional deficiency
    Infectious process
    Neoplasm, primary or metastatic

Source: Adapted from JL Cummings and DF Benson, *Dementia: A Clinical Approach* (Stoneham, Mass: Butterworths Publishers, 1983), p 11. With permission from the publisher.

McKhann and associates aid in the evaluation of patients with dementia.[66] Definite diagnosis of Alzheimer's disease requires histopathologic evidence obtained at autopsy, but a diagnosis of "probable" and "possible" Alzheimer's disease can be made clinically using the criteria set forth by the National Institute of Neurological and Communicative Disorders and Stroke–Alzheimer's Disease and Associated Disorders Association (NINCDS-ADADA) Task Force on Alzheimer's Disease; probable Alzheimer's disease may be diagnosed using the following criteria[66]:

- dementia established by clinical examination and by the Folstein Mini-Mental State Examination or similar examination
- deficits in two or more areas of cognition
- progressive worsening of memory and other cognitive functions
- no disturbance of consciousness (unlike delirium)
- onset most often after age 65
- no systemic disorder or other brain disease that could account for the findings

The diagnosis of Alzheimer's disease is supported by progressive deterioration in specific functions such as language, impaired activities of daily living, and evidence of cerebral atrophy on a computed tomography scan. The *DSM-IV* criteria for dementia of the Alzheimer's type include multiple cognitive deficits (memory impairment, aphasia, apraxia, agnosia, and disturbance of executive function) and interference with social and occupational roles (Table 2–4).[52]

A scale developed as a tool to assist in the differential diagnosis of dementia, specifically for the diagnosis of Alzheimer's disease, is the Inventory of Diagnostic Clinical Features of Senile Dementia of the Alzheimer's Type (Exhibit 2–1).[67] The maximum score is 20, attained by patients with uncomplicated dementia of the Alzheimer's type. Higher scores (14 or greater) are consistent with a diagnosis of Alzheimer's disease, and lower scores suggest other diagnoses.

In retrospective and prospective studies, the inventory was accurate in differentiating patients with Alzheimer's disease from patients who have dementia from another etiology. This inventory gives greater weight to loss of intellectual functions than to motor abnormalities. Atypical presentations of dementia of the Alzheimer's type or mixed diagnoses may fail to be identified because of the absence of multiple areas of intellectual impairment assessed by the inventory.[67,68] The scoring scheme of the inventory reflects the generally normal results of motor examination of patients with Alzheimer's disease and the early impairment of language and memory. Evidence of dementia conjoined with signs or symptoms of a movement disorder should suggest to the practitioner a diagnosis other than primary degenerative (cortical) dementia.

Table 2–4 Diagnostic Criteria for Dementia of the Alzheimer's Type

A. The development of multiple cognitive deficits manifested by both
   (1) memory impairment (impaired ability to learn new information or to recall previously learned information)
   (2) one (or more) of the following cognitive disturbances:
      (a) aphasia (language disturbance)
      (b) apraxia (impaired ability to carry out motor activities despite intact motor function)
      (c) agnosia (failure to recognize or identify objects despite intact sensory function)
      (d) disturbance in executive functioning (i.e., planning, organizing, sequencing, abstracting)
B. The cognitive deficits in Criteria A1 and A2 each cause significant impairment in social or occupational functioning and represent a significant decline from a previous level of functioning.
C. The course is characterized by gradual onset and continuing cognitive decline.
D. The cognitive deficits in Criteria A1 and A2 are not due to any of the following:
   (1) other central nervous system conditions that cause progressive deficits in memory and cognition (e.g., cerebrovascular disease, Parkinson's disease, Huntington's disease, subdural hematoma, normal-pressure hydrocephalus, brain tumor)
   (2) systemic conditions that are known to cause dementia (e.g., hypothyroidism, vitamin B_{12} or folic acid deficiency, niacin deficiency, hypercalcemia, neurosyphilis, HIV infection)
   (3) substance-induced conditions
E. The deficits do not occur exclusively during the course of a delirium.
F. The disturbance is not better accounted for by another Axis I disorder (e.g., major depressive disorder, schizophrenia).

Source: Reprinted with permission from the *Diagnostic and Statistical Manual of Mental Disorders, Fourth Edition*. Copyright © 1994 by the American Psychiatric Association.

Patients with Pick's disease, another primary cortical dementia, have personality changes, poor judgment and social graces, but strikingly preserved memory, language, and visuospatial skills early in the course of the dementia. Pathologic changes in Pick's disease occur primarily in the temporal and frontal lobes of the brain.

Is there evidence of a halting progression of the disorder and spotty mental status deficits associated with a history of hypertension or strokes? This is consistent with a multi-infarct or vascular dementia. In the clinical examination, the practitioner should look for spasticity in the limbs, hyperreflexia, plantar extensor reflexes, and an abnormal gait. The personality is relatively preserved.[69] Criteria of *DSM-IV* for vascular dementia are similar to the criteria for dementia of the Alzheimer's type except that focal neurologic signs and symptoms or imaging studies revealing cerebrovascular disease are present.[52]

The Hachinski Ischemic Score (Exhibit 2–2) has been devised to help distinguish vascular dementia from other types of dementia. Patients with a score of 7

Exhibit 2–1 Inventory of Diagnostic Clinical Features of Senile Dementia of the Alzheimer's Type

Mental Functions	0	1	2
Memory	Normal or forgetfulness that improves with cues	Recalls one or two of three words, spontaneous, incompletely aided by prompting	Disoriented, unable to learn three words in three minutes, recall not aided by prompting
Visuospatial	Normal or clumsy drawings, minimal distortions	Flattening, omissions, distortions	Disorganized, unrecognizable copies of models
Cognition	Normal or impairment of complex abstractions and calculations	Fails to abstract simple proverbs and has difficulty with mathematic problems	Fails to interpret even simple proverbs or idioms, acalculia
Personality	Disinhibition or depression	Appropriately concerned	Unaware or indifferent, irritability not uncommon
Language	Normal	Anomia, mild comprehension deficits	Fluent aphasia with anomia, decreased comprehension paraphasia

Motor Functions	0	1	2
Speech	Mute, severely	Slurred, amelodic, dysarthric	Normal hypophonic
Psychomotor speed	Slow, long latency to response	Hesitant responses	Normal, prompt responses
Posture	Abnormal, flexed, extended, or distorted	Stooped or mildly distorted	Normal, erect
Gait	Hemiparetic, ataxic, apractic, or hyperkinetic	Shuffling, dyskinetic	Normal
Movements	Tremor, akinesia, rigidity, or chorea	Imprecise, poorly coordinated	Normal

Source: Reprinted with permission from American Geriatrics Society, "Dementia of the Alzheimer Type: An Inventory of Diagnostic Clinical Features" by J Cummings and D Benson, *Journal of American Geriatrics Society* (1986;34:12–19).

Exhibit 2–2 Hachinski Ischemic Score

1. Abrupt onset (2)
2. Stepwise deterioration (1)
3. Fluctuating course (2)
4. Nocturnal confusion (1)
5. Relative preservation of personality (1)
6. Depression (1)
7. Somatic complaints (1)
8. Emotional incontinence (1)
9. History of hypertension (1)
10. History of strokes (2)
11. Evidence of associated atherosclerosis (1)
12. Focal neurologic symptoms (2)
13. Focal neurologic signs (2)

The score for each feature is noted in parentheses. A score of greater than 7 suggests a vascular component to the dementia.

Source: Adapted with permission from *Archives of Neurology* (1975;32:634), Copyright © 1975, American Medical Association.

or more are said to be more likely to have vascular dementia or at least a vascular component to their dementia.[70] An extensive review of the literature by Liston and LaRue led the authors to the conclusion that a low Hachinski Ischemic Score could help rule out vascular dementia because ischemic lesions severe enough to produce a dementia would be expected to be severe enough to cause the associated neurologic changes and elevate the score.[71]

Recognition of vascular dementia assumes particular importance when hypertension is being simultaneously treated. Some investigators believe there is a "therapeutic window" within which blood pressure should be controlled. As discussed in Chapter 7, when blood pressure is lowered below this optimal range, patients with vascular dementia exhibit further cognitive decline. Patients who stop smoking also benefit.[72]

Senile dementia of the Binswanger type is a vascular dementia recognized with increasing frequency because of the availability of magnetic resonance imaging. Patients with this kind of dementia suffer from gait disturbance and urinary incontinence and exhibit neurologic signs early in the course of the illness. The pathologic lesion may be infarctions in the white matter just below the cortex, resulting in isolation of the cortex from deeper structures. Risk factors for small artery disease (diabetes, hypertension) may predispose to senile dementia of the Binswanger type.[73,74]

Is there evidence of a movement disorder? Parkinson's disease is an example of a subcortical process associated with a dementia. The patient's intellectual processes, along with his or her movements, seem to be "slowed." Frequently there is a superimposed depression. Subcortical dementias classically are associated with abnormalities of the motor system such as stooped posture, increased muscle tone, and abnormal movements and gait.[65] Other subcortical dementias are associated with Huntington's disease, progressive supranuclear palsy, and Wilson's disease. The difference between cortical and subcortical types of dementia is not as clear-cut as it would seem. Some of the features generally reported to be characteristic of one type may be found in the other (e.g., aphasia is sometimes present in patients with subcortical dementia).[75]

Is there an affective component to the dementia? Patients who vigorously complain of memory impairment are often depressed, have early Alzheimer's disease, or both. These patients, on close continued observation, may be able to learn new facts and to give a detailed account of their memory loss. Depression as a symptom of intellectual impairment is discussed more fully later in this chapter.

Is the classic triad of symptoms of normal pressure hydrocephalus present? Normal pressure hydrocephalus is characterized by gait disturbance, urinary incontinence, and dementia. Physical examination reveals spasticity in the legs and hyperreflexia and plantar extension reflexes. Of course the classic triad need not be present. The computed tomography examination will show dilated ventricles, but there may be considerable symptomatic overlap with other dementias.[76]

Is there evidence of a toxic process? Prescription medications would be the greatest offenders, but hidden alcohol abuse might also be the cause.[77-82] Commonly used medicines (e.g., propranolol or digoxin) may cause an altered mental state as the only side effect. Discontinuation of some medicines (e.g., the benzodiazepines) can precipitate a delirium or seizures.

Is there evidence of a metabolic abnormality? Electrolyte imbalance, such as hyponatremia, can result in a confused mental state. Calcium abnormalities can cause lethargy. Hypoxia or hypercarbia, as could result from pulmonary or cardiac disease, may also cause cognitive impairment.

Is there evidence of an endocrine abnormality? Testing for apathetic hyperthyroidism or for occult hypothyroidism is probably part of the complete workup for dementia. Are the electrolytes suggestive of an adrenal problem? Is there evidence of a nutritional deficiency, such as deficiency of thiamine, niacin, or vitamin B_{12}? Thiamine deficiency, which is associated with alcohol abuse, may result in Wernicke's encephalopathy or organic amnestic syndrome. Niacin deficiency is associated with dementia. Vitamin B_{12} deficiency may result in psychologic changes without concomitant macrocytosis.

Is there evidence of an infectious process such as meningitis? Of course, reliable diagnosis would require lumbar puncture. Lumbar puncture would not be very helpful for the diagnosis of dementia if used indiscriminately, but it could be reserved for specific circumstances, such as acute deterioration with fever. Neurosyphilis is an unusual cause of dementia today but can be present even with a negative rapid plasma reagin or VDRL test. Jakob-Creutzfeldt disease is a rapidly progressing dementia caused by a slow virus and characterized by myoclonus in its late stages and a burst-silence pattern on an electroencephalogram. Dementia secondary to human immunodeficiency virus is perhaps the newest addition to the list. The possibility of acquired immunodeficiency syndrome (AIDS) should be kept in mind, particularly when risk factors, such as sexual exposure to high-risk persons or the use of blood products, are present.[83,84]

Are there focal neurologic signs suggestive of an intracranial process such as a neoplasm or a chronic subdural hematoma? Is there a history of trauma followed by changes in mental state? A complete mental status examination may reveal deficits that point to involvement of an otherwise "silent" area of the brain. Cranial computed tomography rarely uncovers a mass lesion presenting as dementia when focal signs are absent.

Finally, is there more than one process occurring simultaneously? Are there concurrent medical illnesses that could be more optimally treated? In other words, is delirium resulting in the deterioration of the mental status of a patient with a pre-existing dementia? Over 30% of patients with dementia have more than one disorder contributing to the persistence of the dementia.[85]

MENTAL STATUS ASSESSMENT INSTRUMENTS

A number of short mental status instruments have been devised to assist clinicians. As mentioned earlier, some assessment instruments for intellectual functioning are designed for the sole purpose of evaluating mental status, and others form part of a more comprehensive instrument that includes measures of functional status or of psychiatric illness as well as of functional status (see Figure 1–1), as discussed in the next chapter. Further information on instruments for assessing mental state may be found in the *Geropsychology Assessment Resources Guide.*[86]

The sensitivity and specificity of a test are used to assess performance of the test at specific cutpoints. Sensitivity and specificity are characteristics of tests that do not change with the prevalence of the disease in a population. The *sensitivity* of a test is the proportion of those persons with a disease who are detected by the test. *Specificity* is the proportion of those who are free of the disease who are identified as such by the test. A related concept is the predictive value of a test result. The predictive value of a positive test result is the proportion of persons who have positive test results and truly have the disease (persons who have positive results but do not have the disease are said to have false-positive results). The predictive value of a negative test result is the proportion of persons who have negative test results and truly do not have the disease (persons who have negative test results but have the disease are said to have false-negative results).

The *predictive value* of a test varies as the prevalence of the disease in the population varies. The more prevalent (common) the disease is in the population to be tested, the greater is the predictive value of a positive test, but the predictive value of a negative result goes down (the proportion of false-negative results increases). This makes intuitive sense, because it would seem that the more common the disease, the more likely it is that a positive test result is true. Conversely, it will be less likely that a negative test result represents a "true" negative. In a nursing home, for example, where the prevalence of dementia is presumably higher than in the general elderly population, the predictive value of a negative test result is less than the predictive value of a negative result in the general elderly population.

The reverse is true for a less prevalent disease. The less prevalent (rarer) the disease is in the population to be tested, the greater is the predictive value of a negative test result, but the predictive value of a positive result goes down (the proportion of false-positive results increases). Again, it seems intuitive that the rarer a disease is, the more likely a positive test result is "wrong."

In developing and evaluating the mental status instruments to be described, investigators generally compare scores on a test administered to a group of healthy older adults to scores of patients diagnosed with dementia, probing whether the instrument discriminates between the groups. Performance characteristics such as sensitivity and specificity are therefore essentially determined in a sample with a high proportion of persons with cognitive impairment. For example, in a study involving 75 healthy older adults and 75 patients with dementia, the proportion affected is 50%. In community settings, the prevalence of dementia is likely to be much lower than in such studies, so that false-positive test results are a potential problem (positive predictive value declines despite high specificity demonstrated when the instruments were evaluated). We shall see that numerous factors unrelated to cognitive impairment (e.g., impaired vision or hearing, education effects) may influence test scores. Furthermore, not all cognitive impairment is dementia (e.g., delirium associated with abnormal scores). Proper interpretation of test results requires that information from other domains (e.g., functional status, physical examination) be considered.

In addition to detection of cognitive impairment, mental status assessment instruments can stratify patients with regard to degree of impairment. Many of the instruments designed specifically for this purpose also include some assessment of functional ability (e.g., "dementia rating scales," which are discussed in Chapter 3). Because a score is generated by some of the mental status assessment instruments discussed in this section, stratification is possible based on total score. Mental status assessment instruments may exhibit "threshold" or "ceiling" effects. In other words, patients beyond a certain level of severity of dementia score the same despite some differences in degree. If the population tested has a predominance of severely demented patients, for example, an instrument will not be useful for tracking changes if all severely affected patients perform equally poorly. By the same token, in a population of relatively well elders, a test that is too easy will not pick out mildly demented patients, who may be able to perform well on an easy test but have difficulties when the tasks are made more discriminating. A vivid illustration is provided by a case of a patient who "studied" for a short mental status questionnaire (the Folstein Mini-Mental State Examination). An elderly woman who was being admitted to a retirement home was disappointed when the physician did not ask her "those questions" her friend had told her about. She had studied the "answers" to the examination based on information from her friend, who was a resident in the home.[87]

Folstein Mini-Mental State Examination

The Folstein Mini-Mental State Examination (MMSE)[88] is one of the most widely employed tests of cognitive function and one of the best studied.[89,90] The MMSE consists of two parts (Exhibit 2–3). The first part requires verbal responses only and assesses orientation, memory, and attention. The three words used to test memory are left up to the examiner, leaving the possibility that this question could vary in difficulty. The items "apple, table, penny" were used in the Epidemiologic Catchment Area Program. In addition to serial 7s, the patient is asked to spell "world" backwards, and the best score may be taken for calculating the total score. A "chess-move" strategy is used to score the "world" item (the number of *transpositions* required to spell "dlrow" yields the number of errors).[91] The second part evaluates the ability to write a sentence, name objects, follow verbal and written commands, and copy a complex polygon design. The maximum score is 30. The test is not timed. A telephone version of the MMSE is available for special purposes.[92]

In the original work with the MMSE, normal elderly persons scored a mean of 27.6. Patients with dementia, depression with cognitive impairment, and affective disorders formed a continuum with the mean scores for these groups of 9.7, 19, and 25, respectively. Not only did the demented patients score the lowest and the depressed patients the highest, but after treatment of depression, the depressed patients with cognitive impairment showed improvement in their scores. The demented patients had no change, as would be expected.[88]

The MMSE was administered to patients undergoing cranial computerized tomographic scanning referred from neurologic and psychiatric services at the University of Iowa. Patients whose CT scan showed no cerebral atrophy had a mean score of 26.4. Those with focal brain lesions had a score of 25.3, which was not significantly different from the group without atrophy. Patients with atrophy

Exhibit 2–3 The Folstein Mini-Mental State Examination

Maximum Score		
	Orientation	
5	What is the (year) (season) (date) (day) (month)?	
5	Where are we (state) (county) (town) (hospital) (floor)?	
	Registration	
3	Name three objects: one second to say each. Then ask the patient all three after you have said them. Give one point for each correct answer. Repeat them until he learns all three. Count trials and record number.	
	Attention and Calculation	
5	Begin with 100 and count backward by 7 (stop after five answers). Alternatively, spell "world" backward.	
	Recall	
3	Ask for the three objects repeated above.	
	Language	
2	Show a pencil and a watch and ask the patient to name them.	
1	Repeat the following: "No ifs, ands, or buts."	
3	A three-stage command: "Take a paper in your right hand, fold it in half, and put it on the floor."	
1	Read and obey the following: (show written item) CLOSE YOUR EYES	
1	Write a sentence.	
1	Copy a design (complex polygon).	
30	Total score possible	

Source: Adapted with permission from *Journal of Psychiatric Research* (1975;12:196–197), Copyright © 1975, Pergamon Journals Ltd.

alone had a score of 18.0. Thus MMSE results correlate to some degree with structural changes in the brain.[93]

Although one report failed to show a difference in sensitivity between the MMSE and the Short Portable Mental Status Questionnaire (SPMSQ),[94] others have suggested that the sensitivity of the MMSE is better than that of the SPMSQ,[95,96] since it identifies potential cognitive impairment at a rate of 90 percent rather than 50 percent (Table 2–5). The sensitivity of an instrument such as the MMSE, which, unlike the SPMSQ, tests recent memory, written and spoken language, and construction ability (drawing) in addition to orientation, would be expected to be more sensitive because a broader range of intellectual functions is sampled.

In any case, when the MMSE reveals a patient is impaired, additional follow-up and evaluation are indicated to further define the difficulty, as would be true for any brief screening instrument. It is acceptable practice in general medical settings to use the MMSE for initial evaluation of older persons.[13]

Table 2–5 Sensitivity, Specificity, and Predictive Value of the Mini-Mental State Examination (MMSE)

	Clinical Examination Consistent with Dementia	Clinical Examination Not Consistent with Dementia	
Score indicates impairment	Agrees	False positive	Predictive value of a positive test is 60%–93%
Score indicates no impairment	False negative	Agrees	Predictive value of a negative test is 77%–95%
	Sensitivity is 50%–87%	Specificity is approximately 90%	

A cutoff score of 24 is used to indicate dementia.

Sources: Journal of the American Geriatrics Society (1980;28:381–384), Copyright © 1980, American Geriatrics Society; *Psychological Medicine* (1982;12:397–408), Copyright © 1982, Cambridge University Press; *Journal of Neurology, Neurosurgery, and Psychiatry* (1984;47:496–499), Copyright © 1984, British Medical Association.

The sensitivity of the MMSE was 76% when 126 patients on neurosurgical and neurologic wards were tested and a cutoff score of 23 was used to differentiate impaired from normal patients.[97] The mean age of these patients was 49.9. Patients with bilateral hemispheric damage or with left hemispheric damage scored around 23, whereas control subjects and patients with right hemispheric damage scored around 28. Thus the instrument detects left hemispheric dysfunction better than it does right hemispheric dysfunction. This asymmetrical detection of dysfunction was also shown to be true for the Cognitive Capacity Screen,[98] discussed later in this chapter. In the study of Dick and associates, there was excellent agreement between the results of the MMSE and those of the Wechsler Adult Intelligence Scale.[97]

Results of scores on mental status instruments reflect the educational level of the subjects. Low scores may imply more severe intellectual impairment among persons with high educational attainment. As the education level increases, one expects the specificity of an instrument to rise (an abnormal test result probably really is abnormal because an educated person would be more likely to perform well). Conversely, sensitivity goes down as the education level increases (a normal or negative test score might still be achieved by an impaired educated person). For example, the sensitivity of the MMSE was 93% in a population of patients with less than an eighth grade education but fell to 71% in a population of patients with more than eight grades of schooling.[96,99]

Lower scores may be acceptable among patients with less education.[90,100] Normative data on the MMSE based on age and educational attainment were provided by Crum and her colleagues.[90] For persons with 0 to 4 years of education, a cutpoint of 19 and below is used to identify those scoring at a level less than 75% of individuals in the same educational stratum. Corresponding cutpoints are, for persons with 5 to 8 years of schooling, 23 and below; for persons with 9 to 12 years of schooling, 27 and below; for persons with schooling at the college level and beyond, 29 and below.[90]

Short Portable Mental Status Questionnaire

One of the simpler tests widely used to assess mental status is the Short Portable Mental Status Questionnaire (SPMSQ; Exhibit 2–4) developed by Pfeiffer.[101] This test comprises 10 questions dealing with orientation, personal history, remote memory, and calculation. The Kahn-Goldfarb Mental Status Questionnaire[102] is also a 10-item instrument; it is the prototype of short mental state examinations and is similar to the SPMSQ.

The final error score of the SPMSQ is modified by various factors. One is subtracted from the error score if the patient has less than a high school education. More than three errors would identify the person as impaired. In the administration of this test, the examiner must keep in mind that the date must be exact, the birthdate must be exact, the mother's maiden name does not require verification, and the calculations must be done in their entirety and correctly.

Exhibit 2–4 Short Portable Mental Status Questionnaire

1. What is the date today?
2. What day of the week is it?
3. What is the name of this place?
4. What is your telephone number? (If the patient does not have a phone: What is your street address?)
5. How old are you?
6. When were you born?
7. Who is the president of the United States now?
8. Who was the president just before that?
9. What was your mother's maiden name?
10. Subtract 3 from 20 and keep subtracting 3 from each new number you get, all the way down.

Source: Copyright © 1974 by E Pfeiffer. All rights reserved.

The SPMSQ is compact, is easy to use, and requires no special materials. It would appear to meet the minimal criteria for face validity, being a mental status examination covering orientation, remote memory, and calculation. There is no task to assess short-term memory. How does it compare with a neuropsychiatric examination?

To evaluate the SPMSQ, it is necessary to return to the statistical concepts of sensitivity, specificity, and predictive value of test results. When administered to community-dwelling elders, the specificity was found to be better than 90%.[94,103] The sensitivity, the ability of the test to detect impairment, is much less, perhaps as low as 50%.[94] In another study, the sensitivity was found to be 82%, but the SPMSQ could not clearly differentiate mildly impaired from normal elders.[104] It is necessary to consider functional and other factors in interpreting the mental status test. Other studies have found the SPMSQ performs well in clinical settings.[105,106]

Unlike the sensitivity and specificity, the predictive value of a positive and of a negative test result will vary depending on the prevalence of cognitive impairment in the study or practice population. In some published data,[94,101] the predictive value of a positive test result was around 90%; that of a negative result is 70% to 80% (Table 2–6). The predictive value of a normal (negative) SPMSQ test result was about 80% in one community-dwelling elderly population; 20% of those who test negative will have detectable cognitive impairment on more thorough testing. In a nursing home setting, where the prevalence of dementia is presumably higher,

Table 2–6 Sensitivity, Specificity, and Predictive Value of the Short Portable Mental Status Questionnaire

	Clinical Examination Consistent with Dementia	Clinical Examination Not Consistent with Dementia	
Score indicates impairment	Agrees	False positive	Predictive value of a positive test is up to 90%
Score indicates no impairment	False negative	Agrees	Predictive value of a negative test is 70%
	Sensitivity is 50%–82%	Specificity is approximately 9(	

Four errors are used as a cutoff score to indicate dementia.

Sources: Journal of the American Geriatrics Society (1975;23:433–4 (1980;28: 381–384), Copyright © 1975, 1979, 1980, American Geriatrics S

the predictive value of a negative test result falls to around 70%; thus, 30% with a satisfactory score do not have normal cognitive functioning.

The SPMSQ is entirely oral and easy to memorize. The clinician may consider supplementing the SPMSQ with the written parts of the mental status examination (e.g., signature, writing a sentence, drawings) discussed earlier in this chapter. A more complete examination would be warranted if the SPMSQ detects cognitive impairment or if the presenting complaint is related to confusion or personality change.

Orientation and Nonorientation Items

The SPMSQ and the MMSE rely heavily on questions of orientation. As indicated by the low sensitivity of both tests, the common practice of using orientation-type questions to screen for cognitive impairment may miss as many as half of the patients with dementia. A brief example illustrates the pitfall of using an interview heavily weighted toward orientation-type questions. A 66-year-old woman was tested for dementia at the request of her family because of memory difficulties. The patient's daughter stated that on several occasions the patient had forgotten the names of some family members and friends. The patient was still driving, keeping her checkbook, cooking, and performing the usual activities of daily living. Her SPMSQ score was 10 (no errors). Further mental status testing revealed she could not recall three items, copy a simple diagram, or write an organized sentence. Thus orientation-type questions alone failed to identify any problem. Had just the SPMSQ been done, the intellectual deficits would have remained undetected.

Klein and associates reported on the sensitivity and specificity of various components of the mental status examination.[107] The components of the examination were divided into two broad categories: orientation items (does the patient know the day, month, year, city, and hospital?) and nonorientation items (can the patient subtract 7 serially from 100, spell the word "world" backward, and recall three items after five minutes?).

Orientation items uniformly exhibited low sensitivity. Demented patients not uncommonly were oriented to time and place and therefore would have been missed by the unwary examiner using orientation questions exclusively. Recall that low sensitivity means a low proportion of those with dementia are actually detected by the test. On the other hand, nonorientation items were highly sensitive, but since many normal elders also encountered difficulty with these items, the specificity was low. Recall that low specificity means a low proportion of normal persons are identified as normal by the test. This distinction between orientation and nonorientation items must be kept in mind when interpreting the answers of ants to the items (Table 2–7). The patient who knows where he or she is and e it is may still be cognitively impaired.

Table 2–7 Sensitivity and Specificity of Orientation and Nonorientation Items of the Mental Status Examination

Item	Sensitivity (%)	Specificity (%)
Orientation items		
Day	52.8	91.7
Month	56.9	96.5
Year	51.4	98.6
City	15.3	100.0
Hospital	20.8	100.0
Nonorientation items		
Serial 7s (to 79)	97.2	50.0
"World" spelled backward	94.4	61.8
Recall of all three items	97.2	43.1
Recall of at least two items	80.6	74.3
Serial 7s (to 79) or "world" backward and recall of at least two items	100.0	49.3

Source: Reprinted with permission from American Geriatrics Society, "Univariate and Multivariate Analyses of the Mental State Examination" by LE Klein et al in *Journal of the American Geriatrics Society* (1985;33:483–488).

Cognitive Capacity Screen

In one study, a 30-question Cognitive Capacity Screen was used for the detection of cognitive impairment in patients with medical illness (Exhibit 2–5). Patients with scores less than 20 (maximum score of 30) were more likely to meet clinical criteria for dementia. A low test score could reflect a condition other than dementia, of course, such as a low educational level. Conversely, a high test score did not rule out the possibility of a focal abnormality. Most psychiatric patients tested scored greater than 20 on the test. The Cognitive Capacity Screen is a bit more cumbersome than the SPMSQ or the MMSE, but it includes some areas not tested by other instruments such as abstraction ability (questions 18 and 19 deal with similarities).

A high proportion of hospitalized patients given the Cognitive Capacity Screen were found to be impaired (indicated by a score of less than 20). The same study found that 11 patients in the control group (18%) also scored less than 20; however, when these patients were examined carefully, only one met the criteria for dementia.[108] The investigators did not examine the patients with normal scores to see if any demented patients were missed.

On a neuropsychologic service, the Cognitive Capacity Screen had a sensitivity of 49% and a specificity of 90%.[98] The sensitivity was increased when the ex-

Exhibit 2–5 Cognitive Capacity Screen

1. What day of the week is this?
2. What month?
3. What day of the month?
4. What year?
5. What place is this?
6. Repeat the numbers 8 7 2.
7. Say them backward.
8. Repeat these numbers: 6 3 7 1.
9. Listen to these numbers: 6 9 4. Count 1 through 10 out loud, then repeat 6 9 4. (Help if needed. Then use numbers 5 7 3).
10. Listen to these numbers: 8 1 4 3. Count 1 through 10 out loud, then repeat 8 1 4 3.
11. Beginning with Sunday, say the days of the week backward.
12. 9 plus 3 is?
13. Add 6 (to the previous answer or "to 12").
14. Take away 5 ("from 18").

Repeat these words after me and remember them; I will ask for them later: HAT, CAR, TREE, TWENTY-SIX.

15. The opposite of fast is slow. The opposite of up is _____ .
16. The opposite of large is _____ .
17. The opposite of hard is _____ .
18. An orange and a banana are both fruits. Red and blue are both _____ .
19. A penny and a dime are both _____ .
20. What were those words I asked you to remember? (HAT)
21. (CAR)
22. (TREE)
23. (TWENTY-SIX)
24. Take away 7 from 100, then take away 7 from what is left and keep going: 100 minus 7 is ____ .
25. Minus 7 ____ .
26. Minus 7 ____ . (Write down answers; check correct subtraction of 7)
27. Minus 7 ____ .
28. Minus 7 ____ .
29. Minus 7 ____ .
30. Minus 7 ____ .

Total correct (maximum score: 30) ____ .

Source: Reprinted with permission from "Screening for Organic Mental Syndromes in the Medically Ill" by J Jacobs et al in *Annals of Internal Medicine* (1977;86:40–46), Copyright © 1977, American College of Physicians.

amination was combined with a Memory for Designs test, which identified the patients with right hemispheric lesions missed by the Cognitive Capacity Screen. It was suggested that the Cognitive Capacity Screen tends to miss right hemispheric lesions (only two of the seven patients with such lesions were detected by the test).

Patients with diffuse brain injury may be easier to detect with screening instruments, since patients with focal lesions may have deficits that the test does not aid in identifying.

The propensity to miss structural lesions was emphasized in a study comparing results on the Cognitive Capacity Screen with those found through neurologic examination. The sensitivity in consecutive admissions to a neurologic service was 73%, specificity 90%.[109] The predictive value of a positive test result was 93%, that of a negative test result 67%. Of nine patients with a false-negative test, five were found to have a moderate degree of dementia, and all nine had focal (or multifocal) cerebral disease, such as a brain tumor or abscess. Seven of these patients had obvious neurologic deficits, such as hemiparesis.

Kokmen Short Test of Mental Status

The Kokmen Short Test of Mental Status (Exhibit 2–6) attempts to sample a wide range of intellectual tasks, including some not tested by the SPMSQ and the MMSE, such as abstraction.[37] This assessment instrument was given to 93 nondemented patients on a general neurologic consult service and to 87 demented patients living at home. The latter group included 67 patients with Alzheimer's disease. When a score of 29 points or less was used to classify a patient as demented (total maximum score is 38), the sensitivity was 95.5% and the specificity was 91.4%. This instrument may warrant further study.

Orientation-Memory-Concentration Test

In one study, 90% of mentally unimpaired elderly persons taking a six-item Orientation-Memory-Concentration Test (Exhibit 2–7) had a weighted error score of 6 or less.[110] Weighted error scores of 10 or more were consistent with the presence of dementia in most patients. The memory phrase and the months backward questions are among the first items to be answered wrong as dementia develops. This certainly is an example of a test that is short and convenient to use by primary care practitioners; however, it may be too easy for most outpatients.

Category Fluency

The test of category fluency, or the set test, is a simple test in which the patient is asked to name as many items as he or she can in each of four sets or categories.[111] The four sets are fruits, animals, colors, and towns. A maximum of 10 is allowed in each set, for a maximum score of 40. The test is not timed. A score of less than

Exhibit 2–6 The Kokmen Short Test of Mental Status

Orientation
Full name, address, building, city, state, day of the week or month, month, year. Score one point for each correct response.
Maximum: 8

Attention
Digit repetition (start with five, go to six and then seven if correct). Record the best performance and score the number of digits repeated forward correctly.
Maximum: 7

Learning
Remember the following: apple, Mr. Johnson, charity, tunnel. Give a maximum of four trials to learn all words and record the number of words learned and the number of trials to learn them. Score one point per word learned but subtract one less than the number of trials to do so from the number of words learned.
Maximum: 4

Arithmetic Calculation
Do the following: 5 times 13, 65 minus 7, 58 divided by 2, and 11 plus 29. Score one point for each correct answer.
Maximum: 4

Abstraction
How are the following alike? An orange and a banana, a horse and a dog, a table and a bookcase. Score one point for each definitely abstract answer.
Maximum: 3

Information
Who is the President now?
Who was the first President?
How many weeks are there in a year?
Define "island."
Score one point for each correct answer.
Maximum: 4

Construction
Draw the face of a clock showing 11:15 and copy a picture of a three dimensional cube (which the patient may view while copying). Score, for each drawing, two points for an adequate conceptual drawing, one for a less than complete drawing, and zero if the patient is unable to perform the task.
Maximum: 4

Recall
Recall the four items from the learning task. Score one point for each word recalled.
Maximum: 4

Source: Adapted with permission from Kokmen E, et al, *Mayo Clinics Proceedings* (1987;62:282–283), Copyright © 1987, Mayo Foundation.

Exhibit 2–7 Orientation-Memory-Concentration Test

Items	Maximum Error	Score	Weight	Total
1. What year is it now?	1	_____	× 4	_____
2. What month is it now?	1	_____	× 3	_____
Memory phrase. Repeat this phrase after me: John Brown, 42 Market Street, Chicago				
3. About what time is it? (within one hour)	1	_____	× 3	_____
4. Count backward from 20 to 1.	2	_____	× 2	_____
5. Say the months in reverse order.	2	_____	× 2	_____
6. Repeat the memory phrase.	5	_____	× 2	_____
			Total score:	_____

Score one point for each incorrect response; maximum weighted error score equals 28. Over 90% of normal elders have a weighted score of 6 or less. Scores greater than 10 are suggestive of mental impairment.

Source: American Journal of Psychiatry (1983;140:739), Copyright © 1983, the American Psychiatric Association. Reprinted by permission.

15 is abnormal, and in one study 80% of demented elderly persons scored in this range. Conversely, no one with an affective disorder scored less than 15, and only 2 of 146 ostensibly normal elders did so (1%). These rates compare favorably with those of the tests described above.

The value of the set test was demonstrated in a University of Iowa study.[112] Eight psychologic tests were given to a group of normal elders and to a group with a diagnosis of dementia. The investigators then proceeded to determine which tests best differentiated the two groups. Two tasks stood out as especially helpful for identifying persons with dementia. One task involved remembering designs, and the other was a variation of the set test (the production of a list of words beginning with a given target letter).

Presented as a "school-type" test included as part of the examination of the nervous system, the set test would seem to be less likely to offend most elderly patients.

Mattis Dementia Rating Scale

Most of the tools used to screen for dementia help identify patients with mental impairment but do not indicate the degree of impairment. All demented persons score uniformly poorly, and categorization into types or levels of dementia is not possible. Chapter 3 examines some instruments used in the assessment of dementia that combine aspects of the mental state instruments discussed previously and the functional assessment instruments discussed below (see Figure 1–1).

Mental status assessment instruments exhibit threshold or ceiling effects, as mentioned earlier. Patients beyond a certain level of severity of dementia score the same despite some differences in severity. If the population tested has a predominance of severely demented patients, for example, an instrument will not be useful for tracking changes if all severely affected patients perform equally poorly. By the same token, in a population of relatively well elders, a test that is too easy will not help identify mildly demented patients, who may be able to perform well on an easy test but have difficulties when the tasks are made more discriminating.

The Mattis Dementia Rating Scale is intended to be useful over a broad range of impairment.[38] It may provide a compromise between extensive neuropsychologic batteries and brief screening measures such as the SPMSQ and the MMSE. As a tool for primary care, however, its administration, because of its length, requires a fairly motivated physician or office staff.

The Mattis Dementia Rating Scale is organized so that satisfactory performance on an initial task presumes adequate performance on all tasks within that section. For this reason, administration may take 30 to 45 minutes for a patient with dementia, whereas a normal elderly person can complete the entire test in 10 to 15 minutes. A sample question from the battery is shown in Figure 2–2. It is suggested that this scale will reveal changes over time and can be used for following the course of dementia.[38] The Neurobehavioral Cognitive Status Examination is a shorter instrument that tests numerous domains and employs the strategy of skipping sections if stem questions are answered correctly.[113,114]

Scores on the Mattis Dementia Rating Scale range from 0 to 144. Normal persons with Wechsler Adult Intelligence Scale IQ greater than 85 and with average memory abilities score above 140 on the Mattis Dementia Rating Scale, according to the originator. Some of the control subjects in one study, however, scored less than 140 (range 126 to 139), suggesting that a cutoff of 140 may be too high.[115] Another explanation is that the scale was sensitive to cognitive decline previously undetected in these subjects.

Summary of Mental Status Assessment

Assessing mental status of patients is important, especially on initial work-up for an older adult admitted to a hospital or nursing home, and whenever behavior, mental status, or level of functioning is a cause for concern. Changes in mental status can be more confidently assessed when a baseline has been established.

Question regarding "graphomotor" ability:

2a. Copy:

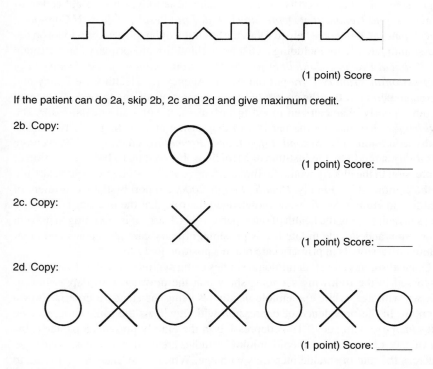

(1 point) Score _____

If the patient can do 2a, skip 2b, 2c and 2d and give maximum credit.

2b. Copy:

(1 point) Score: _____

2c. Copy:

(1 point) Score: _____

2d. Copy:

(1 point) Score: _____

Figure 2–2 Sample question from the Mattis Dementia Rating Scale. *Source:* Excerpted from *Geriatric Psychiatry* (pp 108–110) by L Bellak and TB Karasu (Eds) with permission of Grune & Stratton Inc, © 1976.

Assessment of mental status must be considered within the context of the patient's functional status (see Chapter 3), the physical examination (especially vision and hearing limitations), the history from an informant (see Chapter 7), and the total clinical picture. Mental status questionnaires can be used in combination with the written parts of the mental status examination to provide a record of a patient's performance for the medical chart; the record can then be used for following the progression of cognitive impairment or as a baseline measurement. Some patients will need more careful delineation of mental status and would benefit from formal neuropsychological testing. The reader is referred elsewhere for more detailed discussion of the evaluation of cognitive impairment.[33,61,65,116–119]

ASSESSMENT OF MOOD

The mood disorders include major depression, dysthymia, and bipolar (manic-depressive) disorder. Mood is to affect as climate is to weather.[52] Publication of *Diagnosis and Treatment of Depression in Late Life: Results of the NIH Consensus Development Conference* helped focus the attention of health care providers on depression in late life by including a chapter highlighting the primary care setting.[31] The *Clinical Practice Guidelines for the Detection, Diagnosis, and Treatment of Depression in Primary Care* put out by the Agency for Health Care Policy and Research point out that the course of major depression among the elderly, as well as other poorly characterized mood disturbances, is not well understood.[120] The *Guidelines* also indicate the barriers to diagnosing and treating elderly persons with depression. *The Second Fifty Years: Promoting Health and Preventing Disability,* a report by the Institute of Medicine, observed that a better definition of depression in the elderly would facilitate effective studies of depression in late life in the community.[121] Finally, *Healthy People 2000,* a report by the Department of Health and Human Services, acknowledged the role that the primary care sector plays in maintaining the health of older persons.[122] Clearly, if intervening to prevent depression and suicide in late life is possible, primary care physicians and other health professionals in primary care are in a position to do so.[123,124]

Clinical studies and epidemiologic studies using symptoms scales, like the ones discussed in the following sections, show that the prevalence of depression *increases* with age, while epidemiologic studies using the standard criteria show a *decrease* in the prevalence of depression with age.[125] At the same time, suicide rates *increase* with age.[126] Thus depression in the elderly presents a paradox; the prevalence of depression, if epidemiologic studies are correct, decreases with age, whereas the rate of suicide increases with age. While many factors contribute to suicide in the aged, it seems that (1) the criteria for major depression are *not age specific;* (2) *medical problems* and functional impairment contribute to preoccupation with death and suicide in the elderly; and (3) *hopelessness,* not sadness, may be more pertinent in predicting suicide risk.

Older patients may not feel comfortable discussing concerns of a "psychological" nature with their physicians. An elderly patient may believe raising such concerns is an imposition on the physician, who should be occupied with "real" problems. Therefore, the primary care provider, who has an intimate knowledge of the patient and family, should assess the patient for the possibility of depression. Asking about feelings indicates to the patient that feelings are appropriate subjects for discussion and are not a waste of time. Older adults may view a psychological problem as a sign of weakness, as something to be ashamed of, or as an indication they are "crazy."[127]

Some studies indicate that screening for depression may be useful because recognition by the physician leads to attention to the problem and treatment or referral.[128–131] German and colleagues,[132] working in a general medical outpatient setting, screened patients of all ages using the General Health Questionnaire (GHQ).[132] Feedback regarding a randomized group of patients, consisting of the GHQ scores and their interpretation, was given to the physicians-in-training. Patients were examined six months later. The screening procedure resulted in a significantly increased rate of detection only for the patients aged 65 years and older (63% recognition among the patients for whom the doctor received feedback regarding GHQ scores versus 41% for the patients for whom no feedback was given). There was a trend toward greater efforts to manage depression among the group for whom the doctor received feedback. The resident physicians did not receive any special training to improve skills in detection and management of depression.[132] This study adds weight to the argument that screening for depression among older patients in general medical outpatient settings may be worthwhile.

The diagnostic features of a major depressive episode are delineated in the *DSM-IV* and are reproduced in Table 2–8.[52] These symptoms of depression should be sought in the complete evaluation but especially when mental impairment is a consideration or at the occurrence of a significant life event in which "loss" is a theme (e.g., bereavement or recent diagnosis of cancer). Has the patient felt "blue" or "down in the dumps"? Has the patient lost interest in activities that were enjoyed previously? How is the patient's "energy level"? How well is the patient sleeping? Is the patient eating? Does the patient feel useless or like life is not worth living? Does the family indicate that the patient has withdrawn from usual activities? Is the patient using alcohol, sedatives, or tranquilizers to excess?

Anxious, somatic, or hypochondriacal complaints without sadness in older patients felt to be clinically depressed have been observed by experienced clinicians.[133,134] Feelings of helplessness[135] and hopelessness[136] may be more salient in depression among older persons than among younger persons. Other aspects of depression that may be characteristic for older adults are perceived cognitive deficit[137] and irritability.[138] Anxiety symptoms may accompany depression, persisting even after the patient's mood has improved.[139] Fogel and Fretwell[133] observed that since many depressed older adults do not complain of "depression," a diagnosis of depression emphasizes a symptom that is not relevant to the experience of the older person.

An older adult with numerous somatic complaints may be depressed but may deny feeling "blue." It may then be hard to convince the patient and the family that "depression" is the diagnosis, since mood disturbance is denied by the patient. The family may misinterpret depressive symptoms as grouchiness, hostility, laziness, or mere complaining.[127,140] Hypochondriasis may serve as a plea for help, as a way to displace anxiety, as a manifestation of unresolved guilt, or as a way to manipulate the environment.[141]

In community samples, the dysphoria/anhedonia criterion for major depression was *less likely* to be endorsed by persons 65 years of age and older for the one

Table 2–8 Diagnostic Criteria for a Major Depressive Episode

A. Five (or more) of the following symptoms have been present during the same 2-week period and represent a change from previous functioning; at least one of the symptoms is either (1) depressed mood or (2) loss of interest or pleasure.
   Note: Do not include symptoms that are clearly due to a general medical condition, or mood-incongruent delusions or hallucinations.
   (1) depressed mood most of the day, nearly every day, as indicated by either subjective report (e.g., feels sad or empty) or observation made by others (e.g., appears tearful). *Note:* In children and adolescents, can be irritable mood.
   (2) markedly diminished interest or pleasure in all, or almost all, activities most of the day, nearly every day (as indicated by either subjective account or observation made by others)
   (3) significant weight loss when not dieting or weight gain (e.g., a change of more than 5% of body weight in a month), or decrease or increase in appetite nearly every day. *Note:* In children, consider failure to make expected weight gains.
   (4) insomnia or hypersomnia nearly every day
   (5) psychomotor agitation or retardation nearly every day (observable by others, not merely subjective feelings of restlessness or being slowed down)
   (6) fatigue or loss of energy nearly every day
   (7) feelings of worthlessness or excessive or inappropriate guilt (which may be delusional) nearly every day (not merely self-reproach or guilt about being sick)
   (8) diminished ability to think or concentrate, or indecisiveness, nearly every day (either by subjective account or as observed by others)
   (9) recurrent thoughts of death (not just fear of dying), recurrent suicidal ideation without a specific plan, or a suicide attempt or a specific plan for committing suicide
B. The symptoms do not meet criteria for a Mixed Episode.
C. The symptoms cause clinically significant distress or impairment in social, occupational, or other important areas of functioning.
D. The symptoms are not due to the direct physiological effects of a substance (e.g., a drug of abuse, a medication) or a general medical condition (e.g., hypothyroidism).
E. The symptoms are not better accounted for by Bereavement, i.e., after the loss of a loved one, the symptoms persist for longer than 2 months or are characterized by marked functional impairment, morbid preoccupation with worthlessness, suicidal ideation, psychotic symptoms, or psychomotor retardation.

Source: Reprinted with permission from the *Diagnostic and Statistical Manual of Mental Disorders, Fourth Edition.* Copyright © 1994 by the American Psychiatric Association.

month prior to interview, even adjusting for differences due to level of the symptoms of depression and for characteristics thought to influence the reporting of symptoms, such as educational level and gender.[142] This suggests that the criteria in use for major depression may not be "uniformly valid" across all age groups.[143]

While depression seems to decrease with age in some studies, hopelessness seems to increase with age. This is important because hopelessness, rather than dysphoria, seems to be an important concomitant of suicidal ideation and suicide.[144,145] Community surveys that permit direct age comparisons of the level of hopelessness are uncommon, but employing the Beck Hopelessness Scale, Greene[146] found a clear and statistically significant trend to increasing levels of hopelessness with advancing age in Dublin among 396 community residents. This dovetails with the work showing that dysphoria is less likely to be endorsed by persons aged 65 and older[142] because it means that to identify older persons at risk for suicide, clinicians need to be sensitive to expressions of helplessness and hopelessness. In other words, it is important to ask older patients about feelings of helplessness and hopelessness in the context of physical illness, paying close attention to depression and thoughts of death. Suicide risk may be increased among older persons who live alone, are male, or have a history of psychiatric disorders, including drug or alcohol abuse.

Depression can affect performance on mental status tests. When cognitive impairment is suspected, depression should be considered. The patient with the appearance of cognitive impairment secondary to depression remains oriented and with coaxing can perform cognitive tests. Clues that dementia may be secondary to depression include recent onset and rapid progression, a family history of depressive disorders, a personal history of affective disorders, and onset of the disorder after the age of 60 years.[75] It is helpful to recognize that depression frequently coexists with dementia: Patients can be diagnosed with both Alzheimer's dementia and depression. An observer-rated scale specifically for depression in dementia, the NIMH Dementia Mood Assessment Scale, is available.[147] Patients found to have some cognitive impairment with accompanying depression may be at risk for dementia.[148] A plausible estimate is that 20% of individuals with Alzheimer's disease suffer from a major depressive syndrome.[149,150] Treatment with antidepressants may be the only way to "prove" that a concomitant depression exists.[31,151,152] Treatment of depression could improve cognitive deficits that are mistakenly ascribed to a primary degenerative dementia and could thus improve overall functioning.[153]

The relationship between depression and physical illness and medication effects is particularly important for the elderly, since physical illness and medication use become more common with advancing age. Depression may be a direct manifestation of a physical disorder or medication, may be a reaction to the diagnosis of a chronic illness, or may coexist in a person with physical illness. For example, stroke is especially likely to result in depression if certain brain regions are injured.[154] Depression in persons with cardiovascular disease, on the other hand, may arise as a reaction to functional limitations or to anxiety over sexual issues. The classic lesion associated with depression is carcinoma of the pancreas. Other conditions are pernicious anemia (even without megaloblastic changes or anemia); hypothyroidism; hyperthyroidism; parathyroid and adrenal disease; chronic subdural hematoma; untreated congestive heart failure; systemic vasculitis; infections such as hepatitis, influenza, and encephalitis; drug toxicity from drugs like propranolol and diazepam; and alcoholism.[20,61,77,155]

An argument can be made that some standardized instrument should be used to screen older patients for affective disorders (especially in relation to stressful life events such as institutionalization) in the same way that tests are used to assess cognitive impairment.[156] The instrument might even be used to assess the mood of caregivers who themselves are elderly.[157] The following sections discuss several brief instruments that can be used to uncover depression or psychologic distress.

OTHER PSYCHIATRIC DISORDERS

Dementia and depression have been emphasized in this chapter because these disorders are common in geriatric practice; however, older persons are subject to other psychiatric disorders. Anxiety disorders, alcoholism, and misuse of prescription drugs are not well studied among older adults. Alcohol and drug misuse will be addressed in Chapter 7. Anxiety disorders were among the more common psychiatric disorders found in the Epidemiologic Catchment Area Program.[158] The co-occurrence of anxiety symptoms and depression may explain why depressed older persons tend to be prescribed anxiolytics and hypnotics.[159–161]

DEPRESSION SCALES

Symptom scales can be useful for screening for depression or general psychologic distress. Consideration must be given to two dimensions when trying to define depression: symptom patterns and severity. "Symptom pattern" refers to the type of symptoms that form the items of the scale, for example, somatic complaints, hopelessness, or irritability. When items in a scale are summed to obtain a score, the implicit assumption is that the symptoms are given equal weight. Persons with higher scores are assumed to be more depressed, but this does not necessarily account for the severity of symptoms the patient experiences. While clinical judgment remains paramount, the scales can assist in determining whether the patient is making satisfactory progress or needs further assessment or referral. Finally, when scales are used, the time frame for the assessment (e.g., "in the past two weeks") should be specified.

Geriatric Depression Scale

The Geriatric Depression Scale (GDS) has been recommended for clinical use by the Institute of Medicine,[121] and is included as a routine part of comprehensive geriatric assessment in the Core Curriculum for Geriatrics.[162] Introduced over a decade ago,[163] the GDS is being used increasingly in research on depression in the elderly.

The GDS (Exhibit 2–8) is a questionnaire consisting of 30 items to be answered simply yes or no, a considerable simplification over scales that use a five-category response set. The questionnaire is scored by assigning one point for each answer that matches the yes or no in the parentheses following the written question. A score of 10 or 11 is usually used as the threshold to separate patients into depressed and nondepressed groups.

Exhibit 2–8 Geriatric Depression Scale

1. Are you basically satisfied with your life? (no)
2. Have you dropped many of your activities and interests? (yes)
3. Do you feel that your life is empty? (yes)
4. Do you often get bored? (yes)
5. Are you hopeful about the future? (no)
6. Are you bothered by thoughts that you just cannot get out of your head? (yes)
7. Are you in good spirits most of the time? (no)
8. Are you afraid that something bad is going to happen to you? (yes)
9. Do you feel happy most of the time? (no)
10. Do you often feel helpless? (yes)
11. Do you often get restless and fidgety? (yes)
12. Do you prefer to stay home at night, rather than go out and do new things? (yes)
13. Do you frequently worry about the future? (yes)
14. Do you feel that you have more problems with memory than most? (yes)
15. Do you think it is wonderful to be alive now? (no)
16. Do you often feel downhearted and blue? (yes)
17. Do you feel pretty worthless the way you are now? (yes)
18. Do you worry a lot about the past? (yes)
19. Do you find life very exciting? (no)
20. Is it hard for you to get started on new projects? (yes)
21. Do you feel full of energy? (no)
22. Do you feel that your situation is hopeless? (yes)
23. Do you think that most persons are better off than you are? (yes)
24. Do you frequently get upset over little things? (yes)
25. Do you frequently feel like crying? (yes)
26. Do you have trouble concentrating? (yes)
27. Do you enjoy getting up in the morning? (no)
28. Do you prefer to avoid social gatherings? (yes)
29. Is it easy for you to make decisions? (no)
30. Is your mind as clear as it used to be? (no)

Score one point for each response that matches the yes or no answer after the question.

Source: Adapted with permission from "Development and Validation of a Geriatric Depression Screening Scale: A Preliminary Report" by J A Yesavage and TL Brink in *Journal of Psychiatric Research* (1983;17:41), Copyright © 1983, Pergamon Journals Ltd.

The GDS was devised by choosing from 100 statements felt by its developers to relate to seven common characteristics of depression in later life.[163,164] In particular, the 100 items could be grouped *a priori* into several domains: (1) somatic concern, (2) lowered affect, (3) cognitive impairment, (4) feelings of discrimination, (5) impaired motivation, (6) lack of future orientation, and (7) lack of self-esteem.[163] Based on administration of the items to 46 depressed and normal elders, the best 30 items were selected by noting their correlation to the total score (the total number of the 100 items present). Somatic symptoms such as anorexia and insomnia did not correlate highly with the total score and were dropped from the final instrument. The GDS was then administered to 20 "normal" elders and 51 elders who were in treatment for depression to evaluate the performance of the new 30-item instrument. Using a cutoff score of 11 or above to designate depressed individuals, the test was 84% sensitive and 95% specific for the diagnosis of depression.[163] Subsequent studies have demonstrated the value of the GDS.[165–171]

Persons with dementia were excluded from the formative studies, yet Brink was the first to suggest that the GDS may have uncertain validity in the presence of dementia.[172] Insensitivity of the GDS in the setting of dementia was suggested by a study of patients from a comprehensive evaluation clinic.[173] A total of 72 patients with Alzheimer's disease were compared to 70 cognitively intact patients. Overall, the GDS was found to be useful in the detection of depression, but for a demented group the GDS performance was no better than chance. For the patients with dementia there was no cutoff that yielded a sensitivity and specificity greater than 65%. Another study by Burke and colleagues[174] did not show any difference in the performance of patients with cognitive impairment.[175] In this study, the diagnoses were obtained prospectively (i.e., after the GDS was administered). The authors explain the discrepancy between the studies as due to differences in the case ascertainment. Despite memory impairment, demented patients in this particular study often were consistent in their responses to questions about depression; however, demented patients may deny symptoms of depression in the same way they deny memory difficulties.[175]

Kafonek and associates[176] studied the GDS at an academic nursing home. Of 169 eligible admissions, 134 gave consent for the study, and 70 completed the examination. Patients were classified as depressed or not by a psychiatrist using *DSM-III* criteria and blinded to the results of the GDS. A clinical examination of the patients found 59% to be demented, 19% to be delirious, and 21% to be depressed. Using a cutoff of 13/14, the GDS was 47% sensitive and 75% specific for the diagnosis of depression for the patients as a group. Importantly, the investigators found that GDS sensitivity was markedly diminished in the subset that scored less than 24 on the MMSE. In the study, sensitivity dropped from 75% in the patient subset scoring normally on the MMSE to 25% in the subset scoring in the abnormal range. In other words, the GDS may not be suitable for detecting depression in the presence of dementia (which is a common type of mental impairment in nursing homes).

Finally, Parmelee and associates[177] examined 708 patients of mean age 84 years and found that 43% had symptoms of depression, and 12% met *DSM-III-R* criteria for major depression, even among patients with cognitive impairment. Their paper sets forth very clearly the thorough attempts made at verifying diagnostic accuracy and the reasons for nonparticipation. The GDS showed good agreement with observer ratings of depression whether or not the patient was demented. The investigators felt that the GDS gave reliable data as long as cognitive deficits were not so severe as to preclude comprehension of the questions.

A short version of the GDS has been published.[178] The 15 questions of the shorter version are 1–4, 7–9, 10, 12, 14, 15, 17, and 21–23. Scores of 5 or more may indicate depression, according to the authors. Volunteers ($n = 81$) from a continuing care community and a foster grandparent program were randomized to be tested first using either the long GDS form or the short GDS form and then, two weeks later, the alternative instrument.[179] The correlation coefficient for the scores on the two instruments was 0.66. Using the GDS short form, Cwikel and Ritchie[180] interviewed 285 community respondents aged 65 and older, and a subset of 71 were examined by a clinician. In a preliminary study of 20 cases and 20 controls, the best sensitivity and specificity were attained using a threshold of 6/7. With this threshold, the sensitivity was 72% and specificity was 57% for a *DSM-III* diagnosis of major depression. Persons without formal education were more likely to score in the depressed range on the GDS short form. It remains to be seen how specific the GDS is in regard to "geriatric" depression and how specific in regard to depression as opposed to general psychologic distress; however, the GDS can be usefully applied in general medical settings.

Zung Self-Rating Depression Scale

The Zung Self-Rating Depression Scale (Exhibit 2–9) comprises 10 "positive" and 10 "negative" statements.[181] The statements are answered "a little of the time," "some of the time," "a good part of the time," or "most of the time." The responses are scored from 1 to 4 and in such a way that a higher score indicates greater depression. The score may be expressed as a percentage of 80, which is the maximum score attainable.

The Zung Self-Rating Depression Scale has been validated for a university outpatient psychiatric population.[182,183] Elderly persons apparently score higher than other groups.[184] In one study, community-dwelling elders without psychiatric impairment had a score similar to that which would be considered "borderline" for the population as a whole.[185] Eighty-eight percent of patients with the diagnosis of

Exhibit 2–9 The Zung Self-Rating Depression Scale

1. (−) I feel down-hearted and blue.
2. (+) Morning is when I feel the best.
3. (−) I have crying spells or feel like it.
4. (−) I have trouble sleeping at night.
5. (+) I eat as much as I used to.
6. (+) I still enjoy sex.
7. (−) I notice that I am losing weight.
8. (−) I have trouble with constipation.
9. (−) My heart beats faster than usual.
10. (−) I get tired for no reason.
11. (+) My mind is as clear as it used to be.
12. (+) I find it easy to do the things I used to.
13. (−) I am restless and can't keep still.
14. (+) I feel hopeful about the future.
15. (−) I am more irritable than usual.
16. (+) I find it easy to make decisions.
17. (+) I feel that I am useful and needed.
18. (+) My life is pretty full.
19. (−) I feel that others would be better off if I were dead.
20. (+) I still enjoy the things I used to do.

Statements are answered "a little of the time," "some of the time," "a good part of the time," or "most of the time." The responses are given a score of 1 to 4, arranged so that the higher the score, the greater the depression: the statements designated with (+) are given "1" for response "most of the time," while those with (−) are given a "4" for "most of the time"

Source: Adapted with permission from *Archives of General Psychiatry* (1965;12:65), Copyright © 1965, American Medical Association.

depression by psychiatric examination had a score of 50 or greater, and 88% of patients who were not depressed had a score less than 50.[184,186]

In a study that compared the Zung Self-Rating Depression Scale with psychiatric examination, the scale's sensitivity was 77% and the specificity was 82%. The predictive value of a positive test (for this study, a cutoff of 60 was used) was 65%; for a negative test, it was 89%.[187] The Zung scale contains more "physical" symptoms than other scales, and older adults, even when not depressed, tend to score higher than younger adults.[184]

General Health Questionnaire

The General Health Questionnaire (GHQ) is a 60-item self-administered instrument whose purpose is to detect the presence of psychiatric distress.[188] A scaled version (Exhibit 2–10) has been devised; it consists of 28 items testing four gen-

Exhibit 2–10 Items from the Scaled US Version of the General Health Questionnaire

---

A. *Somatic symptoms*
   A1. Been feeling in need of some medicine to pick you up?
   A2. Been feeling in need of a good tonic?
   A3. Been feeling run down and out of sorts?
   A4. Felt that you are ill?
   A5. Been getting any pains in your head?
   A6. Been getting a feeling of tightness or pressure in your head?
   A7. Been having hot or cold spells?
B. *Anxiety and insomnia*
   B1. Lost much sleep over worry?
   B2. Had difficulty staying asleep?
   B3. Felt constantly under strain?
   B4. Been getting edgy and bad-tempered?
   B5. Been getting scared or panicky for no reason?
   B6. Found everything getting on top of you?
   B7. Been feeling nervous and uptight all the time?
C. *Social dysfunction*
   C1. Been managing to keep yourself busy and occupied?
   C2. Been taking longer over the things you do?
   C3. Felt on the whole you were doing things well?
   C4. Been satisfied with the way you have carried out your tasks?
   C5. Felt that you are playing a useful part in things?
   C6. Felt capable of making decisions about things?
   C7. Been able to enjoy your normal day to day activities?
D. *Depression*
   D1. Been thinking of yourself as a worthless person?
   D2. Felt that life is entirely hopeless?
   D3. Felt that life isn't worth living?
   D4. Thought of the possibility that you might do away with yourself?
   D5. Found at times you couldn't do anything because your nerves were too bad?
   D6. Found yourself wishing you were dead and away from it all?
   D7. Found that the idea of taking your own life kept coming into your mind?

There are four responses for each question: score 1 for either of the two answers consistent with depression and 0 for the other two.

Source: Adapted from *Psychological Medicine* (1979;9:139–145), Copyright © 1979, Cambridge University Press.

---

eral categories (7 questions each): somatic symptoms, anxiety and insomnia, social dysfunction, and depression. The GHQ is unusual in that it was developed specifically for use in the primary care setting.

Using the GHQ, respondents rate the presence of anxious and depressive symptoms "over the past few weeks" into one of four categories: "not at all" (coded 1), "no more than usual" (coded 2), "more than usual" (coded 3), or "much more" (coded 4). Goodchild and Duncan-Jones[189] recommended a modified scoring method in which certain symptoms rated "no more than usual" are considered positive responses, reasoning that the GHQ may otherwise fail to detect *chronic* neurotic illness in persons screened for psychologic distress in general medical settings.

In a British general practice, using a score of 4 or 5 as a cutoff (higher scores indicated psychiatric illness), the scale exhibited an 88% sensitivity (88% of the patients with a psychiatric disorder were correctly classified) and an 84% specificity (84% of the normal patients were correctly classified).[190] Similar results were obtained in an American general practice: when compared with the examination of a psychiatrist who did not know the result of the General Health Questionnaire, the sensitivity was 86% and the specificity was 77%.[191]

As mentioned previously, the use of a screening instrument to detect depression in primary medicine can help increase awareness of depression.[158] Contrary to expectations, elderly patients as a group did not have any more somatic symptoms on the scale than did the younger subjects. Despite the use of idioms such as "strung up" and "keyed up," the GHQ appears to be sensitive to both anxiety and depression in outpatients and has been used all over the world.[130,131,192-200]

Beck Depression Inventory

The Beck Depression Inventory (BDI) contains questions on 21 characteristics associated with depression: mood, pessimism, sense of failure, satisfaction, guilt, sense of punishment, disappointment in oneself, self accusations, self-punitive wishes, crying spells, irritability, social withdrawal, indecisiveness, body image, function at work, sleep disturbance, fatigue, appetite disturbance, weight loss, preoccupation with health, and loss of libido.[201,202] It is administered by an interviewer, although it has been adapted for use as a self-administered instrument. The items were selected on the basis of extensive clinical work with depressed patients. Individual items are scored as 0, 1, 2, or 3. As reported in a study by Beck and associates, a score greater than 21 was indicative of severe depression, with about 75% sensitivity and 92% specificity; the value of a positive test in that population (only 5% of the subjects were over 55 years of age) was 75%, and that of a negative test was 92%.[203] Compared with the *DSM-III* criteria for depression, the instrument was 100% sensitive (no missed cases) and 90% specific when a cutoff score of 10 was used to indicate depression in an adult population with a mean age of about 40 years.[204]

Older adults participating in a psychiatric inpatient program were administered the Beck Depression Inventory with good results. Using a score of 11 or greater as indicative of depression, the instrument had a 93% sensitivity and an 81% specificity. The predictive value of a positive test was 93%.[205] Medically ill older adults over the age of 60 years were administered the BDI on referral to a geriatric clinic. With a cutoff score of 10, the BDI was 89% sensitive and 82% specific when compared with a standardized diagnostic interview.[168]

In a study involving 526 patients in a primary care medical setting, a cutoff score of 13 was used as indicative of depression; with this cutoff score, the sensitivity was 79% and the specificity was 77% for all age groups.[206] The authors suggested using a cutoff score of 10 despite the greater number of false-positive results in order to avoid missing any cases of depression. In another study, a cutoff score of 10 was used for a group of 31 elderly medical outpatients; the BDI proved to be 89% sensitive and 82% specific as regards the detection of depression.[168] In a study population with a prevalence of depression estimated at about 12%, using 10 as a cutoff score was estimated to miss few depressed subjects.[156]

A short version of the Beck Depression Inventory (the 21 items are reduced to 13) was shown to identify cases of depression as well as the longer instrument. This self-administered 13-item Beck Depression Inventory takes 5 minutes to complete. The questions are identical to those in the larger instrument except that the order of the responses is reversed—the patient reads the most negative statements first. Scores of 5 to 7 are consistent with mild depression, scores of 8 to 15 indicate moderate depression, and scores of 16 or greater indicate severe depression.[202]

The number of responses for each item in the Beck instruments is a potential source of confusion to the older patient, especially when some degree of mental impairment is present. Like with other instruments, elderly persons with numerous somatic complaints and difficulties may answer the items in such a way as to reflect these multiple physical complaints rather than depression. The value of a positive test could be lower in a primary care population, where the prevalence of major depression would presumably be lower than among the patients of a psychiatric practice.[156]

Center for Epidemiologic Studies Depression Scale

The Center for Epidemiologic Studies Depression Scale (CES-D; Exhibit 2–11) was developed by the Center for Epidemiologic Studies at the National Institute of Mental Health for use in studies of depression in community samples.[207–209] The CES-D contains 20 items. Respondents are asked to report the amount of time they have experienced symptoms during the past week. Typically, a threshold of 17 and above is taken as defining "caseness,"[210] although higher cutoff points (e.g., 24 and above) have been suggested.[211] Among patients in a medical setting, an inordinate number of false positives was generated with higher thresholds on the CES-D, but a higher threshold, of 27, was associated with greater specificity.[212] The CES-D did not seem to be biased by somatic complaints in a large community survey of persons aged 55 years and older.[213]

Exhibit 2–11 Center for Epidemiologic Studies Depression Scale

INSTRUCTIONS FOR QUESTIONS: Below is a list of the ways you might have felt or be-
haved. Please tell me how often you have felt this way during the past week.

> Rarely or None of the Time (Less than 1 Day)
> Some or a Little of the Time (1–2 Days)
> Occasionally or a Moderate Amount of Time (3–4 Days)
> Most or All of the Time (5–7 Days)

During the past week:
1. I was bothered by things that usually don't bother me.
2. I did not feel like eating; my appetite was poor.
3. I felt that I could not shake off the blues even with help from my family or friends.
4. I felt that I was just as good as other people.
5. I had trouble keeping my mind on what I was doing.
6. I felt depressed.
7. I felt that everything I did was an effort.
8. I felt hopeful about the future.
9. I thought my life had been a failure.
10. I felt fearful.
11. My sleep was restless.
12. I was happy.
13. I talked less than usual.
14. I felt lonely.
15. People were unfriendly.
16. I enjoyed life.
17. I had crying spells.
18. I felt sad.
19. I felt that people dislike me.
20. I could not get "going."

Source: Center for Epidemiologic Studies, National Institute of Mental Health.

Zimmerman and Coryell called attention to the lack of correlation to *DSM* criteria and proposed a revision that would include criteria such as suicidal ideation
and psychomotor agitation or retardation.[214]

Other Instruments

The focus of this chapter has been on questionnaires that can be used in outpatient, inpatient, and nursing home settings. Most of these instruments have been
employed in research as well. Several other instruments that are used primarily in

research will be mentioned here. The Diagnostic Interview Schedule (DIS) was developed for the National Institute of Mental Health Epidemiologic Catchment Area Program.[215] The DIS is a structured interview designed to be administered by trained lay interviewers; its purpose is to check whether diagnostic criteria for disorders as defined in the *DSM* have been met. The Composite International Diagnostic Interview (CIDI) is the World Health Organization's version of the DIS. It is compatible with both the *DSM* and the *International Classification of Diseases.*[216]

The Cambridge Mental Disorders of the Elderly Examination (CAMDEX) is a multidomain instrument used in the diagnosis and quantification of dementia. A "depression severity scale" consisting of 20 items dealing with mood forms part of the first section.[95] The Canberra Interview for the Elderly (CIE) is a lay-administered interview specifically designed for assessment of elderly persons in epidemiologic research.[217,218] The SIDAM is a structured interview for the differential diagnosis of the dementias.[219]

Finally, employing informant interviews may be appropriate for research on mental disorders, especially cognitive impairment, among the aged (the Informant Questionnaire on Cognitive Decline in the Elderly is one instrument that has sometimes been used for this purpose).[220-222] The Life Chart Interview employed in the 13-year follow-up of the Baltimore sample of the Epidemiologic Catchment Area Program uses personal landmarks to fix the timing of psychopathology.[223] Additional discussion regarding cognitive and psychological assessment as well as considerations involved in research on the aged can be found in the works cited in references 86 and 224–227.

CONCLUSION

The instruments discussed in this chapter can be used in clinical settings to improve the recognition and evaluation of dementia and depression. It must be emphasized that the instruments are supplemental to clinical assessment. An abnormal score on a short mental status test may be due to something other than dementia, such as an acute confusional state (delirium), vision or hearing impairment, or low educational level. The patient must be examined carefully and appropriate historical data sought before a diagnosis of dementia is made. If dementia is diagnosed, an attempt should be made to characterize the etiology.

Regardless of the specific properties of the instrument used, the important point is to use some standardized method of mental status testing when assessing elderly persons. The assessment instruments make data collection uniform, and many have been well studied. In addition, many are brief enough to administer at intervals to assess changes in the patient's condition. Regular examinations can provide baseline data of great value, particularly at the time of nursing home placement or hospitalization.

Yet, mental status testing should be viewed as one of several facets in the assessment of elderly patients. Despite stability or deterioration in scores on cognitive tests, patients may improve in other ways, such as diminished behavioral or psychotic symptoms. For example, despite achieving the same score on the Folstein Mini-Mental State Examination as was achieved a year ago, a demented older patient might rest better at night, cause less worry to caregivers, and enjoy socializing when enrolled in a day care program.[228] This type of example does not negate the value of systematic mental status evaluation, but suggests that deficits be kept in perspective.

REFERENCES

1. Shepherd M, Cooper B, Brown AC, Kalton GW. *Psychiatric Illness in General Practice.* London: Oxford University Press, 1966.

2. Regier DA, Goldberg ID, Taube CA. The de facto US mental health services system. *Arch Gen Psychiatry* 1978;35:685–693.

3. Regier DA, Goldberg ID, Burns BJ, Hankin J, Hoeper EW, Nycz GR. Specialist/generalist division of responsibility for patients with mental disorders. *Arch Gen Psychiatry.* 1982;39:219–224.

4. Regier DA, Narrow WE, Rae DS, Manderscheid RW, Locke BZ, Goodwin FK. The de facto US mental and addictive disorders system: Epidemiologic Catchment Area prospective 1-year prevalence rates of disorders and services. *Arch Gen Psychiatry.* 1993;50:85–94.

5. Hankin J, Oktay JS. *Mental Disorder and Primary Medical Care: An Analytic Review of the Literature.* Washington, DC: Superintendent of Documents, US Government Printing Office, National Institute of Mental Health, Series D, No. 5, 1979. DHEW publication (ADM) 78-661.

6. Wilkinson G. *Overview of Mental Health Practices in Primary Care Settings, with Recommendations for Further Research.* Washington, DC: Superintendent of Documents, US Government Printing Office, National Institute of Mental Health, Series DN, No. 7, 1986. DHEW publication (ADM) 86-1467.

7. Miranda J, Hohmann AA, Attkisson CC, Larson DB, eds. *Mental Disorders in Primary Care.* San Francisco, Calif: Jossey-Bass Publishers, 1994.

8. Sager MA, Dunham NC, Schwantes A, Mecum L, Halverson K, Harlowe D. Measurement of activities of daily living in hospitalized elderly: a comparison of self-report and performance-based methods. *J Am Geriatr Soc.* 1992;40:457–462.

9. Jacobs J, Bernhard MR, Delgado A, et al. Screening for organic mental syndromes in the medically ill. *Ann Intern Med.* 1977;86:40–46.

10. McCartney JR, Palmatee LM. Assessment of cognitive deficit in geriatric patients: a study of physician behavior. *J Am Geriatr Soc.* 1985;33:467–471.

11. Williamson J, Stokoe IH, Gray S, et al. Old people at home: their unreported needs. *Lancet.* 1964;1:1117–1120.

12. Knights EB, Folstein MF. Unsuspected emotional and cognitive disturbance in medical patients. *Ann Intern Med.* 1977;87:723–724.

13. Iliffe S, Booroff A, Gallivan S, Goldenberg E, Morgan P, Haines A. Screening for cognitive impairment in the elderly using the Mini-Mental State Examination. *Br J Gen Pract.* 1990;40:277–279.

14. Cooper B, Eastwood R. *Primary Health Care and Psychiatric Epidemiology.* New York, NY: Tavistock/Routledge, 1992.

15. Cooper B, Bickel H. Population screening and the early detection of dementing disorders in old age: a review. *Psychol Med.* 1984;14:81–95.

16. Schneider LS, Reynolds CF, Lebowitz BD, Friedhoff AJ, eds. *Diagnosis and Treatment of Depression in Late Life: Results of the NIH Consensus Development Conference.* Washington, DC: American Psychiatric Association, 1994.

17. Francis J, Kapoor WN. Prognosis after hospital discharge of older medical patients with delirium. *J Am Geriatr Soc.* 1992;40:601–606.

18. Marcantonio ER, Goldman L, Mangione CM, et al. A clinical prediction rule for delirium after elective noncardiac surgery. *JAMA.* 1994;271:134–139.

19. Fields SD, MacKenzie R, Charlson ME, et al. Cognitive impairment: can it predict the course of hospitalized patients? *J Am Geriatr Soc.* 1986;34:579–585.

20. Murray AM, Levkoff SE, Wetle TT, et al. Acute delirium and functional decline in the hospitalized elderly patient. *J Gerontol.* 1993;48:M181–186.

21. Cooper JK, Mungas D, Weiler PG. Relation of cognitive status and abnormal behaviors in Alzheimer's disease. *J Am Geriatr Soc.* 1990;38:867–870.

22. Henderson AS, Huppert FA. The problem of mild dementia. *Psychol Med.* 1984;14:5–11.

23. Warshaw G. Are mental status questionnaires of clinical value in everyday office practice? An affirmative view. *J Fam Pract.* 1990;30:194–197.

24. Kapp MB, Bigot A. *Geriatrics and the Law.* New York, NY: Springer Publishing Co, 1985.

25. Broadhead WE, Blazer DG, George LK, Tse CK. Depression, disability days, and days lost from work in a prospective epidemiologic survey. *JAMA.* 1990;264:2524–2528.

26. Horwath E, Johnson J, Klerman GL, Weissman MM. Depressive symptoms as relative and attributable risk factors for first-onset major depression. *Arch Gen Psychiatry.* 1992;49:817–823.

27. Johnson J, Weissman MM, Klerman GL. Service utilization and social morbidity associated with depressive symptoms in the community. *JAMA.* 1992;267:1478–1483.

28. Pearson JL, Teri L, Reifler BV, Raskind MA. Functional status and cognitive impairment in Alzheimer's patients with and without depression. *J Am Geriatr Soc.* 1989;37:1117–1121.

29. Wells KB, Stewart A, Hays RD, et al. The functioning and well-being of depressed patients: results from the Medical Outcomes Study. *JAMA.* 1989;262:914–919.

30. NIH Consensus Development Conference on Depression in Late Life. Diagnosis and treatment of depression in late life. *JAMA.* 1992;268:1018–1024.

31. Reynolds CF, Schneider LS, Lebowitz BD, Kupfer DJ. Treatment of depression in elderly patients: guidelines for primary care. In: Schneider LS, Reynolds CF, Lebowitz BD, Friedhoff AJ, eds. *Diagnosis and Treatment of Depression in Late Life: Results of the NIH Consensus Development Conference.* Washington, DC: American Psychiatric Association, 1994:463–490.

32. Auerbach SH, Cicerone KD, Levin HS, Tranel D. What you can learn from neuropsychologic testing. *Patient Care.* July 15, 1994;28:97–116.

33. Strub RL, Black FW. *The Mental Status Examination in Neurology.* 2nd ed. Philadelphia, Penn: FA Davis Co, 1985.

34. Jones TV, Williams ME. Rethinking the approach to evaluating mental functioning of older persons: the value of careful observations. *J Am Geriatr Soc.* 1988;36:1128–1134.

35. Fry PS. *Depression, Stress, and Adaptations in the Elderly: Psychological Assessment and Intervention.* Gaithersburg, Md: Aspen Publishers, 1986.

36. Feher EP, Doody R, Pirozzolo FJ, Appel SH. Mental status assessment of insight and judgment. *Clin Geriatr Med.* 1989;5:477–498.

37. Kokmen E, Naessens JM, Offord KP. A short test of mental status: description and preliminary results. *Mayo Clin Proc.* 1987;62:281–288.

38. Mattis S. Mental status examination for organic mental syndrome in the elderly patient. In: Bellak L, Karasu TB, eds. *Geriatric Psychiatry.* New York, NY: Grune & Stratton, 1976:77–121.

39. LaRue A. Memory loss and aging: distinguishing dementia from benign senescent forgetfulness and depressive pseudodementia. *Psychiatr Clin North Am.* 1982;5:89–103.

40. Blum JE, Jarvik LF, Clark ET. Rate of change on selective tests of intelligence: a twenty-year longitudinal study of aging. *J Gerontol.* 1970;25:171–176.

41. Gallo JJ, Stanley L, Zack N, Reichel W. Multidimensional assessment of the older patient. In: Reichel W, ed. *Clinical Aspects of Aging.* 4th ed. Baltimore, Md: Williams & Wilkins, 1995:15–30.

42. Erilsen CW, Hamlin RM, Daye C. Aging adults and rate of memory scan. *Bull Psychonom Soc.* 1973;1:259–260.

43. Smith ME. Delayed recall of previously memorized material after fifty years. *J Gen Psychol.* 1963;102:3–4.

44. Grut M, Jorm AF, Fratiglioni L, Forsell Y, Viitanen M, Winblad B. Memory complaints of elderly people in a population survey: variation according to dementia stage and depression. *J Am Geriatr Soc.* 1993;41:1295–1300.

45. Crook T, Bartus RT, Ferris SH, et al. Age-associated memory impairment: Proposed diagnostic criteria and measures of clinical change: report of a National Institute of Mental Health Work Group. *Dev Neuropsychol.* 1986;2:261–276.

46. Kral VA. Senescent forgetfulness: benign and malignant. *J Can Med Assoc.* 1962;86:257–260.

47. Rediess S, Caine ED. Aging-associated cognitive changes: how do they relate to the diagnosis of dementia? *Curr Opin Psychiatry.* 1993;6:531–536.

48. Working Party of the International Psychogeriatric Association in Collaboration with the World Health Organization. Aging-associated cognitive decline. *Int Psychogeriatr.* 1994;6:63–68.

49. Blackford RC, La Rue A. Criteria for diagnosing age-associated memory impairment: proposed improvements from the field. *Dev Neuropsychol.* 1989;5:295–306.

50. Small GW, Okonek A, Mandelkern MA, et al. Age-associated memory loss: initial neuropsychological and cerebral metabolic findings of a longitudinal study. *Int Psychogeriatr.* 1994;6:23–44.

51. Huppert FA, Brayne C, O'Connor DW, eds. *Dementia and Normal Aging.* Cambridge: Cambridge University Press, 1994.

52. American Psychiatric Association. *Diagnostic and Statistical Manual of Mental Disorders, DSM-IV.* 4th ed. Washington, DC: American Psychiatric Association, 1994.

53. Blazer DG. *Depression in Late Life.* 2nd ed. St. Louis, Mo: CV Mosby, Co, 1993.

54. Damasio AR. Aphasia. *N Engl J Med.* 1992;326:531–539.

55. Wolf-Klein GP, Silverstone FA, Levy AP, Brod MS. Screening for Alzheimer's disease by clock drawing. *J Am Geriatr Soc.* 1989;37:730–737.

56. Sunderland T, Hill JL, Mellow AM, et al. Clock drawing in Alzheimer's disease: a novel measure of dementia severity. *J Am Geriatr Soc.* 1989;37:725–729.

57. Mendez MF, Ala T, Underwood KL. Development of scoring criteria for the clock drawing task in Alzheimer's disease. *J Am Geriatr Soc.* 1992;40:1095–1099.

58. Tuokko H, Hadjistavropoulos T, Miller JA, Beattie BL. The clock test: a sensitive measure to differentiate normal elderly from those with Alzheimer disease. *J Am Geriatr Soc.* 1992;40:579–584.

59. Watson YI, Arfken CL, Birge SJ. Clock completion: an objective screening test for dementia. *J Am Geriatr Soc.* 1993;41:1235–1240.

60. Shuttleworth EC. Memory function and the clinical differentiation of dementing disorders. *J Am Geriatr Soc.* 1982;30:363–366.

61. Lipowski ZJ. Delirium (acute confusional states). *JAMA.* 1987;258:1789–1792.

62. Inouye SK, van Dyck CH, Alessi CA, Balkin S, Siegal AP, Horwitz RJ. Clarifying confusion: the confusion assessment method: a new method for detection of delirium. *Ann Intern Med.* 1990;113:941–948.

62a. Albert MS, Levkoff SE, Reilly C, et al. The delirium symptom interview: an interview for the detection of delirium symptoms in hospitalized patients. *J Geriatr Psychiatry Neurol.* 1992;5:14–21.

63. Larson EB, Reifler BV, Featherstone HJ, et al. Dementia in elderly outpatients: a prospective study. *Ann Intern Med.* 1984;100:417–423.

64. Maletta GJ. The concept of "reversible" dementia: how nonreliable terminology may impair effective treatment. *J Am Geriatr Soc.* 1990;38:136–140.

65. Cummings JL, Benson DF. *Dementia: A Clinical Approach.* 2nd ed. Stoneham, Mass: Butterworth-Heinemann, 1992.

66. McKhann G, Drachman D, Folstein M, et al. Clinical diagnosis of Alzheimer's disease: Report of the NINCDS-ADRDA work group under the auspices of Department of Health and Human Services Task Force on Alzheimer's Disease. *Neurology.* 1984;34:939–944.

67. Cummings JL, Benson DF. Dementia of the Alzheimer type: an inventory of clinical features. *J Am Geriatr Soc.* 1986;34:12–19.

68. Coen RF, O'Mahoney D, Bruce I, Lawlor BA, Walsh JB, Coakley D. Differential diagnosis of dementia: a prospective evaluation of the DAT Inventory. *J Am Geriatr Soc.* 1994;42:16–20.

69. Gorelick PB, Mangone CA. Vascular dementias in the elderly. *Clin Geriatr Med.* 1991; 7:599–615.

70. Hachinski VC, Iliff LD, Zilhka E, et al. Cerebral blood flow in dementia. *Ann Neurol.* 1975;32:632–637.

71. Liston EH, LaRue A. Clinical differentiation of primary degenerative and multi-infarct dementia: a critical review of the evidence: II. Pathological studies. *Biol Psychiatry.* 1983;18:1467–1484.

72. Meyer JS, Judd BW, Tawakina T, et al. Improved cognition after control of risk factors for multi-infarct dementia. *JAMA.* 1986;256:2203–2209.

73. Roman GC. Senile dementia of the Binswanger type: a vascular form of dementia in the elderly. *JAMA.* 1987;258:1782–1788.

74. Mahler ME, Cummings JL, Tomiyasu U. Atypical dementia syndrome in an elderly man. *J Am Geriatr Soc.* 1987;35:1116–1126.

75. Whitehouse PJ. The concept of subcortical and cortical dementia: another look. *Ann Neurol.* 1986;19:1–6.

76. Clarfield AM, Larson EB. Should a major imaging procedure (CT or MRI) be required in the workup of dementia? An opposing view. *J Fam Pract.* 1990;31:405–410.

77. Beresford TP. Alcoholism in the elderly. *Int Rev Psychiatry.* 1993;5:477–483.

78. Brody JA. Aging and alcohol abuse. *J Am Geriatr Soc.* 1982;30:123–126.

79. Gottheil E, Druley KA, Skoloda TE, eds. *The Combined Problems of Alcoholism, Drug Addiction, and Aging.* Springfield, Ill: Charles C Thomas, 1985.

80. Wattis JP. Alcohol problems in the elderly. *J Am Geriatr Soc.* 1981;29:131–134.

81. Zimberg S. Alcohol abuse among the elderly. In: Carstensen LL, Edelstein BA, eds. *Handbook of Clinical Gerontology.* New York, NY: Pergamon Press, 1987:57–65.

82. Widner S, Zeichner A. Alcohol abuse in the elderly: review of epidemiology research and treatment. *Clin Gerontologist.* 1991;11:3–18.

83. Moss RJ, Miles SH. AIDS and the geriatrician. *J Am Geriatr Soc.* 1987;35:460–464.

84. Sabin TD. AIDS: the new "great imitator." Editorial. *J Am Geriatr Soc.* 1987;35:467–468.

85. Larson EB, Reifler BV, Sumi SM, et al. Diagnostic evaluation of 200 elderly outpatients with suspected dementia. *J Gerontol.* 1985;40:536–543.

86. National Center for Cost Containment. *Geropsychology Assessment Resource Guide.* Milwaukee, Wis: US Department of Commerce, National Technical Information Service, 1993.

87. Keating HJ. "Studying" for the Mini-Mental Status Exam. Letter. *J Am Geriatr Soc.* 1987;35:594–595.

88. Folstein MF, Folstein SE, McHugh PR. "Mini-Mental State": a practical method for grading the cognitive state of patients for the clinician. *J Psychiatr Res.* 1975;12:189–198.

89. Tombaugh TN, McIntyre NJ. The Mini-Mental State Examination: a comprehensive review. *J Am Geriatr Soc* 1992;40:922–935.

90. Crum RM, Anthony JC, Bassett SS, Folstein MF. Population-based norms for the Mini-Mental State Examination by age and educational level. *JAMA.* 1993;269:2386–2391.

91. Gallo JJ, Anthony JC. Misperception in the scoring of the MMSE. Letter. *Can J Psychiatry.* 1994;39:382–385.

92. Brandt J, Spencer M, Folstein M. The Telephone Instrument for Cognitive Status. *Neuropsychiatry Neuropsychol Behav Neurol.* 1988;1:11–17.

93. Tsai L, Tsuang MT. The Mini-Mental State test and computerized tomography. *Am J Psychiatry.* 1979;136:436–439.

94. Fillenbaum G. Comparison of two brief tests of organic brain impairment, the MSQ and the short portable MSQ. *J Am Geriatr Soc.* 1980;28:381–384.

95. Roth M, Tym E, Mountjoy CQ, et al. CAMDEX: a standardised instrument for the diagnosis of mental disorder in the elderly with special reference to the early detection of dementia. *Br J Psychiatry.* 1986;149:698–709.

96. Anthony JC, LeResche L, Niaz U, Von Korff M, Folstein MF. Limits of the "Mini-Mental State" as a screening test for dementia and delirium among hospital patients. *Psychol Med.* 1982;12:397–408.

97. Dick JPR, Guiloff RJ, Stewart A, et al. Mini-Mental State Examination in neurological patients. *J Neurol Neurosurg Psychiatry.* 1984;47:496–499.

98. Webster JS, Scott RR, Nunn B, et al. A brief neuropsychological screening procedure that assesses left and right hemispheric function. *J Clin Psychol.* 1984;40:237–240.

99. Kittner SJ, White LR, Farmer ME, et al. Methodological issues in screening for dementia: the problem of education adjustment. *J Chronic Dis.* 1986;39:163–170.

100. Uhlmann RF, Larson EB. Effect of education on the Mini-Mental State Examination as a screening test for dementia. *J Am Geriatr Soc.* 1991;39:876–880.

101. Pfeiffer E. A short portable mental status questionnaire for the assessment of organic brain deficit in elderly patients. *J Am Geriatr Soc.* 1975;23:433–441.

102. Kahn RL, Goldfarb AI, Pollack M. Brief objective measures for the determination of mental status in the aged. *Am J Psychiatry.* 1960;117:326–328.

103. Erkinjuntt T, Sulkava R, Wikstrom J, et al. Short Portable Mental Status Questionnaire as a screening test for dementia and delirium among the elderly. *J Am Geriatr Soc.* 1987;35:412–416.

104. Smyer MA, Hofland BF, Jonas EA. Validity study of the Short Portable Mental Status Questionnaire for the elderly. *J Am Geriatr Soc.* 1979;27:263–269.

105. Dalton JE, Pederson SL, Blom BE, et al. Diagnostic errors using the Short Portable Mental Status Questionnaire with a mixed clinical population. *J Gerontol.* 1987;42:512–514.

106. Wolber G, Romaniuk M, Eastman E, et al. Validity of the Short Portable Mental Status Questionnaire with elderly psychiatric patients. *J Consult Clin Psychol.* 1984;52:712–713.

107. Klein LE, Roca RP, McArthur J, et al. Univariate and multivariate analyses of the mental state examination. *J Am Geriatr Soc.* 1985;33:483–488.

108. Omer H, Foldes J, Toby M, et al. Screening for cognitive deficits in a sample of hospitalized geriatric patients: a re-evaluation of a brief mental status questionnaire. *J Am Geriatr Soc.* 1983;31:266–268.

109. Kaufman DM, Weinberger M, Strain JJ, et al. Detection of cognitive deficits by a brief mental status examination: the Cognitive Capacity Screening Examination. *Gen Hosp Psychiatry.* 1979;1:247–254.

110. Katzman R, Brown T, Fuld P, et al. Validation of a short orientation-memory-concentration test of cognitive impairment. *Am J Psychiatry.* 1983;140:734–739.

111. Issacs B, Kennie AT. The set test as an aid to the detection of dementia in old people. *Br J Psychiatry.* 1973;123:467–470.

112. Eslinger PJ, Damasio AR, Benson AL, et al. Neuropsychologic detection of abnormal mental decline in older persons. *JAMA.* 1985;253:670–674.

113. Kierman RJ, Mueller J, Langston JW, et al. The Neurobehavioral Cognitive Status Examination: a brief but differentiated approach to cognitive assessment. *Ann Intern Med.* 1987;107:481–485.

114. Schwamm LH, Van Dyke C, Kierman RJ, et al. The Neurobehavioral Cognitive Status Examination: comparison with the Cognitive Capacity Screening Examination and the Mini-Mental State Examination in a neurosurgical population. *Ann Intern Med.* 1987;107:486–491.

115. Vitaliano P, Brien AR, Russo J, et al. The clinical utility of the dementia rating scale for assessing Alzheimer patients. *J Chron Dis.* 1984;37:743–753.

116. Council on Scientific Affairs. Dementia. *JAMA.* 1986;256:2234–2238.

117. Arnold SE, Kumar A. Reversible dementias. *Med Clin North Am.* 1993;77:215–230.

118. Siu AL. Screening for dementia and investigating its causes. *Ann Intern Med.* 1991; 115:122–132.

119. Gugel RN. Behavioral approaches for managing patients with Alzheimer's disease and related disorders. *Med Clin North Am.* 1994;78:861–867.

120. Depression Guideline Panel. *Depression in Primary Care.* Vol. 1, *Detection and Diagnosis: Clinical Practice Guideline, Number 5.* Rockville, Md: US Department of Health and Human Services, Public Health Service, Agency for Health Care Policy and Research, 1993. AHCPR publication 93-0550.

121. Institute of Medicine. *The Second Fifty Years: Promoting Health and Preventing Disability.* Washington, DC: National Academy Press, 1992.

122. Department of Health and Human Services. *Healthy People 2000: National Health Promotion and Disease Prevention Objectives.* Washington, DC: US Government Printing Office, 1991. DHHS publication PHS 91-50213.

123. Rabins PV. Prevention of mental disorders in the elderly: Current perspectives and future prospects. *J Am Geriatr Soc.* 1992;40:727–733.

124. Conwell Y. Suicide in elderly patients. In: Schneider LS, Reynolds CF, Lebowitz BD, Friedhoff AJ, eds. *Diagnosis and Treatment of Depression in Late Life: Results of the NIH Consensus Development Conference.* Washington, DC: American Psychiatric Association, 1994:397–418.

125. Newmann JP. Aging and depression. *Psychol Aging.* 1989;4(2):150–165.

126. National Center for Health Statistics. *Vital Statistics of the United States, 1988.* Vol. 2, *Mortality.* Washington, DC: US Public Health Service, 1991. pt. A.

127. Chaisson-Stewart GM. The diagnostic dilemma. In: Chaisson-Stewart GM, ed. *Depression in the Elderly: An Interdisciplinary Approach.* New York, NY: John Wiley & Sons, 1985:18–43.

128. Johnstone A, Goldberg DP. Psychiatric screening in general practice: a controlled trial. *Lancet.* 1976;1:605–609.

129. Hoeper E, Nycz G, Cleary P, et al. Estimated prevalence of RDC mental disorder in primary care. *Int J Ment Health.* 1979;8:6–15.

130. Rand EH, Badger LW, Coggins DR. Toward a resolution of contradictions: utility of feedback from the GHQ. *Gen Hosp Psychiatry.* 1988;10:189–196.

131. Ormel J, Van den Brink W, Koeter MWJ, et al. Recognition, management and outcome of psychological disorders in primary care: a naturalistic follow-up study. *Psychol Med.* 1990;20:909–923.

132. German PS, Shapiro S, Skinner EA, et al. Detection and management of mental health problems of older patients by primary care providers. *JAMA.* 1987;257:489–493.

133. Fogel BS, Fretwell M. Reclassification of depression in the medically ill elderly. *J Am Geriatr Soc.* 1985;33:446–448.

134. Salzman C, Shader RI. Depression in the elderly: I. Relationship between depression, psychologic defense mechanisms and physical illness. *J Am Geriatr Soc.* 1978;26:253–260.

135. Depure RA, Monroe SM. Learned helplessness in the perspective of the depressive disorders: concepts and definitional issues. *Abnorm Psychol.* 1978;87:3–20.

136. Abramson LY, Metalsky GI, Alloy LB. Hopelessness depression: a theory based subtype of depression. *Psychol Rev.* 1989;96:358–372.

137. Weiss IK, Nagel CL, Aronson MK. Applicability of depression scales to the old old person. *J Am Geriatr Soc.* 1986;34:215–218.

138. Rohrbaugh RM, Siegal AP, Giller EL. Irritability as a symptom of depression in the elderly. *J Am Geriatr Soc.* 1988;36:736–738.

139. Blazer D, Hughes DC, Fowler N. Anxiety as an outcome symptom of depression in the elderly and middle-aged adults. *Int J Geriatr Psychiatry.* 1989;4:273–278.

140. Roth M. Differential diagnosis of psychiatric disorders in old age. *Hosp Pract.* July 1986:111–138.

141. Blazer D, Siegler IC. *A Family Approach to Health Care of the Elderly.* Menlo Park, Calif: Addison-Wesley Publishing Co, 1984.

142. Gallo JJ, Anthony JC, Muthen BO. Age differences in the symptoms of depression: a latent trait analysis. *J Gerontol Psychol Sci.* 1994;9:251–264.

143. Henderson AS. Does ageing protect against depression? *Soc Psychiatry Psychiatr Epidemiol.* 1994;29:107–109.

144. Beck AT, Steer RA, Beck JS, Newman CF. Hopelessness, depression, suicidal ideation, and clinical diagnosis of depression. *Suicide Life Threat Behav.* 1993;23:139–145.

145. Beck AT, Steer RA, Kovacs M. Hopelessness and eventual suicide: a 10-year prospective study of patients hospitalized with suicidal ideation. *Am J Psychiatry.* 1985;142:559–563.

146. Greene SM. Levels of measured hopelessness in the general population. *Br J Clin Psychol.* 1981;20:11–14.

147. Sunderland T, Alterman IS, Yount D, et al. A new scale for the assessment of depressed mood in demented patients. *Am J Psychiatry.* 1988;145:955–959.

148. Rabins PV, Merchant A, Nestadt G. Criteria for diagnosing reversible dementia caused by depression: validation by 2-year follow-up. *Br J Psychiatry.* 1984;144:488–492.

149. Rovner B, Broadhead J, Spencer M. Depression in Alzheimer's disease. *Am J Psychiatry.* 1989;146:350–353.

150. Wragg RE, Jeste DV. Overview of depression and psychosis in Alzheimer's disease. *Am J Psychiatry.* 1989;146:577–589.

151. Reynolds CF, Kupfer DJ, Hoch CC, et al. Two-year follow-up of elderly patients with mixed depression and dementia: clinical and electroencephalographic sleep findings. *J Am Geriatr Soc.* 1986;34:793–799.

152. Caine ED. Pseudodementia. *Arch Gen Psychiatry.* 1981;38:1359–1364.

153. Reifler BV, Larson E, Hanley R. Coexistence of cognitive impairment and depression in geriatric outpatients. *Am J Psychiatry.* 1982;139:623–626.

154. Morris PLP, Robinson RG, Raphael B. Prevalence and course of post-stroke depression in hospitalized patients. *Int J Psychiatry Med.* 1990;20:327–342.

155. Lehmann HE. Affective disorders in the aged. *Psychiatr Clin North Am.* 1982;5:27–48.

156. Kamerow DB, Campbell TL. Is screening for mental health problems worthwhile in family practice? *J Fam Pract.* 1987;25:181–187.

157. Gallo JJ. The effect of social support on depression in caregivers of the elderly. *J Fam Pract.* 1990;30:430–436.

158. German PS, Shapiro S, Skinner EA. Mental health of the elderly: use of health and mental health services. *J Am Geriatr Soc.* 1985;33:246–252.

159. Thompson TL, Moran MG, Nies AS. Psychotropic drug use in the elderly: part I. *N Engl J Med.* 1983;308:134–138.

160. Thompson TL, Moran MG, Nies AS. Psychotropic drug use in the elderly: part II. *N Engl J Med.* 1983;308:194–199.

161. Finch J. Prescription drug abuse. *Prim Care.* 1993;20:231–239.

162. Beck JC, ed. *Geriatric Review Syllabus: A Core Curriculum in Geriatric Medicine.* New York, NY: American Geriatrics Society, 1991.

163. Brink TL, Yesavage JA, Lum O, et al. Screening tests of geriatric depression. *Clin Gerontol.* 1982;1:37–43.

164. Yesavage JA, Brink TL. Development and validation of a geriatric depression screening scale: a preliminary report. *J Psychiatr Res.* 1983;17:37–49.

165. O'Riordan TG, Hayes JP, O'Neill D. The effect of mild to moderate dementia on the Geriatric Depression Scale and on the General Health Questionnaire. *Age Ageing.* 1990;19:57–61.

166. Hyer L, Blount J. Concurrent and discriminant validities of the Geriatric Depression Scale with older psychiatric patients. *Psychol Rep.* 1984;54:611–616.

167. Magni G, Shifano F, de Leo D. Assessment of depression in an elderly medical population. *J Affective Disord.* 1986;11:121–124.

168. Norris JT, Gallagher D, Wilson A, Winograd CH. Assessment of depression in geriatric medical outpatients: the validity of two screening measures. *J Am Geriatr Soc.* 1987;35:989–995.

169. Koenig HG, Meador KG, Cohen HJ. Self-rated depression scales and screening for major depression in the older hospitalized patient with medical illness. *J Am Geriatr Soc.* 1988;36:699–706.

170. Rapp SR, Parial SA, Walsh DA. Detecting depression in elderly medical inpatients. *J Consult Clin Psychol.* 1988;56:509–513.

171. Harper RG, Kotik-Harper D, Kirby H. Psychometric assessment of depression in an elderly general medical population: over- or underassessment? *J Nerv Ment Dis.* 1990;178:113–119.

172. Brink TL. Limitations of the GDS in cases of pseudodementia. *Clin Gerontol.* 1984;2:60–61.

173. Burke WJ, Houston MJ, Boust SJ. Use of the Geriatric Depression Scale in dementia of the Alzheimer type. *J Am Geriatr Soc.* 1989;37:856–860.

174. Burke WJ, Nitcher RL, Roccaforte WH, Wengel SP. A prospective evaluation of the Geriatric Depression Scale in an outpatient geriatric assessment center. *J Am Geriatr Soc.* 1992;40:1227–1230.

175. Feher EP, Larrabee GJ, Crook TH. Factors attenuating the validity of the Geriatric Depression Scale in a dementia population. *J Am Geriatr Soc.* 1992;40:906–909.

176. Kafonek S, Ettinger WH, Roca R. Instruments for screening for depression and dementia in a long-term care facility. *J Am Geriatr Soc.* 1989;37:29–34.

177. Parmelee PA, Katz IR, Lawton MP. Depression among institutionalized aged: assessment and prevalence estimation. *J Gerontol.* 1989;44:M22–29.

178. Yesavage JA. The use of self-rating depression scales in the elderly. In: Poon LW, ed. *Clinical Memory Assessment of Older Adults.* Washington, DC: American Psychological Association, 1986:213–217.

179. Alden D, Austin C, Sturgeon R. A correlation between the Geriatric Depression Scale long and short forms. *J Gerontol.* 1989;4:P124–125.

180. Cwikel J, Ritchie K. Screening for depression among the elderly in Israel: an assessment of the short Geriatric Depression Scale (S-GDS). *Isr J Med Sci.* 1989;25:131–137.

181. Zung WWK. A self-rating depression scale. *Arch Gen Psychiatry.* 1965;12:63–70.

182. Zung WWK, Richards DB, Short MF. Self-rating depression scale in an outpatient clinic: further validation of the SDS. *Arch Gen Psychiatry.* 1965;13:508–515.

183. Zung WWK. Factors influencing the self-rating depression scale. *Arch Gen Psychiatry.* 1967;16:543–547.

184. Zung WWK. Depression in the normal aged. *Psychosomatics.* 1967;8:287–292.

185. Freedman N, Bucci W, Elkowitz E. Depression in a family practice elderly population. *J Am Geriatr Soc.* 1982;30:372–377.

186. Moore JT, Silimperi DR, Bobula JA. Recognition of depression by family medicine residents: the impact of screening. *J Fam Pract.* 1978;7:509–513.

187. Okimoto JT, Barnes RF, Veith RC, et al. Screening for depression in geriatric medical patients. *Am J Psychiatry.* 1982;139:799–802.

188. Goldberg DP. *The Detection of Psychiatric Illness by Questionnaire.* London: Oxford University Press, 1972.

189. Goodchild ME, Duncan-Jones P. Chronicity and the General Health Questionnaire. *Br J Psychiatry.* 1985;146:55–61.

190. Goldberg DP, Hillier VF. A scaled version of the General Health Questionnaire. *Psychol Med.* 1979;9:139–145.

191. Goldberg DP, Rickels K, Downing R, Hesbacher P. A comparison of two psychiatric screening tests. *Br J Psychiatry.* 1976;129:61–67.

192. Clarke DM, Smith GC, Herrman HE. A comparative study of screening instruments for mental disorders in general hospital patients. *Int J Psychiatry Med.* 1993;23:323–337.

193. Cleary PD, Goldberg ID, Kessler LG, Nycz GR. Screening for mental disorder among primary care patients. *Arch Gen Psychiatry.* 1982;39:837–840.

194. Ford DE, Anthony JC, Nestadt GR, Romanoski AJ. The General Health Questionnaire by interview: performance in relation to recent use of health services. *Med Care.* 1989;27:367–375.

195. Lindsay J. Validity of the General Health Questionnaire (GHQ) in detecting psychiatric disturbance in amputees with phantom pain. *J Psychosom Res.* 1986;30:277–281.

196. Lobo A, Perez-Echeverria M, Jimenez-Aznarez A, et al. Emotional disturbances in endocrine patients: validity of the scaled version of the General Health Questionnaire (GHQ-28). *Br J Psychiatry.* 1990;152:807–812.

197. Marino S, Bellantuono C, Tansella M. Psychiatric morbidity in general practice in Italy: a point-prevalence survey in a defined geographical area. *Soc Psychiatry Psychiatr Epidemiol.* 1990; 25:67–72.

198. Samuels JF, Nestadt G, Anthony JC, Romanoski AJ. The detection of mental disorders in the community setting using a 20-item interview version of the General Health Questionnaire. *Acta Psychiatr Scand.* 1994;89:14–20.

199. Simon GE, Von Korff M, Durham ML. Predictors of outpatient mental health utilization by primary care patients in a health maintenance organization. *Am J Psychiatry.* 1994;151:908–913.

200. Von Korff M, Shapiro S, Burke JD, et al. Anxiety and depression in a primary care clinic: comparison of Diagnostic Interview Schedule, General Health Questionnaire, and practitioner assessments. *Arch Gen Psychiatry.* 1987;44:152–156.

201. Gallagher D. The Beck Depression Inventory and older adults: review of its development and utility. In: Brink TL, ed. *Clinical Gerontology: A Guide to Assessment and Intervention.* New York, NY: Haworth Press, 1986:149–163.

202. Beck AT, Beck RW. Screening depressed patients in family practice: a rapid technique. *Postgrad Med.* 1972;52:81–85.

203. Beck AT, Ward CH, Mendelson M, et al. An inventory for measuring depression. *Arch Gen Psychiatry.* 1961;4:53–63.

204. Oliver JM, Simmons ME. Depression as measured by the DSM-III and the Beck Depression Inventory in an unselected adult population. *J Consult Clin Psychol.* 1984;52:892–898.

205. Gallagher D, Breckenridge J, Steinmetz J, et al. The Beck Depression Inventory and research diagnostic criteria: congruence in an older population. *J Consult Clin Psychol.* 1983;51:945–946.

206. Nielsen AC, Williams TA. Depression in ambulatory medical patients: prevalence by self-report questionnaire and recognition by nonpsychiatric physicians. *Arch Gen Psychiatry.* 1980; 37:999–1004.

207. Radloff LS. The CES-D Scale: a self-report depression scale for research in the general population. *Appl Psychol Meas.* 1977;1:385–401.

208. Comstock GW, Helsing KJ. Symptoms of depression in two communities. *Psychol Med.* 1976;6:551–563.

209. Eaton WW, Kessler LG. Rates of symptoms of depression in a national sample. *Am J Epidemiol.* 1981;114:528–538.

210. Katon W, Schulberg HC. Epidemiology of depression in primary care. *Gen Hosp Psychiatry.* 1992;14:237–247.

211. Husaini BA, Neff JA, Harrington JB, et al. Depression in rural communities: validating the CES-D Scale. *J Community Psychol.* 1980;8:20–27.

212. Schulberg HC, Saul M, McClelland M, Ganguli M, Christy W, Frank R. Assessing depression in primary medical and psychiatric practices. *Arch Gen Psychiatry.* 1985;42:1164–1170.

213. Foelker GA, Shewchuk RM. Somatic complaints and the CES-D. *J Am Geriatr Soc.* 1992;40:259–262.

214. Zimmerman M, Coryell W. Screening for major depressive disorder in the community: a comparison of measures. *Psychol Assess.* 1994;6:71–74.

215. Robins LN, Helzer JE, Croughan J, Ratcliff KS. National Institute of Mental Health Diagnostic Interview Schedule: its history, characteristics, and validity. *Arch Gen Psychiatry.* 1981;38:381–389.

216. Robins LN, Wing JK, Wittchen HU, et al. The Composite International Diagnostic Interview. In: Mezzich JE, Jorge MR, Salloum IM, eds. *Psychiatric Epidemiology: Assessment Concepts and Methods.* Baltimore, Md: The Johns Hopkins University Press, 1994:249–267.

217. Mackinnon A, Christensen H, Cullen JS, et al. The Canberra Interview for the Elderly: assessment of its validity in the diagnosis of dementia and depression. *Acta Psychiatr Scand.* 1993; 87:146–151.

218. Social Psychiatry Research Unit. The Canberra Interview for the Elderly: a new field instrument for the diagnosis of dementia and depression by ICD-10 and DSM-III-R. *Acta Psychiatr Scand.* 1992;85:105–113.

219. Zaudig M, Mittelhammer J, Hiller W, et al. SIDAM—a structured interview for the diagnosis of dementia of the Alzheimer type, multi-infarct dementia and dementias of other aetiology according to ICD-10 and DSM-III-R. *Psychol Med.* 1991;21:225–236.

220. Jorm AF, Jacomb PA. The Informant Questionnaire on Cognitive Decline in the Elderly (IQ-CODE): sociodemographic correlates, reliability, validity and some norms. *Psychol Med.* 1989; 19:1015–1022.

221. Jorm AF, Scott R, Cullen JS, MacKinnon AJ. Performance of the Informant Questionnaire on Cognitive Decline in the Elderly (IQCODE) as a screening test for dementia. *Psychol Med.* 1991;21:785–790.

222. Jorm AF. A short form of the Informant Questionnaire on Cognitive Decline in the Elderly (IQ-CODE): development and cross-validation. *Psychol Med.* 1994;24:145–153.

223. Lyketsos CG, Nestadt G, Cwi J, Heithoff K, Eaton WW. The Life Chart Interview: a standardized method to describe the course of psychopathology. *Int J Methods Psychiatr Res.* 1994; 4:143–145.

224. Suzman RM, Willis DP, Manton KG, eds. *The Oldest Old.* New York, NY: Oxford University Press, 1992.

225. Pirozzolo FJ, ed. New developments in neuropsychological evaluation. *Clin Geriatr Med.* 1989:5:425–632.

226. Wallace RB, Woolson RF, eds. *The Epidemiologic Study of the Elderly.* New York, NY: Oxford University Press, 1992.

227. Lawton MP, Herzog AR, eds. *Special Research Methods for Gerontology.* Amityville, NY: Baywood Publishing Co, 1989.

228. Erickson RC, Howieson D. The clinician's perspective: measuring change and treatment effectiveness. In: Poon LW, ed. *Clinical Memory Assessment of Older Adults.* Washington, DC: American Psychological Association, 1986:69–80.

3

Functional Assessment

The preservation of function has become a prominent theme in geriatrics.[1] A major goal of the *Healthy People 2000* initiative is to increase the span of healthy life for all Americans.[2] The emphasis has appropriately changed from an exclusive concern with delaying mortality to a focus on avoiding morbidity; that is, to preserving function[3,4] and extending "active" life expectancy.[5] Functional status captures the concept of "quality of life" in ways that an emphasis on medical diagnoses does not.[6,7] Functional assessment is the key to understanding the impact of medical illness on the older patient and family and is the cornerstone of geriatric rehabilitation.[8,9] The typical catalog of medical problems used to describe the patient is not sufficient to answer questions about functional abilities, such as the ability to dress or to use the toilet. Brief methods are emphasized in this chapter to encourage ongoing functional assessment in the office and in other settings.

FOCUS ON FUNCTION

There are several levels of functioning in daily life. Performance in social and occupational roles is at one level.[10,11] The tasks demanded every day, such as driving or using public transportation, constitute another. Activities necessary for functioning in a modern society, such as using the telephone or an automated teller machine, are commonplace. On another plane are personal care tasks such as dressing, bathing, and toileting. Older adults and others who have difficulty with these tasks must compensate for their disabilities.

The capacity to function independently is poorly indicated by the constellation of medical diagnoses alone. Performance on mental status testing does not necessarily predict functional status.[12,13] For example, patients' scores on the Short Portable Mental Status Questionnaire (SPMSQ) were only weakly correlated with the ability of the patients to care for themselves. Of 32 patients with moderate to severe impairment on the SPMSQ, 9 were living completely independently and another 10 needed assistance only with dressing.[14] Even severely impaired patients may perform quite well in a familiar home setting. Similarly, the severity of disease as measured by standard laboratory tests does not necessarily imply disability. Functional status should be assessed directly and *independently* of the assessment of medical and laboratory abnormalities or cognitive impairment.

Consider a 70-year-old woman who suffered from diabetes mellitus, hypertension, and congestive heart failure and was hospitalized for urinary incontinence. Urologic studies were normal, and the patient was discharged home in her husband's care. Two weeks later she was again admitted for "mental status changes," since she was noted to be increasingly disoriented and incontinent. Her daughter gave an account of slowly increasing intellectual impairment over the course of at least one year. Mental status testing revealed global intellectual deficits in orientation, memory, calculation ability, and visuospatial skills. Review of the chart from the previous hospitalization showed no documented mental status examination with which to compare findings. It was believed the patient had Alzheimer's disease with superimposed delirium secondary to medication.

Specific functional loss in the elderly is not determined by the locus of disease—urinary incontinence can occur in conjunction with problems beyond those of the urinary tract. Because of the family's difficulty in caring for this patient, she required nursing home care. In a situation where the patient had better functional ability or where social support was available, she may have been able to stay at home. Thus, the problem list alone did not give all the information needed to make recommendations regarding this patient's treatment.

Functional assessment can help the practitioner focus on the patient's capabilities, and when there is a change, appropriate resources can be rallied and a search for medical illness initiated. The sometimes delicate state of homeostasis makes the older adult vulnerable to disability from a variety of sources, both internal and external to the patient. Going beyond the medical model is critical, since medical or psychiatric illness may present as a nonspecific deterioration in functional status. It is not enough to enumerate the medical problems and treat them in isolation. When a medical illness is diagnosed, how it affects the elder's functional capacity must always be considered. Conversely, the patient's functional status must be considered in formulating the treatment plan.

Consider an 83-year-old man who lives alone, has been paraplegic since an early age, is confined to a wheelchair, and has osteoarthritis, scoliosis, atrial fibrillation with controlled ventricular response on digoxin, a suprapubic catheter for a neurogenic bladder, cataracts, poor dental hygiene, and full dentures. This patient's mental status is normal. Despite his physical limitations and medical problems, he lives in his home alone, being visited periodically by his niece and visiting nurses. Now in addition, suppose that the patient was not able to transfer from his wheelchair to the toilet or to the bed or that he was incapable of taking his medication properly. It is easy to see how difficulty in one of these areas might change the situation and alter one's judgment as to the patient's ability to reside at home. Yet except for his inability to walk, the patient's functional status was good.

The multitude of medical, social, and psychological challenges presented by some older patients can overwhelm health care professionals. The best strategy, therefore, is first to attack small problems with major consequences. Problems that interfere with safe driving and ambulation would be one important focus for intervention. Among the illnesses or complaints of the older patient, which one or two are causing the greatest reduction in functional capacity? For example, cataracts might present a greater obstacle to shopping, preparing meals, and eating than the patient's osteoarthritis.

It is also essential to look closely at less serious although treatable conditions that might be contributing to disability. Correction of minor problems could enhance the person's quality of life. Something as simple as modifying the diuretic drug dosing schedule to obviate the need for evening and nightly trips to the bathroom may enhance the sleep of the patient and the caregiver alike.

Asking about accidents and driving habits is an important inquiry in its own right, but it also can provide evidence as to whether more basic tasks, such as shopping, dressing, and bathing, are being adequately performed. Difficulties with the telephone or improper use of medications may signal cognitive impairment[15] or depression.[16]

The information gathered from functional assessments can play an important role in advising and counseling patients and their families and in following patients after significant medical events.[10] A functional scale has been used to determine the need for institutionalization (at least on a temporary basis) after hip fracture.[17] This scale consists of components for assessing physical health (vision, hearing, and mental status), ambulatory ability, ability to perform daily activities, social situation (lives alone, with spouse, or in nursing home), and "disabilities" (e.g., incontinence, paralysis, amputation, decubiti, and contractures). The Functional Rating Scale for the Symptoms of Dementia, which is discussed below, is a functional assessment questionnaire that evaluates the need for nursing home placement in the patient with dementia.[18]

Functional ability correlates with mortality. For example, a retrospective study compared patients who died within one year of placement in a nursing home with those who survived. The latter group were found to be more independent, especially in bathing and dressing.[19] Mortality was also associated with poor functioning following hospitalization.[20] The inability to perform tasks such as traveling, shopping, meal preparation, housework, and handling money predicts mortality as well.[21,22] Inability to perform simple tasks such as carrying a bag of groceries predicts further functional decline[23] and institutionalization.[24]

In evaluating function, it is necessary to consider the source of information about functional impairment.[25] Patients may perceive their level of functioning to be at a higher level than the evaluation of nurses familiar with them would suggest. In one study, patients rated their functional status higher than attending nurses did, whereas families rated it lower than the nurses.[26] Self-ratings were found to reflect most closely the direct observations of research staff.[27] Pincus and colleagues found that self-reports on a simple questionnaire of functional status were significantly correlated with objective measures of physical impairment due to rheumatoid arthritis.[28] In the Framingham follow-up, older residents did not seem reluctant to assent to functional limitations.[29] In clinical settings, it is best to use information from both the patient and the caregiver. Is the activity performed? Could the activity be performed if necessary? That data from self-reporting of functional impairment predicts mortality lends validity to self-reported information.

Direct observation of the patient would seem desirable to confirm information given by the patient or caregiver about functional status, and some combination of self-reporting and performance measurement may be optimal.[30] Measures adequate for primary care practice are few.[31] One performance test uses props—much like the Denver Developmental Screening Examination for children. Examples of tasks include drinking from a cup, lifting food on a spoon to the mouth (props: spoon and candy), making a telephone call, brushing teeth (prop: toothbrush), and telling the time.[32] Performance tests focusing on manual dexterity can uncover a need for formal support services and appear to be unaffected by age or educational level.[33–36]

The Physical Performance Test permits direct assessment of performance on a set of basic tasks that simulate the activities of daily living.[37,38] The tasks include (1) writing a sentence, (2) simulated eating, (3) lifting a book and putting it on a shelf, (4) putting on and removing a jacket, (5) picking up a penny from the floor, (6) turning 360 degrees, (7) walking, and (8) climbing stairs. Explicit instructions for administration and scoring are provided. Bed mobility, transfer skills, standing up from a chair, standing balance, stepping up one step with a handrail, and walking are the activities rated in another performance measure suitable for hospitalized elderly patients.[39] The observation of performance may produce a more accurate assessment of capability than relying on reports of functional ability by patients or caregivers.

The patient's home can speak volumes about the performance of activities of daily living. How well arranged is the home for bathing and toileting? Are there obvious safety hazards (frayed wires, ashtrays near the bed, slippery floors or rugs, firearms stored in the home of a patient with dementia)? How well does the elderly person maneuver about the home (transfer, ambulation)? How well are nutritional needs met (food in the refrigerator, shopping, cooking)? How well is the home maintained (cleanliness, clutter)? In addition to the other benefits of home visits, such as the assessment of social support available to the patient, they can provide first-hand information about the functional ability of the elder.[40,41]

Functional impairment can be listed independently of the problem list in the problem-oriented medical record. For example, two patients with rheumatoid arthritis may differ in their ability to eat. One may then list "difficulty with feeding" independently of the medical diagnosis of rheumatoid arthritis. This helps quantify functional impairment and alerts the clinician to the implications of the functional impairment (in this case, a problem with nutrition).

A complete problem-oriented medical record, which lists and organizes functional as well as undefined problems, can help establish priorities for solution. Seen as "building blocks," efforts to assist the patient are cumulative, because some problems are selected for immediate attention whereas others are set aside for eventual consideration. Medical diagnosis remains important, but functional assessment keeps the problems in perspective and provides a complementary viewpoint. Functional impairment should prompt a timely, thorough search for evidence of cognitive impairment, depression, substance abuse, adverse medication effects, and sensory impairment.[7]

Functional assessment can be a positive force in caring for the elderly. Since so much of the training of many health professionals deals with the negative aspects of age and its losses, taking care to determine what functional capacity exists makes the task of evaluation appear in a more positive light. Questions to be asked include these: How well does the patient function in his or her own environment? What adaptations and concessions have been made to make up for deficiencies? How can health professionals and other caregivers initiate and promote adaptations to allow the most independent, fulfilling life possible?

THE COMPONENTS OF FUNCTIONAL STATUS

Using a systematic approach to each domain of geriatric assessment, including functional assessment, is desirable. The activities generally agreed on as constituting the proper focus of functional assessment are divided into the activities of daily living (ADLs) and the instrumental activities of daily living (IADLs), although other categorizations are possible.[42] The ADLs are the functions that are fundamental to independent living, such as dressing and bathing. The IADLs include more complex daily activities, such as using the telephone, housekeeping, and managing money. Statistical methods applied to self-reported data on difficulty with activities resulted in similar groupings: (1) activities related to mobility and exercise, such as walking; (2) complex tasks, such as paying bills and shopping; (3) self-care activities, such as toileting; and (4) upper extremity tasks, such as grasping and reaching.[43] Driving and sexual functioning are also important to consider when doing a functional assessment (see Chapter 7).

Evaluation of functional status is not limited to the assessment of specific activities and tasks, although that is the emphasis here. Assessment may also include significant happenings in a person's life or family that have a bearing on the health status or situation (events of daily living); demands placed on the person from within or by the family and society (demands of daily living); the nature of the physical environment (environment of daily living); and the values and beliefs of the person that determine decisions and responses regarding health care (values and beliefs of daily living).[44,45]

ACTIVITIES OF DAILY LIVING

Like mental status testing instruments, ADL scales may have "ceiling" or "threshold" effects.[46] In other words, if the activities chosen for assessment are too easy, so many persons would perform well that the scale would not be helpful in identifying those with functional impairment, except among the "frail elderly."[47] Asking about driving and instrumental activities of daily living is apt to be more fruitful in the functional assessment of the ambulatory elderly.

The term "frailty" has been used to describe elderly persons whose management of day-to-day tasks is tenuous. The frail elderly have been defined in functional terms—as elders who need help performing ADLs,[48,49] and whose impairment has effects on their behavior and quality of life.[50] A dynamic model assumes that it is the balance between assets and deficits that determines frailty and that geriatric assessment should focus on these assets and deficits, such as caregiver burden, resources, attitudes, and health status.[51] A change in status in one domain may tip the balance and push the elder into frailty. Frail elders may need to rely heavily on neighbors or family members to perform routine jobs that fully independent persons do for themselves. Frailty implies health conditions that require frequent hospitalizations, medication, and visits to the physician.

Ideally, practitioners need a set of questions that are quick and easy to administer periodically to detect elders who are beginning to experience difficulty in the activities usually associated with independent living. Something similar to the Apgar score used to evaluate newborns might be desirable for this purpose. Details regarding the use of indexes of function and measurement theory can be found in the works cited in references 1, 46, and 50–56. Further theoretical considerations can be found in the Institute of Medicine Report *Disability in America*.[57] Specific instruments used to assess ADLs and IADLs are discussed below.

Katz Index of Activities of Daily Living

The Katz Index of Activities of Daily Living (Exhibit 3–1) covers bathing, dressing, toileting, transfer, continence, and feeding.[58] It provides a framework for assessing the ability to live independently or, if deficiencies are found, a focal point for remediation. A person dependent in a single activity might need assis-

Exhibit 3–1 Katz Index of Activities of Daily Living

1. Bathing (sponge, shower, or tub):
   I: receives no assistance (gets in and out of tub if tub is the usual means of bathing)
   A: receives assistance in bathing only one part of the body (such as the back or a leg)
   D: receives assistance in bathing more than one part of the body (or not bathed)

2. Dressing:
   I: gets clothes and gets completely dressed without assistance
   A: gets clothes and gets dressed without assistance except in tying shoes
   D: receives assistance in getting clothes or in getting dressed or stays partly or completely undressed

3. Toileting:
   I: goes to "toilet room," cleans self, and arranges clothes without assistance (may use object for support such as cane, walker, or wheelchair and may manage night bedpan or commode, emptying it in the morning)
   A: receives assistance in going to "toilet room" or in cleansing self or in arranging clothes after elimination or in use of night bedpan or commode
   D: doesn't go to room termed "toilet" for the elimination process

4. Transfer:
   I: moves in and out of bed as well as in and out of chair without assistance (may be using object for support such as cane or walker)
   A: moves in and out of bed or chair with assistance
   D: doesn't get out of bed

5. Continence:
   I: controls urination and bowel movement completely by self
   A: has occasional "accidents"
   D: supervision helps keep urine or bowel control; catheter is used, or is incontinent

6. Feeding:
   I: feeds self without assistance
   A: feeds self except for getting assistance in cutting meat or buttering bread
   D: receives assistance in feeding or is fed partly or completely by using tubes or intravenous fluids

Abbreviations: I, independent; A, assistance; D, dependent

Source: Adapted with permission from *Journal of the American Medical Association* (1963;185:915), Copyright © 1963, American Medical Association.

tance at isolated times of the day (such as for bathing), but more help might be needed by persons dependent on assistance in many activities. A three-tiered scale for ADLs is found to be more reliable and is reproducible even when scored by personnel with minimal training. The scale might use the ratings "independent," "semi-independent" (needs a part-time assistant), and "dependent" rather than a checklist with four or five gradations defining how much assistance is required.[59]

Considering the basic ADL items in evaluation of an elderly person has several important advantages. For one thing, focusing on functional abilities allows a start to be made on the matching of services to needs. For example, someone requiring only assistance in bathing may need an aide to visit the home just once a week. In addition, keying in on specific tasks allows interventions to be more focused. In dealing with difficulties in dressing, a caregiver might try putting picture labels on drawers, grouping items that belong together, and taking the patient by the hand and starting a desired action as a cue to the patient. In other cases, multiple areas of dependence may make it impossible to provide sufficient help to maintain the patient at home.[58,60,61]

Subjective estimates of disease severity or mere use of a diagnostic label may not be as helpful as a functional assessment in determining proper treatment. A patient with rheumatoid arthritis may have major functional deficits that could be improved through physical therapy, appliances, or help with key ADLs such as bathing. For a patient who has recently had a stroke, following the patient's progress in the performance of ADLs can be useful.[62] It can help, for example, in the matching of services to needs. Also, if the patient is unable to perform one or more ADLs, he or she may require hospitalization or nursing home placement.

Barthel Index

The Barthel Index has also been used to assess the ability of patients to care for themselves, but the items are weighted to account for the amount of physical assistance that would be required if a patient is unable to carry out a given function. In one study in a rehabilitative setting for patients with neuromuscular disorders, the Barthel Index was used to document improvement. Patients who did not improve their score during rehabilitation were believed to have poor potential for recovery.[63]

A modified Barthel Index (Exhibit 3–2) has been devised. When it was used to assess the need for home health services in one study, the scores correlated with the number of activities patients were able to do independently.[55,64] Patients scoring less than 60 on the modified Barthel Index were able to perform no more than 10 of the defined ADL and IADL tasks. A score of less than 60 was associated with the need for help in feeding, bathing, grooming, dressing, toileting, trans-

Exhibit 3–2 Modified Barthel Index

	Independent		Dependent	
	Intact	Limited	Helper	Null
Drink from cup/feed from dish	10	5	0	0
Dress upper body	5	5	3	0
Dress lower body	5	5	2	0
Don brace or prosthesis	0	0	−2	0
Grooming	5	5	0	0
Wash or bathe	4	4	0	0
Bladder incontinence	10	10	5	0
Bowel incontinence	10	10	5	0
Care of perineum/clothing at toilet	4	4	2	0
Transfer, chair	15	15	7	0
Transfer, toilet	6	5	3	0
Transfer, tub or shower	1	1	0	0
Walk on level 50 yards or more	15	15	10	0
Up and down stairs for one flight or more	10	10	5	0
Wheelchair 50 yards (only if not walking)	15	5	0	0

Source: Adapted with permission from *Medical Care* (1981;19:491), Copyright © 1981, JB Lippincott Company.

ferring, doing housework, and preparing meals.[64] The modified Barthel Index may be a good indicator of the need for support in ADLs.

INSTRUMENTAL ACTIVITIES OF DAILY LIVING

Another set of activities required for independent living are the so-called instrumental activities of daily living (IADLs).[65,66] These include more complex and demanding activities than the ADLs, such as using the telephone, traveling, shopping, preparing meals, doing housework, taking medicine properly, and managing money (Exhibit 3–3). The set of IADLs may be slanted toward tasks traditionally performed by women, especially for the current cohort of elderly persons.[67] This bias notwithstanding, these chores are required daily activities for most persons, and if an elderly patient is unable to perform them, the tasks must be performed by a caregiver.

The IADLs can be distilled into five items to create a simple screening test to determine who may require a more comprehensive assessment.[21] The five items include travel, shopping, meal preparation, housework, and handling money (Exhibit 3–4). The five-item IADL scale has some interesting features.

Exhibit 3–3 Instrumental Activities of Daily Living

1. Telephone:
   I: able to look up numbers, dial, receive and make calls without help
   A: able to answer phone or dial operator in an emergency but needs special phone or help in getting number or dialing
   D: unable to use the telephone

2. Traveling:
   I: able to drive own car or travel alone on bus or taxi
   A: able to travel but not alone
   D: unable to travel

3. Shopping:
   I: able to take care of all shopping with transportation provided
   A: able to shop but not alone
   D: unable to shop

4. Preparing meals:
   I: able to plan and cook full meals
   A: able to prepare light foods but unable to cook full meals alone
   D: unable to prepare any meals

5. Housework:
   I: able to do heavy housework (like scrub floors)
   A: able to do light housework, but needs help with heavy tasks
   D: unable to do any housework

6. Medication:
   I: able to take medications in the right dose at the right time
   A: able to take medications but needs reminding or someone to prepare it
   D: unable to take medications

7. Money:
   I: able to manage buying needs, write checks, pay bills
   A: able to manage daily buying needs, but needs help managing checkbook, paying bills
   D: unable to manage money

Abbreviations: I, independent; A, assistance; D, dependent

Source: Adapted from *Multidimensional Functional Assessment Questionnaire,* ed 2 (pp 169–170) by Duke University Center for the Study of Aging and Human Development with permission of Duke University, 1978.

First, as mentioned previously, inability to perform these tasks correlates with mortality. Second, when the items are arranged vertically, performance by a person of one type of activity (e.g., shopping) indicates that person can probably perform all the activities listed below it on the scale but not above it. When rated from the most difficult to the least difficult, the five items are ordered thus: housework, travel, shopping, finances, and cooking.[21,68]

Exhibit 3–4 The Five-Item Instrumental Activities of Daily Living Screening Questionnaire

1. Can you *get to places* out of walking distance:
   1 Without help (can travel alone on bus, taxi, or drive your own car)
   0 With some help (need someone to help you or go with you when traveling) or are you unable to travel unless emergency arrangements are made for a specialized vehicle such as an ambulance?
   – Not answered

2. Can you *go shopping* for groceries or clothes (assuming you have transportation):
   1 Without help (taking care of all your shopping needs yourself, assuming you have transportation)
   0 With some help (need someone to go with you on all shopping trips), or are you completely unable to do any shopping?
   – Not answered

3. Can you *prepare your own meals:*
   1 Without help (plan and cook meals yourself)
   0 With some help (can prepare some things but unable to cook full meals yourself), or are you completely unable to prepare any meals?
   – Not answered

4. Can you do your *housework:*
   1 Without help (can scrub floors, etc.)
   0 With some help (can do light housework but need help with heavy work), or are you unable to do any housework?
   – Not answered

5. Can you *handle your own money:*
   1 Without help (write checks, pay bills, etc.)
   0 With some help (manage day-to-day buying but need help with managing your checkbook and paying your bills), or are you completely unable to handle money?
   – Not answered

Source: Reprinted with permission from American Geriatrics Society, "Screening the Elderly: A Brief Instrumental Activities of Daily Living Measure" by G Fillenbaum in *Journal of the American Geriatrics Society* (1985;33:698–706).

This five-item scale can be used to discover changes in status and to identify who needs help. It could be administered, for example, to all elderly patients in a primary care practice on a regular schedule. Imagine a 63-year-old woman who has come in for a routine examination and renewal of blood pressure medications. Last year she had no difficulties getting places, shopping, preparing meals, doing housework, or handling money. Today she admits some recent trouble managing her checkbook and reluctantly relates her worries about declining memory and lack of concentration. The Folstein Mini-Mental State Examination score is normal. On further questioning, vegetative symptoms of depression are found.

How a patient performs on the ADL and IADL items is a good indicator of the services that might be needed. For example, nursing care, personal care, continuous supervision, meal preparation, or homemaker assistance may be required by elders because of recent hospitalization or illness.[69]

Hebrew Rehabilitation Center for Aged Vulnerability Index

Another brief instrument that can be used in assessing functional status is the Hebrew Rehabilitation Center for Aged Vulnerability Index. The ten assessment items include questions on meal preparation; taking out the garbage; housework; negotiating stairs; use of a walker, cane, or wheelchair; time spent outside; and ability to dress. It also requires a self-rating of the extent to which illness interferes with activities.[70] The scale was developed for use by social workers and nurses to help rapidly identify patients in need of resources or further assessment.

CASE STUDY: ASSESSMENT OF FUNCTION

Mrs. Jones is a 72-year-old woman who is recently widowed. She has a history of hypertension, which has been treated with an angiotensin-converting enzyme inhibitor and a mild diuretic, and osteoarthritis, especially of the lower back, which has been treated intermittently with a nonsteroidal anti-inflammatory drug. She lives alone in her own home. A 48-year-old working married daughter lives in the same town and visits on the weekends to run errands and do some light housekeeping. An unmarried son lives in a larger city 400 miles away.

Since her bereavement 4 months ago, the patient, who does not drive, has been socially isolated, especially because she is unable to attend usual functions, such as church meetings and gatherings of her bridge club. Her daughter is quite concerned because of her mother's lack of appetite and neglect of personal care. On questioning, Mrs. Jones admitted to early morning awakening, lack of appetite, weight loss, and crying spells. There was no prior history of depression, but the patient was thought to be depressed as part of her grief reaction.

The daughter was able to rearrange her schedule in order to provide transportation to the bridge club and to church. Counseling was arranged to help her cope with the grieving process. Meals on Wheels was suggested as a means to increase her social contact, but Mrs. Jones rejected that idea. Overall, these efforts to help her mitigated some of her feelings of depression, and she improved considerably over the next several months.

She remained at the same functional level, receiving personal assistance from her daughter and financial assistance from her son, until, at age 77, she sustained a hip fracture after slipping on the ice on the way to her mailbox. She was hospitalized with a fracture of the left femoral neck and made a good recovery after insertion of a pin to stabilize her hip. She spent 2 months in a nursing home receiving physical therapy and rehabilitation and was able to keep her spirits up with the thought of returning home. She was finally discharged home, where she ambulated with a walker.

To accommodate her, her bedroom was moved downstairs, a commode was placed at her bedside, nightlights were obtained, and a ramp to the outside was installed. Her movement, however, was more severely limited than before the accident. Her daughter continued to provide help with shopping and housework and was able to arrange for the postal carrier to check daily to see whether Mrs. Jones was well.

Three years later, Mrs. Jones is now 80 years old. Her daughter, at age 56, is hospitalized for a myocardial infarction and will not be able to keep up the same level of assistance as in the past. At least temporarily, she will no longer be available to help her mother with shopping, housekeeping, laundry, meal planning and preparation, and bathing or to provide emotional support. Mrs. Jones does not wish to leave her home, but some of these activities are not being performed.

When her son visits, he is surprised and a little angry at the "condition Mom is in," although he keeps it to himself, realizing his sister's recent heart attack prevents her from doing what she used to. He believes Mrs. Jones should be immediately placed in a protective environment. Since Mrs. Jones is adamant about staying home, her son makes a compromise agreement with her to arrange for a live-in housekeeper. Although he tries to find a satisfactory live-in helper, none of the applicants are satisfactory both to Mrs. Jones and her son.

Since her son must return to work and her daughter is unable to care for her, Mrs. Jones reluctantly agrees to nursing home placement in an intermediate care facility, at least on a trial basis. For Mrs. Jones, the risk factors for nursing home placement include living alone, old age, lack of a caregiver, and impaired ambulation.

DEMENTIA RATING SCALES

A combination of scores on mental status questions and ADL and IADL items is sometimes used to improve the detection of dementia. Dementia rating scales may be considered hybrid instruments (see Figure 1–1). They have been used not only to identify dementia but also to quantify it, that is, to assign a stage or degree of severity. One example is the Blessed Dementia Score (Exhibit 3–5), which has been shown to correlate with pathologic changes in the brains of demented elderly patients at autopsy.[71]

The ideal dementia rating scale, like the ideal mental status instrument, is short and easy to score to facilitate its use in clinical practice. The rating scale should allow some quantification of dementia and have a few differentiating points for categorization of the severity of dementia. It would also be helpful if the practitioner could use the scale to follow the progression of the dementing illness. Several dementia rating scales are discussed below.

Exhibit 3–5 Blessed Dementia Score

---

1. Inability to perform household tasks
2. Inability to cope with small sums of money
3. Inability to remember short lists of items
4. Inability to find way outdoors
5. Inability to find way about familiar streets
6. Inability to interpret surroundings
7. Inability to recall recent events
8. Tendency to dwell in the past
9. Eating:
     Messily, with spoon only
     Simple solids, such as biscuits (2 points)
     Has to be fed (3 points)
10. Dressing:
     Occasionally misplaced buttons, etc.
     Wrong sequence, forgets items (2 points)
     Unable to dress (3 points)
11. Sphincter control:
     Occasional wet beds
     Frequent wet beds (2 points)
     Doubly incontinent (3 points)
12. Increased rigidity
13. Increased egocentricity
14. Impairment of regard for feelings of others
15. Coarsening of affect
16. Impairment of emotional control
17. Hilarity in inappropriate situations
18. Diminished emotional responsiveness
19. Sexual misdemeanor (de novo in old age)
20. Hobbies relinquished
21. Diminished initiative or growing apathy
22. Purposeless hyperactivity

Total score _____

Scores range from 0 to 27; the higher the score, the greater the degree of dementia. Each item scores 1 except the items noted. A second part, the Information Score, contains items testing orientation and memory.

Source: Adapted with permission from *The British Journal of Psychiatry* (1968;114:808–809), Copyright © 1968, The Royal College of Psychiatrists.

Functional Dementia Scale

The Functional Dementia Scale (Exhibit 3–6) is a brief instrument that can be used to assess the severity of dementia.[72] The questions are to be answered by the caregivers in writing or orally. Not only does the scale help quantify the dementia, but it also provides a sort of "review of systems" (or more accurately "review

Exhibit 3–6 Functional Dementia Scale

1. Has difficulty in completing simple tasks on own, such as dressing, bathing, doing arithmetic
2. Spends time either sitting or in apparently purposeless activity
3. Wanders at night or needs to be restrained to prevent wandering
4. Hears things that are not there
5. Requires supervision or assistance in eating
6. Loses things
7. Appearance is disorderly if left to own devices
8. Moans
9. Cannot control bowel function
10. Threatens to harm others
11. Cannot control bladder function
12. Needs to be watched so does not injure self, such as by careless smoking, leaving the stove on, falling
13. Destructive of materials within reach, such as breaks furniture, throws food trays, tears up magazines
14. Shouts or yells
15. Accuses others of doing him or her bodily harm or stealing his or her possessions when you are sure the accusations are not true
16. Is unaware of limitations imposed by illness
17. Becomes confused and does not know where he or she is
18. Has trouble remembering
19. Has sudden changes of mood, such as gets upset, angered, or cries easily
20. If left alone, wanders aimlessly during the day or needs to be restrained to prevent wandering

Each item is rated by the caregiver as follows: none or little of the time, some of the time, a good part of the time, or most or all of the time.

Source: "A Functional Dementia Scale" by J Moore et al in *The Journal of Family Practice* (1983;16:503). Adapted by permission of Appleton & Lange.

of symptoms") for the problems of dementia. No published guidelines on whether the scale is able to track change over time are available. It would be of interest to know if beyond a certain score patients were more likely to require nursing home placement. Perhaps one would then give certain undesirable or hard-to-deal-with characteristics greater weight, such as incontinence, which is often an especially troublesome problem.

Revised Memory and Behavior Problems Checklist

The Revised Memory and Behavior Problems Checklist (Exhibit 3–7) assesses the frequency of observable problem behaviors and, on a separate dimension, the caregiver's response.[73–75] The frequency of the behavior is rated "never," "not in the past week," "1 to 2 times in the past week," "3 to 6 times in the past week," or

Exhibit 3–7 Revised Memory and Behavior Problems Checklist

The following is a list of problems patients sometimes have. Please indicate if any of these problems have occurred *during the past week.* If so, how much has this bothered or upset you when it happened? Use the following scales for the frequency of the problem and your reaction to it. Please read the description of the ratings carefully.

FREQUENCY RATINGS:

0 = never occurred
1 = not in the past week
2 = 1 to 2 times in the past week
3 = 3 to 6 times in the past week
4 = daily or more often
9 = don't know/not applicable

REACTION RATINGS:

0 = not at all
1 = a little
2 = moderately
3 = very much
4 = extremely
9 = don't know/not applicable

Please answer all the questions below. Please circle a number from 0–9 for both _frequency_ and _reaction._

	Frequency	Reaction
1. Asking the same question over and over.	0 1 2 3 4 9	0 1 2 3 4 9
2. Trouble remembering recent events (e.g., items in the newspaper or on TV).	0 1 2 3 4 9	0 1 2 3 4 9
3. Trouble remembering significant past events.	0 1 2 3 4 9	0 1 2 3 4 9
4. Losing or misplacing things.	0 1 2 3 4 9	0 1 2 3 4 9
5. Forgetting what day it is.	0 1 2 3 4 9	0 1 2 3 4 9
6. Starting, but not finishing, things.	0 1 2 3 4 9	0 1 2 3 4 9
7. Difficulty concentrating on a task.	0 1 2 3 4 9	0 1 2 3 4 9
8. Destroying property.	0 1 2 3 4 9	0 1 2 3 4 9
9. Doing things that embarrass you.	0 1 2 3 4 9	0 1 2 3 4 9

10. Waking you or other family members up at night.	0 1 2 3 4 9	0 1 2 3 4 9
11. Talking loudly and rapidly.	0 1 2 3 4 9	0 1 2 3 4 9
12. Appears anxious or worried.	0 1 2 3 4 9	0 1 2 3 4 9
13. Engaging in behavior that is potentially dangerous to self or others.	0 1 2 3 4 9	0 1 2 3 4 9
14. Threats to hurt oneself.	0 1 2 3 4 9	0 1 2 3 4 9
15. Threats to hurt others.	0 1 2 3 4 9	0 1 2 3 4 9
16. Aggressive to others verbally.	0 1 2 3 4 9	0 1 2 3 4 9
17. Appears sad or depressed.	0 1 2 3 4 9	0 1 2 3 4 9
18. Expressing feelings of hopelessness or sadness about the future (e.g., "Nothing worthwhile ever happens," "I never do anything right").	0 1 2 3 4 9	0 1 2 3 4 9
19. Crying and tearfulness.	0 1 2 3 4 9	0 1 2 3 4 9
20. Commenting about death of self or others (e.g., "Life isn't worth living," "I'd be better off dead").	0 1 2 3 4 9	0 1 2 3 4 9
21. Talking about feeling lonely.	0 1 2 3 4 9	0 1 2 3 4 9
22. Comments about feeling worthless or being a burden to others.	0 1 2 3 4 9	0 1 2 3 4 9
23. Comments about feeling like a failure or about not having any worthwhile accomplishments in life.	0 1 2 3 4 9	0 1 2 3 4 9
24. Arguing, irritability, and/or complaining.	0 1 2 3 4 9	0 1 2 3 4 9

Source: Reprinted with permission of L Teri from "Assessment of behavioral problems in dementia: The Revised Memory and Behavior Problems Checklist" by L Teri et al in *Psychology and Aging* (1992;7:622), Copyright © 1992.

"daily." The degree to which each behavior upsets the caregiver is rated by the caregiver on a five-point scale: "not at all," "a little," "moderately," "very much," and "extremely." The assessment of caregiver distress is an advantage when considering disturbing behaviors sometimes associated with dementia. The development of depression in caregivers is predicted primarily by their subjective evaluation of circumstances rather than objective measures of function of the elder.[76]

Functional Rating Scale for the Symptoms of Dementia

The Functional Rating Scale for the Symptoms of Dementia (Exhibit 3–8) is a questionnaire devised to predict who may require nursing home placement.[18] According to the investigators, this dementia scale can measure severity, can track change, and may be valuable in predicting when nursing home placement is necessary. Its possible use in determining when patients reach a level of functional disability requiring nursing home placement makes it an attractive instrument, because such objective measures are generally lacking in assessment for long-term care.

Scores on the scale range from 0 (not demented) to 42. In one study, patients were tested over a two-year period every few months. Patients were divided at the start of the study into two groups: those with scores above 21 and those with scores of 21 or below. Persons with a score greater than 21 had an average of 7 months until nursing home placement occurred, and those with scores of 21 or below did not require nursing home placement for an average of 18 months. Scores at the time of admission to the nursing home were about the same for both groups (about 32).[18]

Three items on the Functional Rating Scale for the Symptoms of Dementia were especially associated with nursing home placement: incontinence of bowel and bladder, inability to speak coherently, and inability to bathe and groom oneself. Eighty-three percent of the patients who suffered from at least two of these three conditions were in a nursing home before the next evaluation.

The investigators who developed this instrument suggested that scores above 30 may indicate a need for nursing home placement.[18] If the physician can state that most patients reaching a certain level of disability require nursing home placement, it may help alleviate some of the family guilt that is common when the issue of such placement arises. Of course, any functional rating scale should be used in conjunction with other relevant medical, social, psychological, and economic data when determining the advisability of nursing home placement.

Global Deterioration Scale

Another approach to the problem of assessing the severity of cognitive impairment is to use a clinical staging system. In Alzheimer's disease, three stages have been commonly recognized. The first is a forgetfulness stage, in which memory problems and impaired visuospatial skills predominate. Then a confusional stage

Exhibit 3–8 Functional Rating Scale for the Symptoms of Dementia

---

Instructions

1. The scale must be administered to the most knowledgeable informant available. This usually is a spouse or close relative.
2. The scale should be read to the informant one category at a time. The informant is presented the description for behavior in each category. The informant is read each of the responses beginning with zero response. All responses should be read before the informant endorses the highest number response that best describes the behavior of the patient.
3. When responses have been obtained for each category, the circled numbers from each category are summed to give an overall score for functional rating of symptoms of dementia.

Circle the highest number of each category that best describes behavior during the past three months.

Eating:
0 Eats neatly using appropriate utensils
1 Eats messily, has some difficulty with utensils
2 Able to eat solid foods (e.g., fruits, crackers, cookies) with hands only
3 Has to be fed

Dressing:
0 Able to dress appropriately without help
1 Able to dress self with occasionally mismatched socks, disarranged buttons or laces
2 Dresses out of sequence, forgets items, or wears sleeping garments with street clothes, needs supervision
3 Unable to dress alone, appears undressed in inappropriate situations

Continence:
0 Complete sphincter control
1 Occasional bed wetting
2 Frequent bed wetting or daytime urinary incontinence
3 Incontinent of both bladder and bowel

Verbal Communication:
0 Speaks normally
1 Minor difficulties with speech or word-finding difficulties
2 Able to carry out only simple, uncomplicated conversations
3 Unable to speak coherently

Memory for Names:
0 Usually remembers names of meaningful acquaintances
1 Cannot recall names of acquaintances or distant relatives
2 Cannot recall names of close friends of relatives
3 Cannot recall name of spouse or other living partner

Memory for Events:
0 Can recall details and sequences of recent experiences
1 Cannot recall details or sequences of recent events
2 Cannot recall entire events (e.g., recent outings, visits of relatives or friends) without prompting
3 Cannot recall entire events even with prompting

continues

Exhibit 3–8 continued

Mental Alertness:
0 Usually alert, attentive to environment
1 Easily distractible, mind wanders
2 Frequently asks the same questions over and over
3 Cannot maintain attention while watching television

Global Confusion:
0 Appropriately responsive to environment
1 Nocturnal confusion on awakening
2 Periodic confusion during daytime
3 Nearly always quite confused

Spatial Orientation:
0 Oriented, able to find and keep his/her bearings
1 Spatial confusion when driving or riding in local community
2 Gets lost when walking in neighborhood
3 Gets lost in own home or in hospital ward

Facial Recognition:
0 Can recognize faces of recent acquaintances
1 Cannot recognize faces of recent acquaintances
2 Cannot recognize faces of relatives or close friends
3 Cannot recognize spouse or other constant living companion

Hygiene and Grooming:
0 Generally neat and clean
1 Ignores grooming (e.g., does not brush teeth and hair, shave)
2 Does not bathe regularly
3 Has to be bathed and groomed

Emotionally:
0 Unchanged from normal
1 Mild change in emotional responsiveness—slightly more irritable or more passive, diminished sense of humor, mild depression
2 Moderate change in emotional responsiveness—growing apathy, increased rigidity, despon-
  dent, angry outbursts, cries easily
3 Impaired emotional control—unstable, rapid cycling or laughing or crying in inappropriate
  situations, violent outbursts

Social Responsiveness:
0 Unchanged from previous, "normal"
1 Tendency to dwell in the past, lack of proper association for present situation
2 Lack of regard for feelings of others, quarrelsome, irritable
3 Inappropriate sexual acting out or antisocial behavior

Sleep Patterns:
0 Unchanged from previous, "normal"
1 Sleeps, noticeably more or less normal
2 Restless, nightmares, disturbed sleep, increased awakenings
3 Up wandering for all or most of the night, inability to sleep

Source: Reprinted with permission of JT Hutton from "Predictors of Nursing Home Placement of Patients
with Alzheimer's Disease" by JT Hutton et al in *Texas Medicine* (1985;81:41), Copyright © 1985.

ensues, in which language and calculation skills are affected, with some changes in personality. Finally, a dementia stage develops, in which intellectual functions are severely deteriorated.[77]

The Global Deterioration Scale for Primary Degenerative Dementia (Exhibit 3–9) is an example of a staging system.[77] The patient's stage is related to progno-

---

Exhibit 3–9 Global Deterioration Scale for Primary Degenerative Dementia with Four-Year Prognosis Data

---

Stage 1: No cognitive decline

Stage 2: Very mild cognitive decline

> The patient complains of memory loss, especially forgetting where objects were placed or familiar names. There is no objective evidence of memory deficit in the clinical interview and no deficits in employment or social situations.
>
> Prognosis: Benign in 95% over a four-year period*

Stage 3: Mild cognitive decline (early confusion)

> Memory loss is evident on testing. Decreased ability to remember names of new acquaintances. Co-workers are aware of memory problems. Gets lost in travel. Associated anxiety or denial.
>
> Prognosis: >80% show no further decline in four years*

Stage 4: Moderate cognitive decline (late confusion)

> Trouble concentrating on a task. Lessened knowledge of personal history, current events, and recent events. Trouble with travel and finances. Remains oriented to time and place. Denial is a prominent defense mechanism.
>
> Prognosis: In four years, one fourth show no change, one fourth are worse but at home, one fourth are in institutions, and one fourth are dead*

Stage 5: Moderately severe cognitive decline

> The phase of dementia. Unable to recall major events of current life. Disoriented to time and place. Occasionally dresses improperly but feeds and toilets independently.
>
> Prognosis: After four years, most are worse*

Stage 6: Severe cognitive decline

> Incontinent. Sleep-wake cycle disturbances.
>
> Personality changes. Forgets even the names of close relatives and spouse.
>
> Prognosis: One third are dead in four years; two thirds are in institutions*

Stage 7: Very severe cognitive decline

> Late dementia, with no speech or psychomotor skills.

---

* The four-year prognosis data are from *Psychiatric Annals* (1985;15:319–322), Copyright © 1985, Charles B Slack Inc.

Source: American Journal of Psychiatry (1982;139:1136–1139). Copyright © 1982, American Psychiatric Association. Reprinted by permission.

sis, and, as expected, the more advanced the stage, the worse is the prognosis. For example, for patients with mild cognitive decline (stage 3), the prognosis is primarily benign, at least over a 4-year period. Patients in early stages may actually have aging-associated cognitive decline (see Chapter 2). On the other hand, when cognitive decline is severe (stage 6), one-third of the patients usually die within 4 years and most have been placed in institutions by the end of that period.

The stages of the global deterioration scale correlate with results of the Folstein Mini-Mental State Examination. Patients at stage 4 of the Global Deterioration Scale, which indicates mild Alzheimer's disease, scored from 16 to 23 on the Folstein Mini-Mental State Examination.[78] Independent validation of the examination set a cutoff score of 24 for detecting dementia.[79-81] Patients at more impaired stages of the global deterioration scale had correspondingly lower scores on the Folstein Mini-Mental State Examination.[78]

Functional Assessment Staging of Alzheimer's Disease

The global deterioration scale has been expanded into a more elaborate staging system called the Functional Assessment Staging of Alzheimer's Disease (FAST; Exhibit 3–10).[82,83] Stages 1 to 5 of the FAST correspond exactly to stages 1 to 5 of the global deterioration scale. Stages 6 and 7 of the global deterioration scale have been subdivided into five and six substages, respectively, in the FAST.

This hierarchal arrangement accomplishes several objectives. First, when a cognitive deficit yields only a baseline or zero score on a mental status examination, further delineation of severity is possible if stages are employed. Second, and more important clinically, when a patient experiences a type of difficulty that seems inconsistent with the expected sequence for Alzheimer's disease, the clinician will be inclined to deal with it as a possibly remediable condition rather than ascribe it to a progression of the Alzheimer's disease.

Imagine a 75-year-old man whose wife states that he has trouble dressing but still picks out his clothes. Since the ability to pick appropriate items should be lost before dressing becomes difficult (stage 5 versus stage 6a), the clinician might consider superimposed depression or stroke as precipitating the trouble rather than a worsening of the underlying dementia. Similarly, a 60-year-old woman who complains about her inability to handle personal finances but is able to function well in a demanding job may be depressed rather than have Alzheimer's disease. Here the appearance of stage 4 difficulties (problems handling personal finances) before stage 3 difficulties (decreased functioning at work) is a clue the proper diagnosis may be depression. Likewise, premature development of urinary incontinence suggests the presence of a urinary tract infection rather than further decline secondary to Alzheimer's disease. Finally, premature loss of speech in an otherwise uncomplicated setting of Alzheimer's disease may suggest focal cerebral pathology, such as an infarction.[82,83]

Exhibit 3–10 Functional Assessment Staging of Alzheimer's Disease Symptomatology and Differential Diagnostic Considerations

FAST Characteristic	FAST Stage	Differential Diagnosis If FAST Stage Is Early
No functional decrement subjectively or objectively	1	
Complains of forgetting location of objects Subjective work difficulties	2	Anxiety neurosis Depression
Decreased functioning in demanding work settings evident to co-workers Difficulty traveling to new locations	3	Depression Subtle manifestations of medical pathology
Decreased ability to perform complex tasks (e.g., planning dinner, shopping, personal finances)	4	Depression Psychosis Focal process (e.g., Gerstmann)
Requires assistance selecting attire May require coaxing to bathe properly	5	Depression
Difficulty dressing properly	6a	Arthritis Sensory deficit Stroke Depression
Requires assistance bathing (fear of bathing)	b	Same as 6a
Difficulty with mechanics of toileting	c	Same as 6a
Urinary incontinence	d	Urinary tract infection Other causes
Fecal incontinence	e	Infection Malabsorption syndrome Other causes
Vocabulary limited to one to five words	7a	Stroke Other dementing disorder (e.g., space-occupying lesion)
Intelligible vocabulary lost	b	Same as 7a
Ambulatory ability lost	c	Parkinsonism Neuroleptic-induced or other secondary extrapyramidal syndrome Jakob-Creutzfeldt disease Normal pressure hydrocephalus Hyponatremic dementia Stroke Hip fracture

continues

Exhibit 3–10 continued

		Arthritis
		Overmedication
Ability to sit lost	d	Arthritis
		Contractures
Ability to smile lost	e	Stroke
Ability to hold up head lost	f	Head trauma
Ultimately, stupor or coma		Metabolic abnormality
		Overmedication
		Other causes

Source: Adapted with permission from "Dementia: A Systematic Approach to Identifying Reversible Causes" by B Reisberg in *Geriatrics* (1986;41[4]:34), Copyright © 1986, Harcourt Brace Jovanovich.

Clinical Dementia Rating Scale

The Clinical Dementia Rating Scale (CDR) was found to correlate to the patient's Short Portable Mental Status Questionnaire (SPMSQ) and to the Blessed Dementia Score, but the CDR was able to differentiate a greater number of degrees of severity over the range of dementia (Exhibit 3–11). For example, patients in CDR 2 scored 8.4 on the SPMSQ, and in CDR 3, an indistinguishable 8.7.[84] The CDR correlates with screening tests of cognitive function such as the SPMSQ[85] and has good reliability.[86] It also correlates with functional impairment more strongly than do tests of mental status.[12,87]

The clinical stage assigned to the patient depends on the pattern of the answers to the questions on the rating scale form (Figure 3–1). The best description of the patient in each of six domains is checked off or circled on the rating scale form. The six domains to be evaluated are memory, orientation, judgment and problem solving, community affairs, home and hobbies, and personal care. The CDR can be employed as a standard instrument for the assessment of elderly demented patients.

Shaded areas in Figure 3–1 show the defined range into which the scores must fall in order to be assigned a specific CDR stage. Memory is considered the primary category, and if at least three other categories are given the same score as memory, then the rating is the same as the rating that describes the patient's memory function. Otherwise, if three or more secondary categories are given a score greater or less than the memory score, the rating is the score of the majority of the secondary categories. If the secondary assessments lie to either side of the memory score, the rating is the same as the memory score.[84] Alternative algorithms for scoring the CDR have been devised to diminish the influence that the memory assessment has on the final CDR score.[88]

Exhibit 3-11 Clinical Dementia Rating Scale (CDR)

	Healthy CDR 0	Questionable Dementia CDR 0.5	Mild Dementia CDR 1	Moderate Dementia CDR 2	Severe Dementia CDR 3
Memory	No memory loss or slight inconstant forgetfulness	Mild consistent forgetfulness; partial recollection of events; "benign" forgetfulness	Moderate memory loss, more marked for recent events; defect interferes with everyday activities	Severe memory loss; only highly learned material retained; new material rapidly lost	Severe memory loss; only fragments remain
Orientation	Fully oriented		Some difficulty with time relationships, oriented for place and person at examination but may have geographic disorientation	Usually disoriented in time, often to place	Orientation to person only
Judgment, problem solving	Solves everyday problems well, judgment good in relation to past performance	Only doubtful impairment in solving problems, similarities, differences	Moderate difficulty in handling complex problems; social judgment usually maintained	Severely impaired in handling problems, similarities, differences; social judgment usually impaired	Unable to make judgments or solve problems

continues

Exhibit 3–11 continued

	Healthy CDR 0	Questionable Dementia CDR 0.5	Mild Dementia CDR 1	Moderate Dementia CDR 2	Severe Dementia CDR 3
Community affairs	Independent function at usual level in job, shopping, business and financial affairs, volunteer and social groups	Only doubtful or mild impairment, if any, in these activities	Unable to function independently at these activities though may still be engaged in some; may still appear normal to casual inspection	No pretense of independent function outside home	
Home, hobbies	Life at home, hobbies, intellectual interests well maintained	Life at home, hobbies, intellectual interests well maintained or only slightly impaired	Mild but definite impairment of function at home; more difficult chores abandoned; more complicated hobbies and interests abandoned	Only simple chores preserved; very restricted interests, poorly sustained	No significant function in home outside of own room
Personal care	Fully capable of self-care		Needs occasional prompting	Requires assistance in dressing, hygiene, keeping of personal effects	Requires much help with personal care; often incontinent

Note: Score each item as 0.5, 1, 2, or 3 only if impairment is due to cognitive loss.

Source: Reprinted with permission from *The British Journal of Psychiatry* (1982;140:566–572), Copyright © 1982, The Royal College of Psychiatrists.

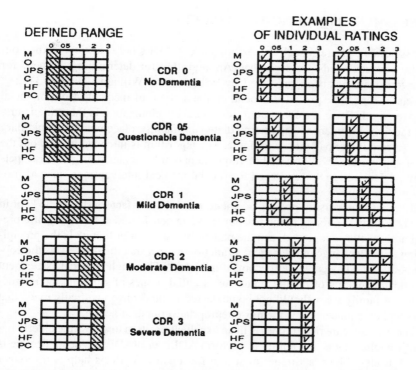

DEFINED RANGE

EXAMPLES OF INDIVIDUAL RATINGS

CDR 0
No Dementia

CDR 05
Questionable Dementia

CDR 1
Mild Dementia

CDR 2
Moderate Dementia

CDR 3
Severe Dementia

Shaded areas indicate defined range within which scores of individual subjects must fall to be assigned a given CDR.

M = Memory; O = Orientation; JPS = Judgment and problem solving; CA = Community affairs; HH = Home, hobbies ; PC = Personal care.

Instructions for assigning the CDR are as follows:

Use all information and make the best judgment. Score each category (M, O, JPS, CA, HH, PC) as independently as possible. Mark in only one box, rating each according to subject's cognitive function. For determining the CDR, memory is considered the primary category; all others are secondary. If at least three secondary categories are given the same numerical score as memory, then CDR = M. If three or more secondary categories are given a score greater or less than the memory score, CDR = score of majority of secondary categories, unless three secondary categories are scored on one side of M and two secondary categories are scored on the other side of M. In this last circumstance, CDR = M.

When M = 0.5, CDR = 1 if at least three of certain others (O, JPS, CA, HH) are scored 1 or greater (PC not influential here). If M = 0.5, CDR cannot be 0; CDR can only be 0.5 or 1. If M = 0, CDR = 0 unless there is slight impairment in two or more secondary categories, in which case CDR = 0.5.

Figure 3–1 How to determine level of dementia using the CDR scale. *Source:* Reprinted with permission from *The British Journal of Psychiatry* (1982;140:566–572). Copyright © 1982, The Royal College of Psychiatrists.

ASSESSMENT FOR LONG-TERM CARE

Assessment of areas such as performance of ADLs helps achieve some congruity between needs and resources. An algorithm for determining the need for long-term care has been suggested by Williams and Williams (Exhibit 3–12).[89] Levels of care to be provided depend on the amount of medical, ADL, or social help required. There is a continuum from acute hospitalization to the skilled nursing facility placement to the intermediate care facility placement to domiciliary care to care in the patient's own home. The algorithm is intended to pick out the most appropriate level of care based on the patient's mental state, ability to perform ADLs and IADLs, and need for special medical interventions, such as provision of oxygen.

If the issue is nursing home placement, precipitating factors should be kept in mind.[90,91] Why is nursing home placement being considered at this time? If a precipitating factor is removed, can the patient be cared for at home? Is the precipitating factor a change in the patient's functioning in a specific ADL? Has the coping ability of a key caregiver become diminished? Thorough physical assessment and documentation of mental status are essential. Issues of guilt and the restructuring of family roles should not be neglected if the decision is finally made that nursing home placement is the most appropriate course of action.[91]

The primary care practitioner is in an excellent position to assess the elderly patient's mental status and ability to perform ADLs and IADLs. When a decline is noted, it alerts the practitioner to search for a cause. Perhaps help is no longer available to perform some necessary function. Recommendations regarding resources or changes in routine may provide a way to accommodate the decline. The line may be crossed when it is no longer possible to provide enough assistance to keep the person functioning adequately at home; then alternative arrangements, such as nursing home placement, would have to be considered.

CASE STUDY: ASSESSMENT FOR LONG-TERM CARE

Mr. Smith is a fit 78-year-old man who lives with his 67-year-old wife in their own home. He exhibits considerable memory impairment and is thought to suffer from Alzheimer's disease (he scores 5 out of a possible 10 on the Short Portable Mental Status Questionnaire). He has no major physical problems. He will perform ADLs with some coaxing from his wife (e.g., bathing, dressing when she lays out his clothes, feeding himself). He has occasional lapses in judgment, including wandering behavior and urinating at inappropriate places or times.

The couple have no children. The patient's sister-in-law lives several blocks away. A next-door neighbor has for years provided assistance with shopping and transportation to the physician's office. In addition, the neighbor has been a source of social interaction for the patient's wife. Mr. Smith's behavior makes it difficult

Exhibit 3–12 Algorithm for Deciding Need for Long-Term Care

I. 1. Is the patient medically unstable?
    2. Is the patient mentally unstable to the extent of being a danger to himself/herself or others?

    NO (continue below)   YES → ACUTE HOSPITAL

II. 1. Is the patient totally disoriented chronically?
    2. Is the patient immobile (i.e., always requires human assistance in locomotion)?
    3. Does the patient have need of special therapy (e.g., intravenous line, tracheostomy, oxygen, ostomy)?
    4. Does the patient require total supervision?
    5. Does the patient require total ADL care?

    NO (continue below)   YES → SKILLED NURSING
                                     FACILITY
                                     or
                             HOME IF SUPPORT
                                 AVAILABLE

III. 1. Does the patient have intermittent disorientation or wandering?
    2. Does the patient fluctuate in ADL ability?
    3. Does the patient require a structured environment—some supervision?
    4. Does the patient require special therapeutics (e.g., complex diet, complex medication schedule, close monitoring)?

    NO (continue below)   YES → INTERMEDIATE LEVEL
                                     FACILITY
                                     or
                             HOME IF SUPPORT
                                 AVAILABLE

IV. Can the patient do all of the following:

1. Feed self	7. Plan meals
2. Bathe	8. Use transportation
3. Dress	9. Use telephone
4. Use the toilet without help	10. Handle finances
5. Change position	11. Manage medications
6. Shop	

    NO (continue below)   YES → HOME

V. Are resources available to meet these needs?

    NO → DOMICILIARY CARE   YES → HOME WITH SUPPORT

Source: Adapted with permission from American Geriatrics Society, "Assessment of the Elderly for Long-Term Care" by TF Williams in *Journal of the American Geriatrics Society* (1982;30:71–73).

for Mrs. Smith to do some of the things she used to do for relaxation. She is able to find a woman in the neighborhood to sit with Mr. Smith so she can run errands and enjoy some respite time.

Over the years Mr. Smith's memory has worsened, and catastrophic reactions occur with increasing frequency and intensity. He hallucinates and talks to himself in the mirror. He frequently does not recognize who his wife is, which of course is very disturbing to her. Mr. Smith's physician helps Mrs. Smith realize that she has become socially isolated, depressed, and even more preoccupied with her husband's care than in years past. Interviewing Mrs. Smith, the physician rates the patient's behavior using the Texas Tech Functional Rating Scale for the Symptoms of Dementia. Mr. Smith's score is 30. On occasion the physician in similar circumstances has used the Moore Functional Dementia Scale as a questionnaire for the family member while the patient is examined.

Because of Mr. Smith's deteriorating ability to perform ADLs, increasing confusion, and catastrophic reactions, including wandering, nursing home placement is recommended. Mrs. Smith is expected to experience guilt and depression, and the physician plans to counsel her to help her deal with the loss of the husband she knew.

Demonstration of a need for alternate living arrangements is more convincing if ADLs are kept in mind or if a scale is employed, such as the Functional Rating Scale for the Symptoms of Dementia. Characteristics associated with nursing home placement include very old age (over 85 years), inability to perform ADLs, incontinence, mental impairment, and lack of a willing, capable family member or caregiver.

CONCLUSION

Functional status assessment of elderly persons is frequently neglected by physicians. For the elderly, however, functional assessment is critical because an elder's ability to remain independent may hinge on his or her ability to perform the activities of daily living.[1,9] The focus on functional needs puts the emphasis on what is important to the patient: how to maximize functioning at home and in the community. This focus directs attention to the health and support services required and possible alternative settings or levels of care.[92]

A systematic approach to functional assessment is helpful because it provides a task-specific framework for checking whether the patient can perform (or has help performing) the tasks that are required to live independently, such as toileting and preparing meals. In fact, problems in performing ADLs could be listed alongside the patient's medical problems, yielding a clearer picture of the spectrum of difficulties encountered by the elderly person and organizing them for possible solution. As Weed suggested, creating a problem list may help the clinician find hitherto unrecognized correlations among physical, mental, and functional spheres.[93] A comprehensive problem-oriented medical record keeps the constellation of medical diagnoses, undiagnosed conditions, and problems of daily living to the fore.

REFERENCES

1. Applegate WB, Blass JP, Williams TF. Instruments for the functional assessment of older patients. *N Engl J Med.* 1990;322:1207–1214.

2. Department of Health and Human Services. *Healthy People 2000: National Health Promotion and Disease Prevention Objectives.* Washington, DC: US Government Printing Office, 1991. DHHS publication PHS 91-50213.

3. Fried LP, Bush TL. Morbidity as a focus of preventive health care in the elderly. *Epidemiol Rev.* 1988;10:48–64.

4. Hadley EC, Ory MG, Suzman R, Weindruch R, Fried L. Physical frailty: a treatable cause of dependence in old age. *J Gerontol.* 1993;48(special issue):1–88.

5. Katz S, Branch LG, Branson MH, et al. Active life expectancy. *N Engl J Med.* 1983;309: 1218–1224.

6. George LK, Bearon LB. *Quality of Life in Older Persons: Meaning and Measurement.* New York, NY: Human Sciences Press, 1980.

7. Rubenstein LV, Calkins DR, Greenfield S, et al. Health status assessment for elderly patients: report of the Society of General Internal Medicine Task Force on Health Assessment. *J Am Geriatr Soc.* 1988;37:562–569.

8. Granger CV, Gresham GE, eds. *Functional Assessment in Rehabilitation Medicine.* Baltimore, Md: Williams & Wilkins, 1984.

9. Mosqueda LA. Assessment of rehabilitation potential. *Clin Geriatr Med.* 1993;9:689–703.

10. Heath JM. Comprehensive functional assessment of the elderly. *Prim Care.* 1989;16:305–327.

11. Guralnik JM, Simonsick EM. Physical disability in older Americans. *J Gerontol.* 1993;48(special issue):3–10.

12. Skurla E, Rogers JC, Sunderland T. Direct assessment of activities of daily living in Alzheimer's disease: a controlled study. *J Am Geriatr Soc.* 1988;36:97–103.

13. Reed BR, Jagust WJ, Seab J. Mental status as a predictor of daily function in progressive dementia. *Gerontologist.* 1989;29:804–807.

14. Brink TL, Capri D, DeNeeve V, et al. Senile confusion: limitations of assessment by the Face-Hand Test, Mental Status Questionnaire, and staff ratings. *J Am Geriatr Soc.* 1978;26:380–382.

15. Barberger-Gateau P, Commenges D, Gagnon M, Letenneur L, Sauvel C, Dartigues JF. Instrumental activities of daily living as a screening tool for cognitive impairment and dementia in elderly community dwellers. *J Am Geriatr Soc.* 1992;40:1129–1134.

16. Iliffe S, Tai SS, Haines A, et al. Assessment of elderly people in general practice, IV: depression, functional ability and contact with services. *Br J Gen Pract.* 1993;43:371–374.

17. Keene JS, Anderson CA. Hip fractures in the elderly. *JAMA.* 1982;248:564–567.

18. Hutton JT, Dippel RL, Loewenson RB, et al. Predictors of nursing home placement of patients with Alzheimer's disease. *Tex Med.* 1985;81:40–43.

19. Lichtenstein MJ, Federspiel CF, Shaffner W. Factors associated with early demise in nursing home residents: a case control study. *J Am Geriatr Soc.* 1985;33:315–319.

20. Incalzi AR, Capparella O, Gemmo A, Porcedda P, Raccis G. A simple method of recognizing geriatric patients at risk for death and disability. *J Am Geriatr Soc.* 1992;40:34–38.

21. Fillenbaum G. Screening the elderly: a brief instrumental activities of daily living measure. *J Am Geriatr Soc.* 1985;33:698–706.

22. Koyano W, Shibata H, Nakazato K, Haga H, Suyama Y, Matsuzaki T. Mortality in relation to instrumental activities of daily living: one year follow-up in a Japanese urban community. *J Gerontol.* 1989;44:S107–109.

23. Mor V, Murphy J, Masterson-Allen S, Willey C, Razmpour A. Risk of functional decline among frail elders. *J Clin Epidemiol.* 1989;42:895–904.

24. Mor V, Wilcox V, Rakowski W, Hiris J. Functional transitions among the elderly: patterns, predictors, and related hospital use. *Am J Public Health.* 1994;84:1274–1280.

25. Branch LG, Meyers AR. Assessing physical function in the elderly. *Clin Geriatr Med.* 1987;3:29–51.

26. Rubenstein LZ, Schairer C, Willard GD, et al. Systematic biases in functional status assessment of elderly adults. *J Gerontol.* 1984;39:686–691.

27. Dorevitch MI, Cossar RM, Bailey FJ, et al. The accuracy of self and informant ratings of physical functional capacity in the elderly. *J Clin Epidemiol.* 1992;45:791–798.

28. Pincus T, Callahan LF, Brooks RH, Fuchs HA, Olsen NJ, Kaye JJ. Self-report questionnaire scores in rheumatoid arthritis compared with traditional physical, radiographic, and laboratory measures. *Ann Intern Med.* 1989;110:259–266.

29. Kelly-Hayes M, Jette AM, Wolf PA, D'Agostino RB, Odell PM. Functional limitations and disability among elders in the Framingham study. *Am J Public Health.* 1992;82:841–845.

30. Myers AM, Holliday PJ, Harvey KA, Hutchinson KS. Functional performance measures: are they superior to self-assessments? *J Gerontol.* 1993;48:M196–206.

31. Guralnik JM, Branch LG, Cummings SR, Curb JD. Physical performance measures in aging research. *J Gerontol.* 1989;44:M141–146.

32. Kuriansky J, Gurland B. The Performance Test of Activities of Daily Living. *International Journal of Aging and Human Development.* 1976;7:343–352.

33. Williams ME, Hadler NM, Earp JAL. Manual ability as a marker of dependency in geriatric women. *J Chron Dis.* 1982;35:115–122.

34. Williams ME. Identifying the older person likely to require long-term care. *J Am Geriatr Soc.* 1987;35:761–766.

35. Williams ME, Gaylord SA, McGaghie WC. Timed manual performance in a community elderly population. *J Am Geriatr Soc.* 1990;38:1120–1126.

36. Williams ME, Gaylord SA, Gerrity MS. The timed manual performance test as a predictor of hospitalization and death in a community-based elderly population. *J Am Geriatr Soc.* 1994;42:21–27.

37. Reuben DB, Siu AL. An objective measure of physical function of elderly outpatients: The Physical Performance Test. *J Am Geriatr Soc.* 1990;38:1105–1112.

38. Rozzini R, Frisoni GB, Bianchetti A, et al. Physical performance test and activities of daily living scales in the assessment of health status in elderly people. *J Am Geriatr Soc.* 1993;41:1109–1113.

39. Winograd CH, Lemsky CM, Nevitt MC, et al. Development of a physical performance and mobility examination. *J Am Geriatr Soc.* 1994;42:743–749.

40. Burton JR. The house call: an important service for the frail elderly. *J Am Geriatr Soc.* 1985;33:291–293.

41. Levy MT. Psychiatric assessment of elderly patients in the home. *J Am Geriatr Soc.* 1985;33:9–12.

42. Reuben DB, Solomon DH. Assessment in geriatrics: of caveats and names. *J Am Geriatr Soc.* 1989;37:570–572.

43. Fried LP, Ettinger WH, Lind B, Newman AB, Gardin J. Physical disability in older adults: a physiological approach. *J Clin Epidemiol.* 1994;47:747–760.

44. Yurick AG, Spier BE, Robb SS, et al. *The Aged Person and the Nursing Process.* 2nd ed. Norwalk, Conn: Appleton-Century-Crofts, 1984.

45. Carnevali DL, Patrick M. *Nursing Management for the Elderly.* 2nd ed. Philadelphia, Pa: JB Lippincott Co, 1986.

46. Applegate WB. Use of assessment instruments in clinical settings. *J Am Geriatr Soc.* 1987; 35:45–50.

47. Siu AL, Reuben DB, Hays RD. Hierarchical measures of physical function in ambulatory geriatrics. *J Am Geriatr Soc.* 1990;38:1113–1119.

48. Blazer D, Siegler IC. *A Family Approach to Health Care of the Elderly.* Menlo Park, Calif: Addison-Wesley Publishing Co, 1984.

49. Woodhouse K, Wynne H, Baillie S, et al. Who are the frail elderly? *Q J Med.* 1988;28:505–506.

50. Schulz R, Williamson GM. Psychosocial and behavioral dimensions of physical frailty. *J Gerontol.* 1993;48(special issue):39–43.

51. Rockwood K, Fox RA, Stolee P, Robertson D, Beattie BL. Frailty in elderly people: an evolving concept. *Can Med Assoc J.* 1994;150:489–495.

52. Feinstein AR. An additional basic science for clinical medicine, IV: the development of clinimetrics. *Ann Intern Med.* 1983;99:843–848.

53. Feinstein AR, Josephy BR, Wells CK. Scientific and clinical problems in indexes of functional disability. *Ann Intern Med.* 1986;105:413–420.

54. Becker PM, Cohen HJ. The functional approach to the care of the elderly: a conceptual framework. *J Am Geriatr Soc.* 1984;32:923–929.

55. Granger CV, Albrecht GL, Hamilton BB. Outcome of comprehensive medical rehabilitation: measurement by PULSES profile and the Barthel index. *Arch Phys Med Rehabil.* 1979;60:145–154.

56. Kane RA, Kane RL. *Assessing the Elderly: A Practical Guide to Measurement.* Lexington, Mass: Lexington Books, 1981.

57. Pope AM, Tarlov AR, eds. *Disability in America: Toward a National Agenda for Prevention.* Washington, DC: National Academy Press, 1991.

58. Katz S, Ford AB, Moskowitz RW, et al. Studies of illness in the aged: the index of ADL. *JAMA.* 1963;185:914–919.

59. Bruett TL, Overs RP. A critical review of 12 ADL scales. *Phys Ther.* 1969;49:857–862.

60. Katz PR, Dube DH, Calkins E. Use of a structured functional assessment format in a geriatric consultative service. *J Am Geriatr Soc.* 1985;33:681–686.

61. Katz S, Downs TD, Cash HR, et al. Progress in development of the index ADL. *Gerontologist.* Spring 1970 (part 1):20–30.

62. Kelly JF, Winograd CH. A functional approach to stroke management in elderly patients. *J Am Geriatr Soc.* 1985;33:48–60.

63. Mahoney FI, Barthel DW. Functional evaluation: the Barthel index. *Md Med J.* 1965;14:61–65.

64. Fortinsky RH, Granger CV, Seltzer GB. The use of functional assessment in understanding home care needs. *Med Care.* 1981;19:489–497.

65. Lawton MP, Brody EM. Assessment of older people: self-maintaining and instrumental activities of daily living. *Gerontologist.* 1969;9:179–186.

66. *The OARS Methodology: Multidimensional Functional Assessment Questionnaire.* 2nd ed. Durham, NC: Duke University Center for the Study of Aging and Human Development, 1978: 169–170.

67. Teresi JA, Cross PS, Golden RR. Some applications of latent trait analysis to the measurement of ADL. *J Gerontol.* 1989;44:196–204.

68. Suurmeijer TPBM, Doeglas DM, Moum T, et al. The Groningen Activity Restriction Scale for measuring disability: its utility in international comparisons. *Am J Public Health.* 1994;84:1270–1273.

69. Gallo JJ, Franch MS, Reichel W. Dementing illness: the patient, caregiver, and community. *Am Fam Physician.* 1991;43:1669–1675.

70. Morris JN, Sherwood S, Mor V. An assessment tool for use in identifying functionally vulnerable persons in the community. *Gerontologist.* 1984;24:373–379.

71. Blessed G, Tomlinson BE, Roth M. The association between quantitative measures of dementia and of senile changes in the cerebral grey matter of elderly subjects. *Br J Psychiatry.* 1968; 114:797–811.

72. Moore J, Bobula JA, Short TB, et al. A functional dementia scale. *J Fam Pract.* 1983; 16:499–503.

73. Teri L, Truax P, Logsdon R, Uomoto J, Zarit S, Vitaliano PP. Assessment of behavioral problems in dementia: the revised Memory and Behavior Problems Checklist. *Psychol Aging.* 1992;7:622–631.

74. Zarit SH, Todd PA, Zarit J. Subjective burden of husbands and wives as caregivers: a longitudinal study. *Gerontologist.* 1986;26:260–266.

75. Zarit SH, Anthony CR, Boutselis M. Interventions with care givers of dementia patients: comparison of two approaches. *Psychol Aging.* 1987;2:225–232.

76. Gallo JJ. The effect of social support on depression in caregivers of the elderly. *J Fam Pract.* 1990;30:430–436.

77. Reisberg B, Ferris SH, DeLeon MJ, et al. The global deterioration scale for assessment of primary degenerative dementia. *Am J Psychiatry.* 1982;139:1136–1139.

78. Reisberg B, Ferris SH, Borenstein J, et al. Assessment of presenting symptoms. In: Poon LW, ed. *Clinical Memory Assessment of Older Adults.* Washington, DC: American Psychological Association, 1986:108–128.

79. Smyer MA, Hofland BF, Jonas EA. Validity study of the Short Portable Mental Status Questionnaire for the elderly. *J Am Geriatr Soc.* 1979;27:263–269.

80. Shuttleworth EC. Memory function and the clinical differentiation of dementing disorders. *J Am Geriatr Soc.* 1982;30:363–366.

81. Fillenbaum G. Comparison of two brief tests of organic brain impairment, the MSQ and the Short Portable MSQ. *J Am Geriatr Soc.* 1980;28:381–384.

82. Reisberg B. Dementia: a systematic approach to identifying reversible causes. *Geriatrics.* 1986;41:30–46.

83. Reisberg B, Ferris SH, Franssen E. An ordinal functional assessment tool for Alzheimer-type dementia. *Hosp Community Psychiatry.* 1985;36:593–595.

84. Hughes CP, Berg L, Danziger WL, et al. A new clinical scale for the staging of dementia. *Br J Psychiatry.* 1982;140:566–572.

85. Davis PB, Morris JC, Grant E. Brief screening tests versus clinical staging in senile dementia of the Alzheimer type. *J Am Geriatr Soc.* 1990;38:129–135.

86. Burke WJ, Miller JP, Rubin EH, et al. Reliability of the Washington University clinical dementia rating. *Arch Neurol.* 1988;45:31–32.

87. Winograd CH. Mental status tests and the capacity for self care. *J Am Geriatr Soc.* 1984;32:49–53.

88. Gelb DJ, St. Laurent RT. Alternative calculation of the Global Clinical Dementia Rating. *Alzheimer Dis Assoc Disord.* 1993;7:202–211.

89. Williams TF, Williams ME. Assessment of the elderly for long-term care. *J Am Geriatr Soc.* 1982;30:71–75.

90. Rabins P, Mace NL, Lucas MJ. The impact of dementia on the family. *JAMA.* 1982; 248:333–335.

91. Pace WD, Anstett RE. Placement decisions for the elderly: a family crisis. *J Fam Pract.* 1984;18:31–46.

92. Williams TF. Assessment of the geriatric patient in relation to needs for services and facilities. In: Reichel W, ed. *Clinical Aspects of Aging.* 2nd ed. Baltimore, Md: Williams & Wilkins, 1983: 543–548.

93. Weed L. *Medical Records, Medical Education, and Patient Care.* Cleveland, Ohio: Case Western Reserve Press, 1970.

4

Social Assessment

or most older adults, life is immeasurably enhanced by their relationship with family members. At no other time of life, save perhaps for childhood, does the family play such a pivotal role. The benefits of the relationship are reciprocal: Older members of the family may give gifts and financial aid or may assist with domestic chores such as housekeeping or child care. Grandparents who assume the major role in raising grandchildren have become more common. In addition to tangible help, older family members provide a sense of the life cycle to younger people.

Persons over 85 years of age make up the fastest growing segment of the population of the United States. As a result, children who find themselves caring for elderly parents may themselves be elderly. One-fourth of all caregivers are 65 to 74 years of age, and 10% are over age 75.[1] One in ten persons over age 65 have a child who is at least 65 years of age.[2] Not uncommonly, the caregiver is a woman in her sixties caring for a 90-year-old mother. Because more persons are living to advanced age, the average woman can expect to spend more years caring for an

The authors gratefully acknowledge consultation with representatives from the following organizations in the preparation of this chapter: Adult Protective Services, Arlington, Virginia; the Fairfax Department of Human Services, Fairfax, Virginia; the National Center on Elder Abuse; Legal Services of Northern Virginia; the National Coalition of Nursing Home Reform; and the American Association of Retired Persons.

elderly parent than her counterpart in 1900.[3] The trend toward smaller families (meaning there are fewer adult children to serve as caregivers) and the increasing participation of women in the workplace further strain the support system of the older person.

The assessment of the social situation, particularly of the support available to the person unable to perform independently all the activities of daily living, is intimately intertwined with the issues surrounding nursing home placement. Numerous studies indicate the presence of a caregiver is the most important factor in the disposition of elderly patients following discharge from the hospital.[4–10] For example, a clinic at the University of Wisconsin assessed patients with Alzheimer's disease who were living in the community at the time of assessment. Patients who eventually had to be placed in a nursing home did not differ from the others in ability to perform the activities of daily living or in health status. The major precipitating reason for placement was lack of a willing caregiver.[9] Caregiver burden and degree of functional impairment of the elder were independently associated with the use of health services over the course of a 12-month period in another study.[10]

Despite myths to the contrary, families continue to provide help for their elderly members, sometimes stretching financial and emotional resources to the limit. The clinician may or may not use formal screening instruments analogous to cognitive or functional status tests, but issues of social support cannot be ignored.

Adverse environmental and social situations contribute to stress and illness.[11] The elderly are subject to a great number of significant life stressors. The kinds of physiologic, psychologic, and social resources that are most helpful for dealing with stressful situations are often diminished in older adults. The Holmes and Rahe Social Readjustment Rating Scale was employed to demonstrate the association between life events and illness.[12,13] In the scale, each of 43 life stressors is assigned a value expressed in "life change units" (LCUs). The higher the LCU value, the more stressful the event. The highest LCU (100) is assigned to the death of a spouse, whereas the lowest (11) is assigned to minor violations of the law. (The value assigned to a particular event is based on how the event was rated by about 400 persons from diverse socioeconomic strata.) Subjects check off experiences of the past year, and the total number of LCUs obtained is a measure of the stress experienced.

Many of the highly stressful life events on the Social Readjustment Rating Scale are commonly experienced by older people. Significant life stress, such as the death of a spouse, may portend subsequent health problems.[12–15] Unexpected life events may be more stressful than planned or scheduled events.[16] Perhaps anticipatory guidance regarding common and foreseeable events, such as retirement, could make these events less stressful. Significant life changes should be carefully evaluated to learn the circumstances of an event; the level of anticipation of and preparation for the event; the degree of control exercised by the person over the event; and the social, financial, and health resources available to cope with the event.[16]

Stressful life events not only increase susceptibility to illness but also impair the ability to cope with illness psychologically and physiologically.[17] Elderly persons who have few social and community ties are at increased risk of disease as well as institutionalization.[7] There is a clear correlation between social bonds and mortality even after adjustment for differences due to physical health, smoking, alcohol consumption, obesity, and physical activity.[7,18] In addition, the strength and intensity of contacts may be more important than the total number of relationships, so that an intimate relationship with a spouse would be potentially more influential than affiliation with a church.[7]

SOURCES OF SOCIAL SUPPORT

The support system of older adults comprises three components: the informal network, the formal support system, and semiformal support.[18,19] The informal support network includes family and friends. The formal support system includes Social Security, Medicaid, and social welfare programs. Semiformal support includes assistance and social interaction of the kind provided by neighborhood organizations such as churches and senior citizen centers.[18]

Sources of informal support are generally selected by the elderly persons themselves, often based on longstanding relationships. The informal network is the constellation of social relationships providing not only social interaction and discourse, such as daily phone contact, but also services, such as transportation to the physician's office or to the grocery store. A social network is the constellation of a person's social relationships, but social support is the actual help (financial, emotional, or otherwise) that the social network can provide.[20] Persons in the social network may or may not be helpful (i.e., provide social support). For example, a son who lives nearby may not provide adequate support for an elderly widow.

Neighbors who deal with an elderly person on a daily basis may perform essential chores or errands. The family may be unaware of the extent of the help provided by this "natural helper" network; indeed, the elderly person him- or herself may not fully comprehend it.[21] The postal carrier who sees to it that the mail is picked up, the grocery clerk who helps with bags, and neighbors who bake and share their cooking and company are examples of natural helpers. In rural communities, informal helpers may acquire considerable importance, especially if the elderly person is geographically isolated and reluctant to participate in formal programs.[22] Some rural elderly are not comfortable receiving even informal assistance unless they have accumulated "social credit" (i.e., they have helped others).[23]

The formal support system consists of the Social Security, Medicaid, and social welfare programs. These programs play an important role in the economic as well as social well-being of elderly persons, especially in our mobile industrialized society, in which children move far from their parents. The precise relationship that should exist between the government and the informal support system is a matter of some debate, since it is commonly argued that substantial government involvement would make long-term care even more costly. Studies suggest, however, that families request only the help actually required to care for elderly family members. Furthermore, they generally prefer to have a service provided rather than receive financial aid (e.g., to have access to respite care rather than be given direct financial support).[2]

Semiformal support groups, such as church groups, neighborhood organizations, clubs, and senior citizen centers, are important sources of social support for older adults. For many kinds of support, the older adult must take the initiative to gain access to services and might require encouragement or assistance from health professionals or family members. Professionals who are involved in the care of older people should take heed of the available sources of support and get a sense of what type of informal, formal, and semiformal help has been provided in the past.

THE CAREGIVER

Social assessment for older patients has two dimensions: (1) assessment of the sources and kinds of help available to the elder within the social network, and (2) assessment of the primary caregiver, the "hidden patient," often the patient's spouse.[24] An assessment of the social help available to an elder is incomplete without some evaluation of the physical, mental, emotional, functional, social, and economic condition of the caregiver.

Assessment of caregiver "burden" has been conceptualized into three components.[25] The first is a determination of the impairment of the elder, including an assessment of the elder's ability to perform activities of daily living, sociability, disruptive behavior, and mental status. The severity of symptoms or impairment alone, however, may be a poor predictor of the degree of caregiver stress.[26] Second, the tasks that correspond to the elder's needs are rated as difficult, tiring, or upsetting. Dealing with bowel or bladder incontinence, for example, would probably be considered more difficult, tiring, and upsetting than assisting with meals. Lastly, the impact of the elder's behaviors and the required tasks on the caregiver's life is assessed. For example, situations of caregiving may result in a change of job or the turning down of a promotion or in a redefinition of family relationships.[25]

The tasks that family caregivers undertake are often rigorous—both physically and emotionally demanding. The range of support includes emotional support (such as telephone calls), help with the instrumental activities of daily living (transportation, shopping, housekeeping, and meal preparation), and help with the basic activities of daily living (bathing, feeding, dressing, and toileting). Two-thirds of the caregivers surveyed stated they attended to some personal care needs of the elderly family member.[2]

A lack of social support for the caregiver often exacerbates the caregiver's despair.[27] If the patient's behavior is embarrassing, the caregiver may become further isolated and drop previously enjoyed activities. Administration of a short instrument, such as the Family APGAR or the Zarit Burden Interview, at least broaches the topic of caregiver stress. An argument can be made that the instruments for detecting depression discussed in Chapter 2 might also be used to uncover depression among elderly caregivers. The prevalence of depression among caregivers may be very high, and the perceived burden of care may be greater when depression is present.[27,28]

Making a special effort to include an assessment of how the caregiver is coping validates the person's caregiving effort and sends the clear message that the physician is concerned with the caregiver, not just the older patient; this can be therapeutic for the caregiver.[20] Assessment of the physical health of the caregiver has practical value as well. The caregiver with cardiovascular problems or arthritis cannot be expected to do heavy lifting in the course of caring for an impaired elderly person. The possibility of health problems on the part of caregivers highlights the need to consider the functional status of older patients. In one survey, one-third of caregivers rated their health as "fair or poor."[2] Other investigators showed that caregivers had three times as many stress-related symptoms and used more psychoactive drugs than similar control subjects.[29] The most stressful type of living arrangement was an adult child living in the same household with an elderly parent.[29]

A family-centered approach to medical care is helpful in caring for an elderly patient. It is important, for example, to consider how the family has handled stress in the past. A family that has rallied to the aid of troubled or ill members in the past will continue to do so when the ailing family member is older. Religious or ethnic expectations may also enter into how care is provided. When siblings are involved in caring for an elderly parent, previously uncommunicated feelings or past conflicts may emerge. As Hooyman and Lustbader point out, children who have been family scapegoats or who were abused by parents may have difficulty participating in caregiving.[21]

If the family tends to adhere rigidly to traditional gender roles, the women in the family may find themselves performing all the personal care tasks.[21,30,31] Indeed, 72% of primary caregivers are women. Of these female caregivers, 29% are the daughters of the patients and 23% are wives of patients.[1] Generally speaking, a woman is more likely to help with personal care or housekeeping, a man with transportation, home repair, and financial management.[2]

A woman with a career may suffer considerable stress in trying to balance her work life and her role as a caregiver. She may feel unable to meet all her responsibilities because of limited time, energy, and resources. She may feel guilty that her performance does not meet her high standards (standards that may be unrealistic).[32] Career women may increase their caregiving responsibilities at the expense of their leisure and work time. Daughters are more likely than sons to leave work in order to care for elderly family members: 12% of daughters left their job to care for an ailing parent, whereas only 5% of sons did so.[1] Nationally, about 11% of workers who quit a job did so in order to undertake caregiving responsibilities.[2] These demographic changes may propel the movement toward employee benefits that include "kin care."[33]

Scharlach considered potential benefits and costs of working while caregiving and the implications for workplace support systems.[34] In this study, caregiving was viewed as rewarding and was associated with high life-satisfaction. The positive consequences of combining work with caregiving included these: Work actually served as a form of respite; helped meet the psychosocial needs of the caregiver; and tended to alleviate some of the negative consequences of caregiving, such as role restriction, social isolation, and stress.

CAREGIVERS OF OLDER ADULTS WITH DEMENTIA

When the elder is impaired by dementia, caregiving becomes all the more stressful, as the family must deal with impaired memory, difficult behaviors, and the pain of personality changes in a loved one. If that were not bad enough, the reactions of friends and neighbors may worsen the feelings of hopelessness. Memory disturbance is the most common and disturbing of behaviors exhibited by demented patients. Ninety-three percent of caregivers rated this as a major problem.[35] Caregivers who failed to keep in mind that the patient is brain damaged reported a great deal of stress in caregiving.[26] Violent behavior, such as hitting, was not often reported but was particularly distressing when it occurred.[35] Caregivers may find that a dementia rating scale (see Chapter 3) serves well as a review of systems (or, more accurately, a review of symptoms) for the problems of dementia.

Denial may be the initial response of a caregiver who must deal with the gradual loss of a loved one to Alzheimer's disease.[36] Excuses are made for the patient's memory loss, and the caregiver takes false comfort from the relative preservation of remote memory. Once the memory deficit is so great as to be undeniable, the caregiver helps the patient compensate and may become overinvolved with routine tasks. As difficulty mounts, and deficits become more pervasive, the caregiver feels angered at the disease, the elder, and the health care professionals. There may be guilt about how things were handled and about surreptitious wishes for the patient's death. Lastly, the caregiver may begin to accept that the loved one is no longer the same person. Not all caregivers go through this stereotyped sequence

reminiscent of Kubler-Ross's stages of psychologic change in confronting terminal illness,[37] but the sequence is useful as a rough framework.

Chenoweth and Spencer[38] found that caregivers expressed difficulty convincing
physicians of subtle changes, and once the diagnosis of Alzheimer's disease was
made, no information was given on what to expect. This is particularly unfortunate, since the only "family therapy" that may be required to help the caregivers
cope is information about disease diagnosis and prognosis.[39,40] Prior to the evaluation of patients at a geriatric clinic, caregivers were asked what questions they
wished the evaluation would answer.[41] Most had wanted to know what the future
course of the Alzheimer's disease would be, what the cause of the patient's symptoms was, and whether everything had been done to find out if the symptoms were
treatable. It was noted that 68% of the patients had been diagnosed with dementia
but were brought to the clinic because of an inadequate explanation of how the diagnosis was made or what to expect.[41]

A study of caregiver burden revealed that, when compared with a control group
of noncaregiver elders, the caregivers of demented patients had social networks
similar in size to those of the control group but were less satisfied with the networks' adequacy.[42] They were unable to partake in family and church activities to
the same degree as the control subjects. The caregivers reported poorer health,
more visits to physicians, and greater use of prescription drugs.[42]

Caregiving is not without its challenges, failures, and triumphs. Tremendous
growth occurs in some families as they meet the challenges of caregiving. Parent-
child roles undergo redefinition as children strive to help their ailing parents.
Brothers and sisters work together in new ways and redefine their relationship to
one another.[21] An elderly caregiver may find new meaning in life, a feeling of increased self-worth, and a new role that compensates for other lost roles (e.g., as a
jobholder).[2] Rzetelny and Mellor set forth a caregiver's bill of rights (Table 4–1)
in which the importance of including the caregiver in the assessment of the elderly
patient is recognized.

The 36-Hour Day,[43] a book on caregiving, is aptly titled and can be recommended as a reference for caregivers. Other titles that may benefit caregivers are

---

Table 4–1 The Caregiver's Bill of Rights

1. The right to live a life of one's own.
2. The right to choose a plan for caring.
3. The right to be free from any form of financial or legal coercion when choosing a plan for providing care.
4. The right to be recognized as a vital source of family stability.

Source: Reprinted from *Support Groups for Caregivers of the Aged: A Training Manual for Facilitators* (p 72) by H Rzetelny and J Mellor with permission of Community Service Society of New York.

cited in the references[44-46] and in the *Geriatric Patient Education Resource Manual.*[47] Intensive efforts to educate caregivers, such as programs offered by some community colleges, may pay off for older persons with dementia in terms of decreased utilization of services and even survival.[48]

ELDER ABUSE

Abuse of older adults exists and is a growing problem, as violence is generally more pervasive and the number of older persons is increasing. The American Medical Association defined elder abuse in its Model Elderly Abuse Reporting Act (1985) as follows: "Abuse includes intentional infliction of physical or mental injury; sexual abuse; or withholding of necessary food, clothing, and medical care to meet the physical and mental needs of an elderly person by one having the care, custody, or responsibility of an elderly person."[49] Types of abuse identified by the National Aging Resource Center on Elder Abuse for purposes of state reporting include (1) physical abuse, (2) sexual abuse, (3) emotional or psychological abuse, (4) neglect, (5) financial or material exploitation, and (6) self-abuse/neglect.[50,51]

All 50 states, the District of Columbia, Guam, and the Virgin Islands have legislation to protect elders from abuse in domestic and institutional settings. Mandatory reporting of suspected abuse is required in 42 states, but in 8 states reporting is voluntary. Persons mandated to report suspected elder abuse usually include law enforcement personnel, staff of adult protective services (APS) and aging agencies, health care personnel, and staff in residential facilities. Some states also require ordinary citizens to file a report when abuse is suspected. State statutes vary widely, but generally the state or local APS agency accepts reports of suspected domestic abuse. In most states, the names of persons reporting suspected abuse are to be kept confidential, disclosed only to the APS agency or to the legal system. A person reporting suspected abuse bears no liability as a result of the report unless the report was known to be false. Failure to report suspected elder mistreatment is a misdemeanor in 17 states.[52]

In most states, the APS agencies are responsible for investigating reports of elder abuse and for providing treatment and protective services; however, numerous public and private organizations play an active role in dealing with abuse. For example, the area agency on aging, the state ombudsman's office, law enforcement agencies, medical facilities, and mental health agencies may be involved in investigating cases of alleged abuse.[52] Decision trees may be useful by providing guidelines for the decision-making process. Hawaii has developed a decision tree that can serve as a model.[53]

Major factors predisposing caregivers to engage in elder abuse include impairment of the elder and consequent dependence on the caregiver, caregiver stress, family dynamics and a history of violence, and psychopathology in the caregiver (e.g., substance abuse).[54-60] Frequently mistreatment starts after some event that leaves the elder more dependent on the caregiver. Health care professionals who deal with older patients should remain alert for functional changes in the elderly patient that leave the caregiver reluctant to care for the patient or simply feeling unable to do so.

The elder is even more vulnerable to abuse and neglect when the caregiver has physical or emotional problems.[49,54,59,61] Often the least psychologically prepared and socially integrated child is called upon to assume the caregiver role. Substance abuse on the part of the caregiver may contribute to violent behavior.[49,54] Bendik, investigating personal and situational characteristics of caregivers that may lead to abuse, found that having an external locus of control orientation, inadequate income and social supports, and poor problem-solving skills led to mood disturbance and seemingly irrational behavior.[62] Older adults with cognitive impairment are at particular risk for becoming victims of abuse. Cognitively impaired older patients may put extreme demands on the caregiver, exhibiting aggressive or violent behavior and thereby increasing the burden of care and the strain on the caregiver.[56,61,62]

The possibility of abuse exists in every setting in which older adults receive care, including nursing homes. Pillemer and Moore conducted a telephone survey of 577 nursing home staff.[63] Thirty-six percent witnessed at least one incident of physical abuse in the preceding year. Excessive restraint was especially common, but pushing, grabbing, shoving, pinching, slapping, and hitting residents occurred, and even, in a small number of cases, throwing things at residents and kicking them. Eighty-one percent of the respondents witnessed psychological abuse, especially shouting at or insulting residents, in the previous year.

In evaluating a possible case of abuse, creating trust and rapport with the patient and the family is essential. Information should be gathered from the patient, other involved persons, and agencies in a nonthreatening and nonjudgmental manner.[60,64] When interviewing the caregiver in a possible abuse case, the examiner should focus on the problems of the patient so that the caregiver does not feel his or her response to the situation is being questioned. The examiner should also ask the caregiver about who helps with the caregiving and should attempt to gauge the caregiver's level of perceived burden, depression, and use of medication or alcohol. A home visit is desirable, and the process of evaluation in cases of possible abuse may be facilitated when a multidisciplinary team is consulted.[64-66]

The presence of confusion or a diagnosis of dementia in an older person being evaluated for suspected abuse should not deter the examiner from asking about the circumstances that prompted an evaluation or that gave rise to a suspicion of abuse.[49,60,64] The examiner should include direct questions about injuries and behavior related to the suspected abuse (Exhibit 4–1). The examiner should also assess risk factors and the patient's self-care ability, cognitive and functional status,

Exhibit 4–1 Questions That May Elicit a History of Elder Abuse

1. Has anyone at home ever hurt you?
2. Has anyone ever touched you without your consent?
3. Has anyone ever made you do things you didn't want to do?
4. Has anyone taken anything that was yours without asking?
5. Has anyone ever scolded or threatened you?
6. Have you signed any documents that you didn't understand?
7. Are you afraid of anyone at home?
8. Are you alone a lot?
9. Has anyone ever failed to help you take care of yourself when you needed help?

Source: Adapted from *Elder Mistreatment Guidelines for Health Care Professionals: Detection, Assessment and Intervention,* Mount Sinai/Victim Services Aging Elder Abuse Project, New York, 1988.

and level of dependency on the caregiver.[60] While the patient may not want to name an abuser, the examiner may be able to determine the identity from a description of the patient's activities during a typical day.

The following types of situations may signal abuse:

- The patient is brought to the emergency room by someone other than the usual caregiver.
- The patient is home alone and calls for help.
- The patient becomes fearful, agitated, or overly quiet in the presence of the caregiver.
- A long interval passes between an injury and the seeking of treatment.
- The description of how an injury occurred is inconsistent with physical findings.
- The patient has many unexplained injuries or the oral explanations vary with time and differ from those in the caregiver's report.

The examiner should be particularly wary if the caregiver is quick to answer questions asked of the elder, if the elder looks to the caregiver before and during answering questions, or if the elder yields to the caregiver.[60,64]

The Risk of Elder Abuse in the Home (REAH) instrument (Exhibit 4–2) is designed to evaluate the risk of elder abuse. The REAH index is the sum of two component parts, a score based on a vulnerability assessment of the older adult and a score based on a stress assessment of the caregiver. The higher the REAH index, the greater the potential risk. The REAH index can be calculated regularly to detect changes or for use in hospital discharge planning. At the first indication of a potentially abusive situation, an intervention can be planned and implemented.[67]

Exhibit 4–2 REAH—An Index for Assessing the Risk of Elder Abuse in the Home

The REAH is the sum of two components, the vulnerability assessment score of the aged person (VASAP) and the stress assessment score of the caregiver (SASC). Use the tables below to calculate VASAP and SASC, then add them to find the REAH.

REAH (sum of VASAP and SASC, RANGE 0 to 41)   _____

VASAP—Vulnerability Assessment Score of the Aged Person

A. Personal Data Section (aged person)

	2 points	1 point	0 points	Score
Age	85 or older	75–84	74 or younger	_____
Sex		Female	Male	_____
Health	Frail	Average	Robust	_____

Subtotal, A. Personal Data (sum of above, range 0 to 5)   _____

B. Dependency Needs Section (aged person)

1 point for a "yes," 0 points for a "no" or "don't know"	Score
Intellectual or severe mental impairment?	_____
Lives in home with caregiver?	_____
Needs help bathing?	_____
Needs help dressing?	_____
Needs help toileting? (or is incontinent or has catheter)	_____
Needs help eating?	_____
Depends on caregiver for all social interaction?	_____
Allows caregiver to assume parental role?	_____
Demanding and authoritative to caregiver?	_____
Is financially dependent upon caregiver?	_____

Subtotal, B. Dependency Needs (sub of above, range 0 to 10)   _____

VASAP (sum of subtotals A and B, range 0 to 15)   _____

SASC–Stress Assessment Score of the Caregiver

A. Personal Data Section (caregiver)

	2 points	1 point	0 points	Score
Age	70 and over	45–69	under 45	_____
Phys. health	poor	good	excellent	_____
Ment. health	poor	good	excellent	_____
Finances	under $7000	$7–$14000	$14000 & more	_____
Dependents (not elder)	2 or more	1	none	_____

Subtotal, A. Personal Data (sum of above, range 0 to 10)   _____

continues

Exhibit 4–2 continued

B. Stress Factors Section (caregiver)	
1 point for a "yes," 0 points for a "no" or "don't know"	Score
Alcoholism or substance abuse?	_____
Mental retardation?	_____
History or observation of family violence?	_____
Change in lifestyle to assume care of aged person?	_____
Receives financial help from the elder?	_____
Limited time for own personal activities?	_____
Personal stresses (i.e., marital problems, empty nest)?	_____
Mostly or always at home (unable to leave aged person)?	_____
Absence of support system (family, friends, community)?	_____
Shows frustrations, resentment in care of aged person?	_____
Treats elder as a child?	_____
Has limited knowledge of the aging process?	_____
Believes any care at home is better than nursing home?	_____
Minimizes or denies dependency of aged person?	_____
Shows dependency toward the elder?	_____
Authoritative manner with the elder?	_____
Subtotal, B. Stress Factors (sum of above, range 0 to 16)	_____
SASC (sum of subtotals A and B, range 0 to 26)	_____

For the VASAP, 12–15 represents highest risk, 9–11 high risk, 6–8 medium risk, 3–5 low risk, and 0–2 lowest risk. For the SASC, 20–26 represents highest risk, 15–19 high risk, 10–14 medium risk, 5–9 low risk, and 0–4 lowest risk.

Source: Reprinted with permission from *Journal of Gerontological Nursing* (1989;15:21–26), Copyright © 1989, Slack, Inc.

Elder abuse is a complex problem and requires the expertise of many disciplines if appropriate interventions are to be pursued. The interventions will vary depending on local laws and customs, the willingness of the elder to receive help, the availability of resources, and other circumstances.[52]

INSTRUMENTS FOR ASSESSING SOCIAL SUPPORT

The instruments presented in this section should be viewed as supplementary to the interview, the usual method of collecting data about the elder's social situation. Many primary care physicians prefer not to use such formal instruments. Nonetheless, the instruments focus attention on specific qualities of a social support network that investigators believe constitute the essence of a good social support system, and the questions may be helpful in promoting a discussion of important social support issues with patients and caregivers.

The assessment of family functioning is not a one-time assessment—support available to the elder needs to be periodically re-evaluated. A change in the elder's condition should compel a fresh look at caregiving roles and stresses. The spouse may be able to manage a demented elder until, for example, caregiving becomes too physically demanding. Changes within the family may necessitate a restructuring of social support. A new job may take a child away from an elderly parent. The death or illness of a spouse may leave an elder "stranded." New sources of assistance may need to be rallied in order to provide adequate care for the family member.

The Family APGAR and the Friends APGAR

The Family APGAR (Exhibit 4–3), although not developed exclusively for use with the elderly, is a short screening instrument used to assess social functioning.[68] The five aspects of family functioning selected for assessment are adaptation, partnership, growth, affection, and resolve (APGAR). Scores of 2, 1, or 0 are assigned to each item. Scores of less than 3 of a possible 10 indicate a highly dysfunctional family, at least as perceived by the person. A score of 4 to 6 is indicative of moderate family dysfunction.[68,69]

For an elderly person who has more intimate social relationships with friends than family members, the Friends APGAR (Exhibit 4–4) may be more appropriate.

Exhibit 4–3 Family APGAR

1. I am satisfied that I can turn to my family for help when something is troubling me. (adaptation)
2. I am satisfied with the way my family talks over things with me and shares problems with me. (partnership)
3. I am satisfied that my family accepts and supports my wishes to take on new activities or directions. (growth)
4. I am satisfied with the way my family expresses affection and responds to my emotions, such as anger, sorrow, or love. (affection)
5. I am satisfied with the way my family and I share time together. (resolve)

Statements are answered always (2), some of the time (1), or hardly ever (0).

Source: Adapted with permission from *The Journal of Family Practice* (1982;15:307), Copyright © 1982, Appleton & Lange.

Exhibit 4–4 Friends APGAR

---

1. I am satisfied that I can turn to my friends for help when something is troubling me. (adaptation)
2. I am satisfied with the way my friends talk over things with me and share problems with me. (partnership)
3. I am satisfied that my friends accept and support my wishes to take on new activities or directions. (growth)
4. I am satisfied with the way my friends express affection and respond to my emotions, such as anger, sorrow, or love. (affection)
5. I am satisfied with the way my friends and I share time together. (resolve)

Statements are answered always (2), some of the time (1), or hardly ever (0).

Source: Adapted with permission from *The Journal of Family Practice* (1982;15:307), Copyright © 1982, Appleton & Lange.

Neither of these instruments should be used in isolation to diagnose family dysfunctionality. However, Smilkstein and associates[68] have recommended using a screening instrument such as the Family APGAR in four situations:

1. when interviewing new patients,
2. when interviewing persons who will be caring for a chronically ill family member,
3. following an adverse event (such as a death or diagnosis of cancer), or
4. when the patient's history suggests that a dysfunctional family is itself the problem.

Either of the two instruments could also be used to assess a caregiver's perceptions of the adequacy of emotional and social support following, for example, a new diagnosis of Alzheimer's disease in a relative.

The Social Dysfunction Rating Scale

In scoring the Social Dysfunction Rating Scale (Exhibit 4–5), the rater assigns a score based on the following six gradations: not present (score 1), very mild (score 2), mild (score 3), moderate (score 4), severe (score 5), and very severe (score 6). This instrument was able to categorize 92% of patients correctly when applied to a group of 80 psychiatric and nonpsychiatric outpatients (the original determination of the outpatients' social function was based on the judgment of clinicians unaware of the scale).[70] The Social Dysfunction Rating Scale contains examples of the kinds of questions that assess social situation.

Exhibit 4–5 Social Dysfunction Rating Scale

Self-esteem
1. Low self-concept (feelings of inadequacy, not measuring up to self-ideal)
2. Goallessness (lack of inner motivation and sense of future orientation)
3. Lack of a satisfying philosophy or meaning of life (a conceptual framework for integrating past and present experiences)
4. Self-health concern (preoccupation with physical health, somatic concerns)

Interpersonal System
5. Emotional withdrawal (degree of deficiency in relating to others)
6. Hostility (degree of aggression toward others)
7. Manipulation (exploiting of environment, controlling at other's expense)
8. Overdependency (degree of parasitic attachment to others)
9. Anxiety (degree of feeling of uneasiness, impending doom)
10. Suspiciousness (degree of distrust or paranoid ideation)

Performance System
11. Lack of satisfying relationships with significant persons (spouse, children, kin, significant persons serving in a family role)
12. Lack of friends, social contacts
13. Expressed need for more friends, social contacts
14. Lack of work (remunerative or nonremunerative, productive work activities that normally give a sense of usefulness, status, confidence)
15. Lack of satisfaction from work
16. Lack of leisure time activities
17. Expressed need for more leisure, self-enhancing, and satisfying activities
18. Lack of participation in community activities
19. Lack of interest in community affairs and activities that influence others
20. Financial insecurity
21. Adaptive rigidity (lack of complex coping patterns to stress)

Score from 1 (not present) to 6 (very severe) for each item.

Source: Adapted with permission from "A Social Dysfunction Rating Scale" by MW Linn et al in *Journal of Psychiatric Research* (1969;6:300), Copyright © 1969, Pergamon Journals Ltd.

Social Resources Section of the Older Americans Resources and Services Multidimensional Functional Assessment Questionnaire

One of the domains covered by the Older Americans Resources and Services (OARS) Multidimensional Functional Assessment Questionnaire developed at Duke University is social resources.[71] Items in the social resources section (Exhibit 4–6) include frequency of visitors, satisfaction with social contacts, loneliness, availability of a confidant, and availability of help in case of illness. In its entirety the OARS Multidimensional Functional Assessment Questionnaire also assesses economic resources, mental health, activities of daily living, and

Exhibit 4–6 Social Resources Section of the OARS Multidimensional Functional Assessment Questionnaire

1. Are you single, married, widowed, divorced or separated?
2. Who lives with you?
3. How many persons do you know well enough to visit with in their homes?
4. About how many times did you talk to someone—friends, relatives, or others on the telephone in the past week (either you called them or they called you)?
5. How many times during the past week did you spend some time with someone who does not live with you, that is, you went to see them or they came to visit you or you went out to do things together?
6. Do you have someone you can trust and confide in?
7. Do you find yourself feeling lonely quite often, sometimes, or almost never?
8. Do you see your relatives and friends as often as you want to or are you somewhat unhappy about how little you see them?
9. Is there someone who would give you any help at all if you were sick or disabled, for example your husband/wife, a member of your family, or a friend?

If "yes," answer a and b:
   a. Is there someone who would take care of you as long as needed, or only for a short time, or only someone who would help you now and then (for example, taking you to a physician or fixing lunch occasionally)?
   b. Who is this person? (obtain the name and relationship of this person)

Source: Adapted from *Multidimensional Functional Assessment Questionnaire*, ed 2 (pp 154–156) by Duke University Center for the Study of Aging and Human Development with permission of Duke University, 1978.

instrumental activities of daily living (using some of the instruments described previously). After asking the questions, the interviewer makes a judgment as to social functioning using a scale from 1 to 6, from unimpaired to extremely impaired.

Zarit Burden Interview

The Zarit Burden Interview (Exhibit 4–7) is intended to identify feelings engendered in the caregiver that contribute to the "burden" of caring for an impaired elder. The perception of burden by the caregiver does not correlate closely with the symptoms of the patient. Specifically, reported memory and behavior problems, deficits exhibited in mental status testing, and ability to perform the instrumental activities of daily living do not correlate with the level of burden as defined by the scale.[72]

Feelings of burden seemed more related to the social support available to the caregiver, how the caregiver interprets and responds to the patient's symptoms,

Exhibit 4–7 Zarit Burden Interview

1. Do you feel that your relative asks for more help than he/she needs?
2. Do you feel that because of the time you spend with your relative that you don't have enough time for yourself?
3. Do you feel stressed between caring for your relative and trying to meet other responsibilities for your family or work?
4. Do you feel embarrassed over your relative's behavior?
5. Do you feel angry when you are around your relative?
6. Do you feel that your relative currently affects your relationship with other family members or friends in a negative way?
7. Are you afraid what the future holds for your relative?
8. Do you feel your relative is dependent on you?
9. Do you feel strained when you are around your relative?
10. Do you feel your health has suffered because of your involvement with your relative?
11. Do you feel that you don't have as much privacy as you would like because of your relative?
12. Do you feel that your social life has suffered because you are caring for your relative?
13. Do you feel uncomfortable about having friends over because of your relative?

Source: Adapted with permission from *The Hidden Victims of Alzheimer's Disease: Families Under Stress* by SH Zarit, NK Orr, JM Zarit, New York University Press, 1985. Copyright © 1983 by SH Zarit and JM Zarit.

and the nature of the ongoing relationship between the caregiver and the patient.[26] Emphasis is again given to assessment of the caregiver for the symptoms of depression, which may indicate that the caregiver is overextended.

Caregiver Strain Index

The Caregiver Strain Index (Exhibit 4–8) is a short (13-item) scale for measuring caregiver strain of burden.[73] The scale was shown to be valid when tested in a population of nondemented elderly who were returning home from hospitalization. Again, the types of issues believed to impinge on the lives of caregivers are evident: changing roles, disturbing behavior exhibited by the older patient, the burden of physical help required, and sleep disturbance.

CONCLUSION

The assessment of the social situation of elderly patients forms a vital background for geriatric assessment and therapy. Caregivers must be considered in the management plan of an elderly patient with physical or mental impairment. Specific areas of need may be handled by persons in the patient's informal and

Exhibit 4–8 Caregiver Strain Index

Sleep is disturbed (e.g., because _____ is in and out of bed or wanders around at night)

It is inconvenient (e.g., because helping takes so much time or it's a long drive over to help)

It is a physical strain (e.g., because of lifting in and out of a chair; effort or concentration is required)

It is confining (e.g., helping restricts free time or cannot go visiting)

There have been family adjustments (e.g., because helping has disrupted routine; there has been no privacy)

There have been changes in personal plans (e.g., had to turn down a job; could not go on vacation)

There have been other demands on my time (e.g., from other family members)

There have been emotional adjustments (e.g., because of severe arguments)

Some behavior is upsetting (e.g., because of incontinence; _____ has trouble remembering things; or _____ accuses others of taking things)

It is upsetting to find _____ has changed so much from his/her former self (e.g., he/she is a different person than he/she used to be)

There have been work adjustments (e.g., because of having to take time off)

It is a financial strain

Feeling completely overwhelmed (e.g., because of worry about _____ ; concerns about how you will manage)

Total score (count "yes" responses):

Instructions given to the caregiver: I am going to read a list of things that other persons have found to be difficult in helping out after somebody comes home from the hospital. Would you tell me whether any of these apply to you? (Give the examples)

Score 1 for yes and 0 for no.

Source: Adapted with permission from *Journal of Gerontology* (1983;38[3]:345), Copyright © 1983, Gerontological Society of America.

semiformal support systems if these systems are appropriately evaluated and applied. Older persons can sometimes suggest solutions to their own problems if encouraged to do so, perhaps with some help from family or professionals.[21] The formal support system ideally is employed in such a fashion as to complement the support from other sources. The ultimate aim, to allow the elder patient to function at maximum capacity, is achieved not only through treatment of the patient in the physician's office or the hospital but also by forming a partnership, a therapeutic alliance, with the caregiver and the family.[74]

REFERENCES

1. Stone R, Cafferata GL, Sangl J. Caregivers of the frail elderly: a national profile. *Gerontologist.* 1987;27:616–626.

2. Subcommittee on Human Services of the US House Select Committee on Aging. *Exploding the Myths: Caregiving in America.* Washington, DC: US Government Printing Office, 1987.

3. Preston SH. Children and the elderly in the U.S. *Sci Am.* 1984;250:44–49.

4. Sloane PD. Nursing home candidates: hospital inpatient trial to identify those appropriately assignable to less intensive care. *J Am Geriatr Soc.* 1980;28:511–514.

5. Wachtel TJ, Fulton JP, Goldfarb J. Early prediction of discharge disposition after hospitalization. *Gerontologist.* 1987;27:98–103.

6. Lindsey AM, Hughes EM. Social support and alternatives to institutionalization for the at-risk elderly. *J Am Geriatr Soc.* 1981;29:308–315.

7. Berkman L. The assessment of social networks and social support in the elderly. *J Am Geriatr Soc.* 1983;31:743–749.

8. Williams TF, Williams ME. Assessment of the elderly for long-term care. *J Am Geriatr Soc.* 1982;30:71–75.

9. Fisk AA, Pannill FC. Assessment of the elderly for long-term care. *J Am Geriatr Soc.* 1987; 35:307–311.

10. Brown LJ, Potter JF, Foster BG. Caregiver burden should be evaluated during geriatric assessment. *J Am Geriatr Soc.* 1990;38:455–460.

11. Cohen F. Stress, emotion, and illness. In: Temoshok L, Van Dyke C, Zegans LS, eds. *Emotions in Health and Illness: Theoretical and Research Foundations.* New York, NY: Grune & Stratton, 1983.

12. Holmes TH, Rahe RH. The Social Readjustment Scale. *J Psychosom Res.* 1967;11:213–218.

13. Rahe RH, Arthur RJ. Life change patterns surrounding illness experience. *J Psychosom Res.* 1968;11:341–349.

14. Orrell MW, Davies ADM. Life events in the elderly. *Int Rev Psychiatry.* 1994;6:59–71.

15. Frank E, Anderson B, Reynolds CF, Ritenour A, Kupfer DJ. Life events and the Research Diagnostic Criteria endogenous subtype: a confirmation of the distinction using the Bedford College methods. *Arch Gen Psychiatry.* 1994;51:519–524.

16. Schroots JJF, Birren JE. Concepts of time and aging in science. In: Birren JE, Schaie KW, eds. *Handbook of the Psychology of Aging.* 3rd ed. New York, NY: Academic Press, 1990:45–64.

17. Fry PS. *Depression, Stress, and Adaptations in the Elderly: Psychological Assessment and Intervention.* Rockville, Md: Aspen Publishers, 1986.

18. Rzetelny H, Mellor J. *Support Groups for Caregivers of the Aged.* New York, NY: Community Service Society, 1981.

19. Zarit SH, Pearlin LI, Schaie KW, eds. *Caregiving Systems: Informal and Formal Helpers.* Hillsdale, NJ: Lawrence Erlbaum Associates, 1993.

20. Gallo JJ, Franch MS, Reichel W. Dementing illness: the patient, caregiver, and community. *Am Fam Phys.* 1991;43:1669–1675.

21. Hooyman NR, Lustbader W. *Taking Care: Supporting Older People and Their Families.* New York, NY: The Free Press, 1986.

22. Reichel W. Care of the elderly in rural America. *Md Med J.* May 1980:75.

23. Lozier J, Althouse R. Retirement to the porch in rural Appalachia. *Int J Aging Hum Dev.* 1975;6:7–15.

24. Fengler AP, Goodrich N. Wives of elderly disabled men: the hidden patients. *Gerontologist.* 1979;19:175–183.

25. Poulshock SW, Deimling GT. Families caring for elders in residence: issues in the measurement of burden. *J Gerontol.* 1984;39:230–239.

26. Zarit SH, Orr NK. *Working with Families of Dementia Victims: A Treatment Manual.* Washington, DC: US Government Printing Office, 1984. Publication 84-20816.

27. Gallo JJ. The effect of social support on depression in caregivers of the elderly. *J Fam Pract.* 1990;30:430–436.

28. Drinka TJK, Smith JC, Drinka PJ. Correlates of depression and burden for informal caregivers of patients in a geriatric referral clinic. *J Am Geriatr Soc.* 1987;35:522–525.

29. George LK, Gwyther LP. Caregiver well-being: a multidimensional examination of family care-givers of demented adults. *Gerontologist.* 1986;26:253–259.

30. Stoller EP. Parental caregiving by adult children. *J Marriage Fam.* November 1983:851–858.

31. Horowitz A. Family caregiving for the frail elderly. In: Eisdorfer C, ed. *Annual Review of Gerontology and Geriatrics.* New York, NY: Springer Publishing Co, 1985.

32. Scharlach AE. Role strain in mother-daughter relationships in later life. *Gerontologist.* 1987;27:627–631.

33. Smith DM. *Kin Care and the American Corporation: Solving the Work/Family Dilemma.* Homewood, Ill: Business One Irwin, 1991.

34. Scharlach AE. Caregiving and employment: competing or complementary roles? *Gerontologist.* 1994;34:378–385.

35. Rabins P, Mace NL, Lucas MJ. The impact of dementia on the family. *JAMA.* 1982; 248:333–335.

36. Teusink JP, Mahler S. Helping families cope with Alzheimer's disease. *Hosp Community Psychiatry.* 1984;35:152–156.

37. Kubler-Ross E. *On Death and Dying.* New York, NY: Macmillan Publishing Co, 1969.

38. Chenoweth B, Spencer B. Dementia: the experience of family caregivers. *Gerontologist.* 1986; 26:267–272.

39. Gwyther LP, Blazer DG. Family therapy and the demented patient. *Am Fam Phys.* 1984; 29:149–156.

40. Larson D, Blazer DG. Family therapy with the elderly. In: Blazer DG, Siegler IC, eds. *A Family Approach to the Health Care of the Elderly.* Menlo Park, Calif: Addison-Wesley Publishing Co, 1984:95–111.

41. Simonton LJ, Haugland SM. Assessing caregiver information needs: a brief questionnaire. Presented at Gerontological Society of America Annual Meeting; 1986; Des Moines, Iowa.

42. Haley WE, Levine EG, Brown SL, et al. Psychological, social, and health consequences of caring for a relative with senile dementia. *J Am Geriatr Soc.* 1987;35:405–411.

43. Mace NL, Rabins PV. *The 36-Hour Day.* rev. ed. Baltimore, Md: Johns Hopkins University Press, 1991.

44. Hooyman NR, Lustbader W. *Taking Care of Your Aging Family Members: A Practical Guide.* New York, NY: The Free Press, 1986.

45. Cohen D, Eisdorfer C. *The Loss of Self: A Family Resource for the Care of Alzheimer's Disease and Related Disorders.* New York, NY: W.W. Norton & Co, 1986.

46. Coons DH, Metzelaar L, Robinson A, Spencer B, eds. *A Better Life: Helping Family Members, Volunteers and Staff Improve the Quality of Life of Nursing Home Residents Suffering from Alzheimer's Disease and Related Disorders.* Columbus, Ohio: The Source for Nursing Home Literature, 1986.

47. The Aspen Reference Group, eds. *Geriatric Patient Education Resource Manual.* Gaithersburg, Md: Aspen Publishers, 1994.

48. Brodaty H, Peters KE. Cost effectiveness of a training program for dementia carers. *Int Psychogeriatr.* 1991;3:11–22.

49. American Medical Association, Council on Scientific Affairs. Elder abuse and neglect. *JAMA.* 1987;257:966–971.

50. Fabian DR, Rathbone-McCuan E, eds. *Self-Neglecting Elders: A Clinical Dilemma.* Westport, Conn: Auburn House, 1992.

51. Tatara T. *Summaries of the Statistical Data on Elder Abuse in Domestic Settings for FY 90 and FY 91: A Final Report.* Washington, DC: National Aging Resource Center on Elder Abuse, 1993.

52. National Center on Elder Abuse. *Elder Abuse: Questions and Answers.* Washington, DC: National Center on Elder Abuse, 1994.

53. Braun K, Lenzer K, Schumacher-Mukai C, Snyder P. A decision tree for managing elder abuse and neglect. *J Elder Abuse Neglect.* 1993;5:89–103.

54. Bourland MD. Elder abuse: from definition to prevention. *Postgrad Med.* 1990;87:139–144.

55. Pillemer K, Finkelhor D. The prevalence of elder abuse: a random sample survey. *Gerontologist.* 1988;8:51–57.

56. Andrew CC, Reichman WE, Berbig LJ. The relationship between dementia and elder abuse. *Am J Psychiatry.* 1993;150:643–646.

57. Kurrle SE, Sadler PM, Cameron ID. Patterns of elder abuse. *Med J Aust.* 1992;157:673–676.

58. Douglass RL. *Domestic Mistreatment of the Elderly—Towards Prevention.* Washington, DC: American Association of Retired Persons, 1992.

59. McDowell JD, Kasselbaum DK, Strombos SE. Recognizing and reporting victims of domestic violence. *J Am Dent Assoc.* 1992;123:44–50.

60. All AC. A literature review: assessment and intervention in elder abuse. *J Gerontol Nurs.* 1994;20:25–32.

61. Ehrlich F. Patterns of elder abuse. *Med J Aust.* 1993;158:292–293.

62. Bendik MF. Reaching the breaking point: dangers of mistreatment in elder caregiving situations. *J Elder Abuse Neglect.* 1992;4:39–59.

63. Pillemer K, Moore D. Abuse of patients in nursing homes: findings from a survey of staff. *Gerontologist.* 1989;29:314–320.

64. Quinn MJ, Tomita SK. *Elder Abuse and Neglect: Causes, Diagnosis, and Intervention Strategies.* New York, NY: Springer Publishing Co, 1986.

65. Decalmer P, Marriott A. The multidisciplinary assessment of clients and patients. In: Decalmer P, Glendenning F, eds. *The Mistreatment of Elderly People.* Newbury Park, Calif: Sage Publications, 1993:117–135.

66. Noone JF, Decalmer P, Glendenning F. The general practitioner and elder abuse. In: Decalmer P, Glendenning F, eds. *The Mistreatment of Elderly People.* Newbury Park, Calif: Sage Publications, 1993:136–149.

67. Hamilton GP. Using a prevent elder abuse family systems approach. *J Gerontol Nurs.* 1989; 15:21–26.

68. Smilkstein G, Ashworth C, Montano D. Validity and reliability of the Family APGAR as a test of family function. *J Fam Pract.* 1982;15:303–311.

69. Smilkstein G. The physician and family function assessment. *Fam Syst Med.* 1984;12:263–278.

70. Linn MW, Sculthorpe WB, Evje M, et al. A Social Dysfunction Rating Scale. *J Psychiatr Res.* 1969;6:299–306.

71. *The OARS Assessment Methodology: Multidimensional Functional Assessment Questionnaire.* 2nd ed. Durham, NC: Duke University Center for the Study of Aging and Human Development, 1978:169–170.

72. Zarit SH. Relatives of the impaired elderly: correlates of feelings of burden. *Gerontologist.* 1980;20:649–655.

73. Robinson BC. Validation of a caregiver strain index. *J Gerontol.* 1983;38:344–348.

74. American Medical Association, Council on Scientific Affairs. Physicians and family caregivers: a model for partnership. *JAMA.* 1993;269:1282–1284.

5

The Values History: Assessing Patient Values and Directives Regarding Long-Term and End-of-Life Care

David J. Doukas and Laurence B. McCullough

eriatric assessment focuses on the multidimensional status of the elderly patient. With increasingly complex ethical dilemmas in hospitals and community-based and institutional long-term care, the health care professional should place increased emphasis on prospectively identifying the patient's values and assisting the patient to provide advance directives on the basis of those values. The living will and the durable power of attorney for health care (DPA/HC) can help in this task by addressing the issue of preferences for future health care. Yet use of these legal instruments alone ignores the patient's values regarding such preferences and the impact of values on the patient's decisions. Therefore, an instrument allowing a more systematic evaluation of advance health care decision making by the competent elderly patient has been advocated: the Values History.[1-4] This clinical tool enhances the autonomy of the elderly patient and clarifies for the health care team and the patient's family what the patient's values are and what decisions are to be carried out when decision making by the patient is no longer possible. The Values History helps to achieve the ideal goal of advance directives: the identification of the value-based preferences of the patient prior to the time when the patient can no longer speak for him- or herself. Consequently, the Values History is a valuable adjunct in fulfilling one important object of the Patient Self-Determination Act of 1990: the informing of patients in Medicare- and Medicaid-receiving institutions about their right to refuse medical therapy (through use, for example, of a living will or DPA/HC).[5] The critical decisions that are necessary in the hospital and nursing home setting are prospectively addressed by using the Values History in the outpatient setting, and factors that adversely affect the elderly population, such as sickness and diminished capacity, can be prevented from undermining autonomous decision making by patients. Other adjuncts to advance directives have been proposed, but these do not explicitly address a patient's specific end-of-life values and value-based preferences.[6,7]

THE LIVING WILL

The living will documents the proactive decision of an elderly patient to withhold or withdraw mechanical and other artificial means of health care when the patient is terminally ill and is no longer able to make decisions regarding such interventions. The living will is a tool to be used when the patient has a terminal condition. Many jurisdictions also allow use of a living will for patients in a persistent vegetative state. One of its advantages is that the living will allows a patient to decide broadly that a spectrum of drugs, procedures, and therapies available to treat the terminal disease process and its complications should not be administered. The living will's strength is that it is a written declaration conveying treatment refusal to the health care team in the presence of a terminal condition and the dying process. The instrument cannot be challenged by third parties so long as it has been executed according to the procedures defined in the state statute. The patient may also revoke the living will even when the patient is incompetent.

One widely noted shortcoming of the living will is a vagueness regarding which medical procedures are refused. The living will's imprecision can lead to misinterpretation (either construed too broadly or too narrowly) of what the patient has refused.[8] Also, physician adherence to a living will depends on physician estimates of the probability of the patient's recovery.[8] Furthermore, in most states, the living will must be in the precise form mandated by the statute.[9]

A more serious shortcoming is that no living will statute mandates physicians to work with their patients to identify their values regarding terminal treatment and care or make decisions about terminal care based on those values. Although the living will is a valuable asset in allowing elders to declare themselves noncandidates for some means of life support, it does not address patient values that help patients and health care providers better understand the basis of advance directives. Thus, health care providers' understanding of their patients' reasoning and motivation needs to be augmented. Doing so will help in extrapolating the living will to decisions not specifically addressed in it.

DURABLE POWER OF ATTORNEY FOR HEALTH CARE

The durable power of attorney for health care (DPA/HC) legally empowers an agent to make health care decisions for a person when that person is incapacitated. "Durable" is the crucial term here, as the appointed agent of a person would otherwise lose his or her power of decision upon that person's incapacity (as occurs in the case of a simple power of attorney). The durable power of attorney allows for the assignment of a legally enforceable surrogate decision maker when the patient has lost decision-making capacity. The patient does not have to be terminally ill for the durable power of attorney to take effect, in contrast to a living will (see Table 5–1). In many states, DPA/HC laws have been legislated to specify that this authority applies specifically to health-related decisions. The designated surrogate decision maker considers the medical options available to the patient and then chooses the option that most closely adheres to the previously stated or written preferences of the patient. The use of a DPA/HC may allow a more precise adherence to the patient's preferences than the living will, provided that the patient has expressed relevant preferences. The use of the DPA/HC, when no living will has been signed, allows for a transference of the patient's autonomy to an agent in order to make decisions consenting to or refusing medical therapy when the patient has lost decision-making capacity. Although the living will obviates the need for decision making by others, the DPA/HC, with its enhanced flexibility and reduced vagueness, may represent a better approach.

The main objection to the DPA/HC is that the patient's proxy might not understand all of the patient's health care preferences.[10] Will the proxy be able to determine the patient's likely responses in all health care circumstances? The problem here is that the surrogate decision maker may not have helped the patient identify his or her values and beliefs regarding terminal care or elicited specific preferences based on those values or beliefs.

Table 5–1 Conditions for Applicability of Advance Directives

Living Will
- The patient is, in reasonable medical judgment, terminally ill or, in some state statutes, persistently vegetative (as this phrase is defined in applicable statute or, as in the case of the Department of Veterans Affairs, in applicable policy).
- The patient, in reasonable medical judgment, has lost the capacity to make decisions about his or her own care.

Durable Power of Attorney for Health Care
- The patient, in reasonable medical judgment, has lost the capacity to make decisions about his or her own care.

THE VALUES HISTORY

The Values History (Exhibit 5–1) provides for the identification of end-of-life health care values and the expression of preferences on the basis of those values and thus serves as a useful clinical adjunct to other advance directives. The Values History has two main sections. In the first section, the patient identifies his or her values and beliefs regarding terminal care. In the second, the patient states decisions in advance about such care given those values. The goal of this section is twofold: to facilitate clarification of the patient's end-of-life values and to assist health care providers in understanding, respecting, and implementing the value-based decisions of the Values History in the clinical setting. The physician's goal, though, is not to gauge "validity" of the patient's values or otherwise attempt to force value and preference concordance, as this would be grossly paternalistic.

The Values History Preamble

The Values History begins with a preamble explaining its intent to supplement the patient's pre-existing advance directive (or directives) by providing him or her with the opportunity to articulate explicit, value-based preferences. The Values History directives are reversible as long as the patient is competent and are revokable even when the patient has lost decision-making capacity under the terms of the living will or DPA/HC legislation existing in the relevant jurisdiction. The values and preferences should guide health care providers when a patient without decision-making capacity has been documented as terminally ill and the withholding or withdrawing of life-sustaining measures is contemplated. As is always the case, competent patients can affirm or change advance directives as they choose.

The Values Section

The patient is to identify the values he or she holds that are relevant to the decisions that must be made. The first basic decision is between length of life and quality of life. The patient is then asked to identify and circle the values most important to him or her from a list of 13 common end-of-life values. The patient is also provided an opportunity to add to the list and elaborate on the chosen values. The chosen values should be used to facilitate discussion of how the patient views the advance directives regarding medical care in the next section.

Exhibit 5–1 The Values History

Patient Name: _____

This Values History serves as a set of my specific value-based directives for various medical interventions. It is to be used in health care circumstances when I may be unable to voice my preferences. These directives shall be made a part of the medical record and used as supplementary to my living will and/or durable power of attorney for health care.

I. VALUES SECTION

Values are things that are important to us in our lives and our relationships with others—especially loved ones. There are several values important in decisions about terminal treatment and care. This section of the Values History invites you to identify your most important values.

A. Basic Life Values

Perhaps the most basic values in this context concern length of life versus quality of life. Which of the following two statements is the most important to you?

_____ 1. I want to live as long as possible, regardless of the quality of life that I experience.

_____ 2. I want to preserve a good quality of life, even if this means that I may not live as long.

B. Quality of Life Values

There are many values that help us to define for ourselves the quality of the life that we want to live. Review this list (and feel free to either elaborate on it or add to it) and circle those values that are *most* important to your definition of quality of life.

1. I want to maintain my capacity to think clearly.
2. I want to feel safe and secure.
3. I want to avoid unnecessary pain and suffering.
4. I want to be treated with respect.
5 I want to be treated with dignity when I can no longer speak for myself.
6. I do not want to be an unnecessary burden on my family.
7. I want to be able to make my own decisions.
8. I want to experience a comfortable dying process.
9. I want to be with my loved ones before I die.
10. I want to leave good memories of me to my loved ones.
11. I want to be treated in accord with my religious beliefs and traditions.
12. I want respect shown for my body after I die.
13. I want to help others by making a contribution to medical education and research.
14. Other values or clarification of values above:

continues

Exhibit 5–1 continued

II. PREFERENCES SECTION

Some directives involve simple yes or no decisions. Others provide for the choice of a trial of intervention. Use the values identified above to explain why you made the choice you did. The information will be very useful to your family, to your health care surrogate (or proxy), and to health care providers.

Initials/Date

_____ _____ 1. I want to undergo cardiopulmonary resuscitation.
          _____ YES
          _____ NO
          Why?

_____ _____ 2. I want to be placed on a ventilator.
          _____ YES
          _____ TRIAL for the TIME PERIOD OF _____
          _____ TRIAL to determine effectiveness using reasonable medical judgment.
          _____ NO
          Why?

_____ _____ 3. I want to have an endotracheal tube used in order to perform items 1 and 2.
          _____ YES
          _____ TRIAL for the TIME PERIOD OF _____
          _____ TRIAL to determine effectiveness using reasonable medical judgment.
          _____ NO
          Why?

_____ _____ 4. I want to have total parenteral nutrition administered for my nutrition.
          _____ YES
          _____ TRIAL for the TIME PERIOD OF _____
          _____ TRIAL to determine effectiveness using reasonable medical judgment.
          _____ NO
          Why?

_____ _____ 5. I want to have intravenous medication and hydration administered; regardless of my decision, I understand that intravenous hydration to alleviate discomfort or pain medication will not be withheld from me if I so request them.
          _____ YES
          _____ TRIAL for the TIME PERIOD OF _____
          _____ TRIAL to determine effectiveness using reasonable medical judgment.
          _____ NO
          Why?

continues

Exhibit 5–1 continued

_____ _____ 6. I want to have all medications used for the treatment of my illness continued; regardless of my decision, I understand that pain medication will continue to be administered including narcotic medications.
_____ YES
_____ TRIAL for the TIME PERIOD OF _____
_____ TRIAL to determine effectiveness using reasonable medical judgment.
_____ NO
Why?

_____ _____ 7. I want to have nasogastric, gastrostomy, or other enteral feeding tubes introduced and administered for my nutrition.
_____ YES
_____ TRIAL for the TIME PERIOD OF _____
_____ TRIAL to determine effectiveness using reasonable medical judgment.
_____ NO
Why?

_____ _____ 8. I want to be placed on a dialysis machine.
_____ YES
_____ TRIAL for the TIME PERIOD OF _____
_____ TRIAL to determine effectiveness using reasonable medical judgment.
_____ NO
Why?

_____ _____ 9. I want to have an autopsy done to determine the cause(s) of my death.
_____ YES
_____ NO
Why?

_____ _____ 10. Admission to an intensive care unit.
_____ YES
_____ NO
Why?

_____ _____ 11. For patients in long-term care facilities or receiving care at home who experience a life-threatening change in health status: I want 911 called in case of a medical emergency.
_____ YES
_____ NO
Why?

_____ _____ 12. OTHER DIRECTIVES:

continues

Exhibit 5–1 continued

I consent to these directives after receiving honest disclosure of their implications, risks, and benefits by my physician, free from constraints and being of sound mind.

_____   _____
Signature   Date

_____
Witness

_____
Witness

13. PROXY NEGATION:
    I request that the following persons NOT be allowed to make decisions on my behalf in the event of my disability or incapacity:

    _____
    _____
    _____

_____   _____
Signature   Date

_____
Witness

_____
Witness

14. ORGAN DONATION:
    [Specific state version inserted here]

The Preferences Section

The Preferences Section contains a list of health care interventions. The first three, dealing with acute care situations, are highly pertinent to code/no code decision making. Of note, directives 2–8 also include the option of "trial of intervention," either limited by time or benefit. This approach allows for an intermediate course of action—either attempting a therapy for a designated period of time or ascertaining if medical benefit is present and continued once a therapy is initiated. In each case, a therapy can at least be tried, then possibly discontinued at a later date if it proves ineffective. The use of cardiopulmonary resuscitation is fundamental, since the withholding of resuscitation will usually result in death. Discussion of this topic is important to reduce ambiguity because many physicians presume that patients want this medical intervention unless told otherwise. Code status is of particular importance when the patient soon may be hospitalized and decisions in this regard are of prime concern. Respirator use is also important to consider, particularly if the threat of respiratory arrest is great (e.g., in the case of patients with chronic pulmonary disease). The issue of endotracheal tube use is integral to the first two directives. By discussing endotracheal tube use, concerns or misconceptions about these interventions can be dealt with.

The chronic care directives include the use of total parenteral nutrition, intravenous hydration and medication, medications necessary for the treatment of illnesses by other routes (e.g., by mouth or by intramuscular injection), enteral feeding tubes, and dialysis. Each directive should be discussed in the context of long-term recuperative or vegetative care. Importantly, the patient must be assured that pain medication will be available even if any of the above are refused.

Directive 9 concerns autopsy. Whether to request an autopsy is a highly personal decision often influenced by religious or cultural beliefs. The physician should explain to the patient that an autopsy could possibly benefit the patient's family since it could increase scientific understanding of diseases with a genetic pattern of inheritance.

A place is provided below directive 11 to add other directives not listed (e.g., directives allowing or refusing specific types of surgery).

All the directives are to be initialed by the patient and dated as they are consented to, and reviewed periodically. Importantly, in each case, the patient should elucidate the reasons for his or her decision. Although the values in the first section may constitute the rationale for a directive, other values may also emerge. Information as to the values at the basis of a decision is helpful in eliciting the patient's reasoning and possibly will uncover inconsistent values. The process of filling out the values history may also expose possible depressive or delusional ideation that may prevent truly informed consent on the part of the patient. The health care provider may then be able to help the patient therapeutically restore his or her decision-making capacity.

The preferences expressed by the patient are to be signed and witnessed. Any preferences expressed after this initial signing should be initialed and dated in the Values History by the patient. The physician should make note of any later changes in the medical record for that date. Throughout the process, the assumption is that the patient is able to consent to these decisions unless he or she is reliably shown to be incompetent to do so. The burden is on the health care provider to evaluate the patient and rigorously establish and thoroughly document in the medical record that the patient is unable to make these decisions.

The proxy negation directive allows the patient to name a person or persons who should be excluded from future health care decision making if the patient should become incompetent. This directive is useful for a patient who believes a family member has a differing philosophy regarding medical care or has a potential conflict of interest. Last, the uniform donor card specific to the patient's state should be considered, and the patient should then decide whether to allow the post-mortem use of organs in transplantation, medical therapy, and medical research or education. Like the decision about autopsy, this is a personal decision and should be respected by the family.

THE VALUES HISTORY IN CLINICAL PRACTICE

All competent adult patients should be considered candidates for completing a Values History. This instrument can readily be made part of geriatric assessment. In the primary care office, preliminary questioning about end-of-life care should be directed toward the elderly patient. First, an explanation of the intent of the living will and DPA/HC should be provided by the physician. If the patient decides to sign a living will or DPA/HC, the decision can be documented using the proper form for the specific jurisdiction (with copies placed in the medical record). The physician should then discuss the patient's perspectives on quality of life versus length of life, the issue addressed in the Values Section of the Values History. When the Values Section is complete, the physician should discuss the directives listed in the Preferences Section. The starting point for these discussions would depend on the patient's medical problems. For example, the physician should explain the use of a ventilator to a patient with chronic lung disease as well as the meaning of a trial of intervention. In this way, the specific life-sustaining therapy that might need to be implemented in the patient's near future would be discussed. Just as important are the options of acute care therapy (e.g., cardiopulmonary resuscitation, intubation, and ventilation); these too should be discussed early on.

The physician would do well to discuss the remainder of the Values History with the patient on subsequent patient visits, noting preference decisions as they occur. Such discussion and noting of preferences makes the Values History a better guide if the patient becomes incapacitated and can also serve to initiate patient-agent health care discussions. The assignment of an agent is particularly useful for the patient who has left directives undecided in his or her Values History. However, the patient may take the view that it is preferable to make his or her own decisions rather than oblige a relative or friend to try to determine his or her wishes after incapacitation. If the patient has not signed a Values History or living will and has not assigned an agent, the physician is obliged to inform the elderly patient that using any of these methods will enhance the chances that his or her wishes will be carried out. The physician might, for example, be forced by institutional policy into a presumption in favor of treatment, which may violate the patient's autonomy. In the optimal situation, after the patient has signed a living will or DPA/HC (or both), the patient would discuss his or her values and the advance directives listed in the Values History with his or her physician over time. As a decision is reached in each case, the directive is consented to by the patient's initialing and dating of the directive. Likewise, the patient would reach decisions on the proxy negation and organ donation directives and document those decisions. Perhaps after five visits or within the space of a year the Values History would be completed.

BARRIERS TO THE USE OF THE VALUES HISTORY

Many factors could potentially act as barriers to using the Values History. First, the physician may perceive that revealing the possibility of approaching mortality to the patient is harmful or that he or she wants to wait until the "right time."[11] If the physician is not the regular health care provider, he or she may attempt to avoid honoring it. However, this stand would abrogate the physician's obligation to implement the patient's wishes (especially when a living will or DPA/HC has also been signed). Paternalistic claims to protect the patient are often used when attempting to overrule autonomous preferences of the patient. These attempts to negate patient decision-making are ethically suspect.

Incapacitation of the patient from the beginning of the physician-patient relationship can be a barrier to the Values History. In this case, no valid advance directives can be obtained. Patients who are indecisive or exhibit denial in discussions on end-of-life care can impair efforts to elicit a Values History. In response to these circumstances, the physician should attempt to probe the patient's end-of-life values and preferences as sensitively as possible.

The family of the patient could also impede implementation of the Values History. A family member may disagree with the patient's autonomous request to withhold or withdraw certain therapies. In case of a challenge to the patient's competent decisions, acknowledgment by the physician of the patient's autonomy to refuse specific interventions is helpful.

The possibility of legal barriers to use of the Values History must also be considered. First, although most states now have living will statutes that allow for directives to be appended to them, a few do not.[5] Therefore, in a state without a living will statute containing this type of stipulation, it would seem prudent to append the Values History to a DPA/HC. The use of *both* a Values History and a DPA/HC is not precluded, since both instruments would help the medical team by clarifying the patient's values and preferences toward end-of-life care. The reader is urged to consult applicable state laws.

Organ donation statutes also vary from jurisdiction to jurisdiction. Again, the reader should substitute the statutory wording applicable to the jurisdiction where the Values History will be used. Further, consulting legal counsel about appending to the living will directives that may not be condoned in the reader's jurisdiction (e.g., directives regarding intravenous nutrition and hydration) should be contemplated. If deemed legally necessary, directives may be deleted by the health care provider from the Values History prior to presentation to the patient if required by the jurisdiction. With the investment of some effort toward tailoring the Values History in this way, the clinician will be able to use it confident that it complies with the law.

CONCLUSION

The Values History has been designed to add detail and dimension to the living will and the DPA/HC. Some alterations may be required to make the Values History applicable to a given jurisdiction. By making the necessary adaptations, the health care provider will possess a tool of considerable precision for clarifying the value-based preferences of patients. By using the Values History, the provider will be able to prospectively identify the autonomous decisions of patients and implement them with greater confidence that he or she is acting in accordance with the patients' values and preferences.

REFERENCES

1. Doukas D, McCullough L. Assessing the Values History of the aged patient regarding critical and chronic care. In: Gallo J, Reichel W, Andersen L. *Handbook of Geriatric Assessment.* Rockville, Md: Aspen Publishers, 1988:111–124.

2. Doukas D, Lipson S, McCullough L. Value History. In: Reichel W, ed. *Clinical Aspects of Aging.* 3rd ed. Baltimore, Md: Williams & Wilkins, 1989:615–616.

3. Doukas D, McCullough L. The Values History: the evaluation of the patient's values and advance directives. *J Fam Pract.* 1991;32:145–153.

4. Doukas D, Reichel W. *Planning for Uncertainty: A Guide to Living Wills and Other Advance Directives for Health Care.* Baltimore, Md: Johns Hopkins University Press, 1993.

5. Omnibus Budget Reconciliation Act of 1990. Pub L. No. 101–508 §§4206, 4751.

6. Emanuel LL, Emanuel EJ. The medical directive: a new comprehensive advance care document. *JAMA.* 1989;261:3288–3293.

7. Lambert P, Gibson JM, Nathanson P. The values history: an innovation in surrogate medical decision-making. *Law Med Health Care.* 1990;18(3):202–212.

8. Eisendrath S, Jonsen A. The living will: help or hindrance? *JAMA.* 1983;249:2054–2058.

9. Society for the Right to Die. *The Physician and the Hopelessly Ill Patient: Legal, Medical, and Ethical Guidelines.* New York, NY: Society for the Right to Die, 1985;32–33.

10. Wanzer S, Adelstein J, Cranford R, et al. The physician's responsibility toward hopelessly ill patients. *N Engl J Med.* 1984;310:955–959.

11. Doukas D, Gorenflo D, Coughlin S. The living will: a national survey. *Fam Med.* 1991; 23:354–356.

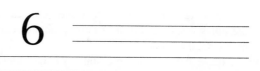

6

Economic Assessment

On the whole, older persons have come a long way toward economic security, particularly if money "in kind," meaning goods and services available free or at a cost below market value, is added to income. In addition, the elderly receive special tax treatment, such as additional personal exemptions and property tax deductions.[1] The major problem areas in terms of public policy, affecting all but the wealthiest of elders, remain catastrophic illness and long-term care, particularly nursing home care. In 1994, health care reform was halted and the outcome of future debate remains uncertain.

Economic factors have an influence on health, nutrition, and place of residence. Although the clinician's inquiry into the area of economic security need not be detailed, it is important to keep in mind that some older persons fail to take prescribed medication or alter the dosage schedule because of financial considerations. For some it is a choice of whether to devote limited dollars to buying food, medication, or heat. Purchase of insurance, dental or podiatric care, and the availability of home health care may all be predicated on financial resources. Financial considerations may figure prominently in availability of the full spectrum of alternatives to nursing home placement, including respite services and adult day care.

Medical complaints that an elder brings to the primary care clinician are occasionally direct results of social and economic factors. Weight loss may occur when the patient cannot afford proper nutrition or dentures that fit. The clinician may not use formal instruments analogous to those discussed for mental status testing;

however, ignoring economic issues creates risk of recommending impractical therapies. Most definitions of comprehensive assessment include some evaluation of financial factors.[2-5]

Although the economic status of the elderly has improved considerably, the poverty rate still tends to be high in the older population, especially among minorities.[6,7] For example, given a definition of poverty as an income of less than $6,503 for an older couple and less than $5,156 for an elderly person, the poverty rate was approximately 12.6%. Another 8% of the elderly are "near poor" (that is, their income was less than 125% of the poverty level). Poverty rates tend to be higher among the unmarried and those who live alone. Persons of advanced age also tend to fall below the poverty line. For example, one-third of persons over the age of 80 have incomes below the poverty line. Finally, rates of poverty tend to be higher for certain groups of elderly: 16% for women compared with 8% for men; 32% for African-Americans compared with 11% for whites; 18% for elderly in rural areas compared with 12% for those in metropolitan areas.[8,9]

FINANCING HEALTH CARE

In the United States, Social Security and pensions are the mainstay of income support for elderly persons. Social Security, established in 1935 during the Depression, when many of today's elders were young and just entering the work force, provides about 40% of the income of elders.[10] The benefit amount for each retiree depends on average yearly earnings, but the initial intent of the Social Security program was not to supply a retiree's entire income. Pensions have become more generous and widespread, supplementing retirement income. Depending on assumptions, the retirement income from Social Security alone ranges from 40% to 70% of preretirement income.[1] For example, Social Security payments constitute 90% of the income for 40% of older African-Americans who live alone.[10]

The Social Security system has undergone significant modifications since its inception. For one thing, more and more workers are included in the program, which initially excluded many industries. Benefits have been significantly increased as well. Social Security provides a "floor" of income for every beneficiary, on top of which is added payment based on earnings.[10]

In 1939, even before the first Social Security payment was made, the first major revision of the Social Security apparatus was legislated: the institution of the survivors' and dependents' benefits program. In 1956, disability insurance was added, and it became possible to retire early with reduced benefits. Medicare was created in 1965 as one of the Johnson administration's "Great Society" programs. In 1975, automatic inflation adjustments in Social Security benefits, legislated in 1972, were begun. In 1983, a new Social Security financing package was enacted by Congress that included, for the first time, the taxation of Social Security benefits. The Supplemental Security Income Program was begun at that time, too. The retirement age was increased to age 67, to be phased in gradually by 2027. Workers may still retire at age 62, but their benefits will be reduced.[1,11]

Medicare, the government health insurance program, consists of two parts: Part A, which deals with hospital insurance and is paid for through payroll deductions of workers, and part B, which is intended to pay physician's bills and other costs and is financed by voluntary participation of workers and a matching contribution from the government. Because of rising health care costs, a gap developed between the cost of health care and the amount of protection afforded by Medicare. For example, acute care costs for the last year of life are estimated to amount to 30% of all Medicare dollars, or 1% of the gross national product.[8] Medicare pays an average of 48% of an elderly person's medical costs at a time when more is spent by the patient on health care than before the enactment of the original Medicare legislation.[1,11]

Medicare pays about 75% of hospital bills, 55% of physician's bills, and, contrary to what many elderly persons think, just 2% of nursing home bills.[12] Some older persons assume, incorrectly, that Medicare will cover their nursing home expenses. Part A of Medicare pays for 90 days of hospitalization and the first 20 days of skilled nursing facility care. The next 80 days of care are partially covered. After that, the resident uses personal resources, which, at current nursing home rates, would rapidly deplete the resources of all but the wealthiest elders.

Part B pays for physician services, up to 80% of "reasonable charges" as determined by the program (after an annual deductible). Physicians who accept "assignment" are paid directly by the program and agree to accept the sum as final payment.[1] In most states, if the physician does not accept assignment, the patient receives the payment from Medicare; the physician must then bill the patient for services. Once a patient is a resident in a nursing home and the Medicare benefits run out, the patient then must "spend down" to a certain level to become eligible for Medicaid, which will then pay the rest of the bills.

Unfortunately, government benefits tend not to encourage home care for elderly family members. For example, Supplemental Security Income benefits, actually financed through Medicaid, may be decreased if the elder moves in with the family.[13] Consequently, tax supports for caregivers have been proposed. As discussed in the previous chapter, however, the emotional and physical aspects of caregiving frequently strain the family more than do financial problems.[14] Nursing home bills create a staggering burden for older Americans who require nursing home care. Nursing home bills average $22,000 per year, and two-thirds of the elderly who live alone would run out of savings in 13 weeks in a nursing home.[11]

Because of the high cost of medical care, older adults have turned to so-called Medigap policies, designed to cover costs that Medicare does not cover.[15] Some policies are sold through the use of high-pressure tactics by unscrupulous persons who sell multiple policies and even forge signatures. One resident of Arkansas told a US House of Representatives subcommittee that his aunt bought 28 worthless policies she thought would protect her from excessive medical care costs.[16] It is estimated that older Americans spend billions of dollars each year on worthless medical insurance that does not cover long-term care.[11]

The private sector is beginning to respond to some of the gaps in the current framework. Some companies now offer special programs for caregivers, including education and training regarding aging, respite care benefits, and economic grants to assist caregivers.[13,17] Potentially a large market exists for insurance that covers the costs of long-term care.[18] Major marketing efforts are directed at older adults to encourage them to join new capitated health care plans that are administered by major managed health care programs with Medicare as the financial basis. The quality and success of these trends will need to be evaluated.

Somers has set forth several principles to guide national policy.[19] These principles espouse continuity of care, multidimensional assessment, better integration of community and institutional programs, and support for family and informal resources. Home health care has received considerable attention in the debate over health care reform, and views on how to integrate long-term and chronic care into a reformed health care system will continue to evolve.

RETIREMENT

Retirement from the work force is a significant life event, for some a "rite of passage" to a new status with new privileges. The loss of social contact at work may leave a retired elder with a void difficult to fill, and without planning, the person may suddenly find lots of time at home with little to do. Although many elderly workers retire for reasons of health, the issues surrounding retirement are intimately related to occupation and financial considerations. A significant number of retirees may not have personally fulfilling jobs and so welcome the chance to leave a boring or even dangerous occupation, wishing to retire as early as financially possible. Better economic conditions, including the proliferation of pension plans and the increased benefits from Social Security, allow a more comfortable retirement for most people.[20,21]

Planning for retirement so as to ensure appropriate arrangements are made is a field in its own right.[22] For most persons, income falls after retirement, but at the same time retirees expect their standard of living not to change. Indeed, an unchanged standard of living is the desirable goal toward which retirement planning strives. It is estimated that about 64% of preretirement income would be needed from interest and dividend income, pensions, and Social Security in order to maintain the same style of life as before retirement.[12]

The elderly constitute a largely untapped resource. This is true from an economic perspective as well as from a personal and societal one. The care of some frail elders might be partially placed in the hands of healthy elders with special or additional training. Elders could also work as teacher's aides or participate in foster grandparent programs. Some might choose to continue working, accepting less than usual pay for performing tasks not yet considered important enough for society to pay full market wages.[23] Since many elders can expect to live one to two decades following retirement, such options could provide a way of using time more productively.[24]

Retirement in the future will reflect changing careers, mobility of the work force, flexible workhours, shortened workweeks, and favorable attitudes toward work and retirement (see Chapter 1). In some settings, retirement is gradually phased in (the older adult works a shorter and shorter workweek). Some older workers may remain in their place of employment as temporary consultants. Mental and physical functioning can be maintained through the pursuit of volunteer activities and hobbies, which should be actively encouraged by health professionals.

Anticipatory guidance with regard to the use of time, maintenance of self-esteem, a positive attitude toward household tasks, and moderate use of alcohol and tobacco may be helpful to the retiree. Dr. Gene Cohen, former Director of the National Institute on Aging, suggests that older adults should develop a "social portfolio" containing four compartments: (1) group active (activities that involve others actively, such as tennis or travel), (2) group passive (e.g., discussion groups centered around movies or books), (3) individual active (e.g., walking and gardening), and (4) individual passive (e.g., reading, woodworking, or knitting). Then when occupational roles wane, the older adult is ready with a portfolio of other pursuits that keep the mind and body active.

ECONOMIC ASSESSMENT IN CLINICAL PRACTICE

Although a clinician may feel uncomfortable asking direct questions about financial status, clues that indicate potential economic difficulty are sometimes overlooked or attributed to other causes. While note can be taken of the condition of shoes, handbags, and clothing (including undergarments) as an indication of economic status, remember that poor condition of these items may reflect frugality, eccentricity, or a visual disorder rather than financial impoverishment. In addition, economic reasons for noncompliance with the treatment regimen should be considered. A home visit may provide a more complete picture of the economic status of the older adult than is possible to achieve elsewhere. A rough indication of the adequacy of financial resources is the ability to spend money on small lux-

Exhibit 6–1 Economic Resources Assessment Scale of the Older Americans Resources and Services Multidimensional Functional Assessment Questionnaire

1. Are you presently employed full time, part time, retired, retired on disability, not employed and seeking work, not employed and not seeking work, a full-time student, or a part-time student?
2. What kind of work have you done most of your life?
3. Does your husband/wife work or did he/she ever work?
4. Where does your income (money) come from (yours and your husband's/wife's)?
    Earnings from employment
    Income from rental, interest from investments, etc.
    Social Security (but not Supplemental Security Income)
    Veterans Administration Benefit
    Disability payments not covered by Social Security, Supplemental Security Income, or the Veterans Administration
    Unemployment compensation
    Retirement pension from job
    Alimony or child support
    Scholarships or stipends
    Regular assistance from family members
    Supplemental Security Income payments
    Regular financial aid from private organizations and churches
    Welfare payments or Aid for Dependent Children
    Other
5. How much income do you and your husband/wife have in a year?
6. How many persons altogether live on this income (that it provides at least half their income)?
7. Do you own your own home?
8. Are your assets and financial resources sufficient to meet emergencies?
9. Are your expenses so heavy that you cannot meet the payments, or can you barely meet the payments, or are your payments no problem to you?
10. Is your financial situation such that you believe you need financial assistance or help beyond what you are already getting?
11. Do you pay for your own food or do you get any regular help at all with costs of food or meals?
12. Do you believe that you need food stamps?
13. Are you covered by any kinds of health or medical insurance?
14. Please tell me how well you think you (and your family) are now doing financially as compared with other persons your age—better, about the same, or worse?
15. How well does the amount of money you have take care of your needs—very well, fairly well, or poorly?
16. Do you usually have enough to buy those little extras, that is, those small luxuries?
17. Do you believe that you will have enough for your needs in the future?

Source: Adapted from *Multidimensional Functional Assessment Questionnaire,* ed 2 (pp 157–162) by Duke University Center for the Study of Aging and Human Development with permission of Duke University, 1978.

uries. Out-of-pocket expenses for health care may cut significantly into the elderly person's ability to use money for other purposes.

Although the total assets of an older person, such as a paid-for house, may be substantial, frequently such assets are not available to pay day-to-day bills. If income is low, the elderly person may choose deprivation rather than sell a familiar house. A home may have fallen into disrepair because taxes and maintenance costs have increased considerably over the years. What the elder once thought were adequate savings for later years may have dwindled.

Many elders who need financial help do not receive available assistance simply because they do not know where or how to receive assistance. The bureaucracy, with its endless forms to complete and numerous telephone calls necessary to coordinate services, can be overwhelming, even for a younger person. Some elders who are illiterate or uneducated may have a poor command of English, which further hampers the capacity for obtaining help. English may be a second language, and the elder person may not understand written material even if it is in the native language. The stigma attached to public assistance may keep some elders from even making an inquiry about obtaining assistance.

One of the domains assessed by the Older Americans Resources and Services (OARS) Multidimensional Functional Assessment Questionnaire is the economic resources of the elder (Exhibit 6–1).[2] Items deal with employment, sources of income, annual income, home ownership, and subjective estimates by the elderly person of the adequacy of financial resources. Under what circumstances Medicare or other benefits will cover respite, home health, or hospice care can be quite complicated, and the physician will want to turn to other professionals for guidance. In light of the complexity of economic and financial issues, an experienced social worker can contribute significantly to the comprehensive assessment.

CONCLUSION

One object of a comprehensive assessment of an elderly patient is to discover whether the patient will be hindered in following the treatment plan because of financial difficulty. If the patient is not financially secure, the provider should offer assistance to the patient in obtaining information and benefits or should be prepared to refer the patient to someone who can provide such assistance.

REFERENCES

1. Schulz JH. *The Economics of Aging.* Belmont, Calif: Wadsworth Publishing Co, 1985.

2. *The OARS Assessment Methodology: Multidimensional Functional Assessment Questionnaire.* 2nd ed. Durham, NC: Duke University Center for the Study of Aging and Human Development, 1978:169–170.

3. Applegate WB. Use of assessment instruments in clinical settings. *J Am Geriatr Soc.* 1987;35:45–50.

4. Williams T. Comprehensive functional assessment: an overview. *J Am Geriatr Soc.* 1983;31:637–641.

5. Kane RA, Kane RL. *Assessing the Elderly: A Practical Guide to Measurement.* Lexington, Mass: Lexington Books, 1981.

6. Radner DB. The economic status of the aged. *Soc Secur Bull.* 1992;55:3–23.

7. Radner DB. Changes in the incomes of age groups, 1984–89. *Soc Secur Bull.* 1991;54:2–18.

8. American Association of Retired Persons. *A Profile of Older Americans.* Washington, DC: American Association of Retired Persons, 1986.

9. American Association of Retired Persons. *Summary of the 1987 National Legislative Policy.* Washington, DC: American Association of Retired Persons, 1987.

10. Achenbaum WA. *Social Security: Visions and Revisions.* New York, NY: Cambridge University Press, 1986.

11. Holzman D. Closing Medicare's coverage gaps. *Insight.* January 26, 1987:52–53.

12. England R. Greener era for gray America. *Insight.* March 2, 1987:8–11.

13. U.S. House Select Committee on Aging, Subcommittee on Human Services. *Exploding the Myths: Caregiving in America.* Washington, DC: US Government Printing Office, 1987.

14. Hooyman NR, Lustbader W. *Taking Care: Supporting Older People and Their Families.* New York, NY: The Free Press, 1986.

15. Morrisey MA. Retiree health benefits. *Annu Rev Public Health.* 1993;14:271–292.

16. McGrath A. The financial agony of long-term illness. *US News and World Report.* February 8, 1987:53.

17. Smith DM. *Kin Care and the American Corporation: Solving the Work/Family Dilemma.* Homewood, Ill: Business One Irwin, 1991.

18. Crown WH, Capitman J, Leutz WN. Economic rationality, the affordability of private long-term care insurance, and the role for public policy. *Gerontologist.* 1992;32:478–485.

19. Somers AR. Insurance for long-term care: some definitions, problems, and guidelines for action. *N Engl J Med.* 1987;317:23–29.

20. Atchley RC, Robinson JL. Attitudes toward retirement and distance from the event. *Res Aging.* 1982;4:299–313.

21. Foner A, Schwab K. Work and retirement in a changing society. In: Riley MW, Hess BB, Bond K, eds. *Aging in Society: Selected Reviews of Recent Research.* Hillsdale, NJ: Lawrence Erlbaum Associates, 1983:71–93.

22. Dennis H, ed. *Retirement Preparation: What Retirement Specialists Need to Know.* Lexington, Mass: Lexington Books, 1984.

23. Morris R, Bass SA. The elderly as surplus people: is there a role for higher education? *Gerontologist.* 1986;26:12–18.

24. Gerontological Society of America. *Higher Education and an Aging Society.* Washington, DC: Gerontological Society of America, 1989.

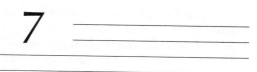

Physical Assessment

Functional, social, values, and economic evaluations lie outside the traditional medical model's catenation of complaint, history, physical examination, investigations, diagnosis, treatment, and cure that permeates medicine and generally serves quite well. In dealing with older adults, however, things may not be so clearly and neatly packaged.[1]

Illness presentation in the elderly corresponding to a single disease process (the "medical presentation") is unusual.[2] Other types of presentations include (1) the *synergistic morbidity* presentation (multiple conditions result in functional decline), (2) the *attribution* presentation (the patient attributes problems to a previously diagnosed condition while a new condition progresses), (3) the *causal chain* presentation (one illness causes another and precipitates decline), and (4) the *unmasking event* presentation (a stressful event exposes an underlying, previously hidden morbidity).[2] The concept of illness presentations facilitates thinking about multiple and interacting illnesses and the inclusion of social and other factors in the medical encounter.

Functional assessment, in particular, may be especially relevant to the elder's circumstances and best suited to delineate the decisions facing the elder regarding appropriate placement or to define how physical problems interfere with the ability to live independently. The social assessment and evaluation of the caregiver plays a pivotal role, too. Emphasis on multiple aspects of assessment, however, is in no way meant to disparage a thorough and thoughtful physical examination. In most respects, the physical examination of an older adult is no different from the examination of a young adult. Consequently, geriatric assessment does not depart to any great degree from physical assessment in general medicine.

The greater prevalence of disease and infirmity in the elder population requires a greater vigilance on the part of health care practitioners to discover abnormalities (separating pathologic processes from "aging" processes) and then to judge their relevance for a particular patient. This process is complicated because the presenting symptom in the elder may be a red herring, that is, a nonspecific signal that something is amiss somewhere but not necessarily in the system expected. Dysfunction in any organ system may only manifest as deteriorating mental status, for example, so that pneumonia (respiratory), appendicitis (gastrointestinal), or congestive heart failure (cardiac) cause confusion (central nervous system). The physical examination of the older person therefore needs to be as complete and systematic as possible, particularly at the time of admission to a hospital or nursing home or prior to surgery.[3,4]

Frequently the precise sequence and timing of the examination must be modified when dealing with an older person because of an older person's impaired hearing, sight, comprehension, or mobility. Rather than rush through the history and physical examination, it may be better to stretch out the process over two or more visits and include an assessment of other domains as well. Unfortunately, physicians, if anything, usually spend less time with their elderly patients than with younger patients.[5]

What makes examination of the elderly different, then, is not the content of the examination per se but rather the need to develop an approach that does an elder person justice without undue discomfort or embarrassment. The best approach patiently takes into account an elder's impaired special senses or diminished mobility and considers the elder's slowed response time in answering questions, respectfully allowing concerns that he or she thinks are most important to be expressed. The caregivers and family may have concerns that need to be addressed within this context as well. Indeed, the "chief complaint" may be formulated by the family rather than by the patient.

COMMUNICATION

It is precisely because the elderly frequently have impaired communication skills as a result of illness or lack of schooling that it is crucial for the examiner to pay special attention to communication issues in history taking and physical examination. During the introduction, the patient is observed for communication problems. For many elderly, particularly the "old old," English may be a second language, and the possibility of difficulty in providing or understanding information in the interview must be kept in mind.

A hearing problem may be easily disguised and can result in misunderstanding if it is not recognized. The patient who is hearing impaired may respond to questions inappropriately, and an erroneous evaluation or diagnostic label of dementia could result. If the patient uses a hearing aid, the volume of both the hearing aid and the examiner's voice must be adjusted. It is important to speak clearly and articulate rather than to shout at the patient.

Eye contact, a handshake, addressing the patient by the last name, and physical contact are the rudiments of good communication with all patients but particularly the elderly. Eye contact is important for establishing a relationship. Prolonged eye contact can seem like staring, however, and in some cultures eye contact is believed to be inappropriate.

Addressing the patient by the last name is a sign of respect. Most of today's elders grew up in a time when one would not think of addressing an older person or the physician by the first name. Using the last name is no barrier to friendliness; professional caregiving relationships are no less loving and warm. A sincere touch on the hand or shoulder is appreciated by many elderly persons. Done in a sincere and caring manner, a touch may allay some of the anxiety associated with a trip to the physician's office or a home visit by a nurse or social worker.

The patient should be spoken to directly. For all but the most cognitively impaired, the clinician should talk to the caregiver only with the permission of the older patient. The family may appreciate some time alone with the clinician to express their concerns without feeling embarrassed by the elderly person's presence. A natural time for this to occur is while the patient undresses in preparation for the physical examination.

The environment of the encounter must be comfortable and as free from noise, distractions, and interruptions as possible. It is helpful to provide the patient and family with a brief explanation and description of what is to be accomplished during the visit and subsequent visits (if the evaluation is to be spread out over several visits).

EXAMINATION OF OLDER ADULTS WITH DEMENTIA

The physical examination of the patient with Alzheimer's disease poses special challenges because the patient may not be able to pinpoint what is wrong. Mental impairment severely limits the ability of many patients to express themselves. One danger is that mental deterioration will be automatically ascribed to the Alzheimer's disease and that a reversible superimposed factor might consequently be overlooked. The physical examination of the older person with mental impairment therefore needs to be particularly thorough.

Not only may the Alzheimer's patient have communication difficulties, but he or she may not be cooperative. Because of memory difficulties, the patient may need to be gently but firmly reminded of what is expected. The patient may be extraordinarily restless. A firm, reassuring touch (holding the hand or a shoulder); giving clear, simple, one-step requests; and eye contact increase the chance that good communication and cooperation will occur. Often the presence of a family member or friend can have a calming, orienting effect on the person being examined.

HISTORY-TAKING

During the initial examination, an elderly person might present to the practitioner a barrage of complaints and difficulties. The family might inform the practitioner of problems of which the elder is unaware. The physical and laboratory evaluation may uncover yet other undisclosed problems. The practitioner could easily begin to feel frustrated and overwhelmed. Where to begin? What is important to address now and what can wait? Just collecting adequate data with which to make a decision, let alone implementing a treatment plan, can be difficult within the time constraints of a primary care practice. At the initial interview, it is probably best to attend to the specific problem, if there is one, be it "medical" or "social," that prompted the evaluation.[6]

Although some elderly persons are reluctant to give information to the interviewer, others are more than willing to share, at length, numerous irrelevant incidents that happened long ago. The interviewer, without showing disinterest or disrespect, must strive to help the elderly patient focus on the issues at hand. Functional assessment helps to direct the clinician's initial efforts to the solution of the problems that have a direct impact on the elder's ability to perform the tasks of daily living.

The trouble is that there often are multiple "chief complaints," the chief complaint is unstated ("Mom just doesn't seem herself"), or the chief complaint is stated but does not fit the usual mold ("Mom just doesn't cook anymore"). Weed[7] has stressed the importance of good problem-oriented medical records to help sort things out.[7] Although not all the "problems" recorded will be addressed in a single visit, spelling them out, even if expressed as "undifferentiated" medical problems or functional difficulties, helps to organize the problems for solution. For the elderly, this is particularly important, because the "parsimony of diagnosis" role may not apply—several diseases (and their treatments) may coexist and interact. By keeping track of diagnosed and undifferentiated medical, social, and functional problems in this way, each visit with the patient may build on the accomplishments since the last evaluation.[7] Undertaking an assessment to decide which problems are to be addressed at each visit is a worthwhile policy.

Although it is generally a good idea to use open-ended questions to obtain information from patients (and the elderly are no exception), it is sometimes necessary to supply an elder with specific words to choose from to help describe the problem. For example, "Describe your chest pain" is open-ended; "Was the pain sharp, stabbing, dull, or crushing?" may help the older patient along if there is trouble describing the pain.

The elderly have the reputation of answering yes to all the questions in the review of systems. Still, there are problems that may otherwise remain "hidden" unless specifically asked about by the examiner. Ham[8] has identified several: sexual dysfunction, depression, incontinence, musculoskeletal stiffness, alcoholism, hearing loss, and dementia. A suggested review of systems is presented in Table 7–1. It is important to realize that a problem such as dyspnea may not be new but merely altered in quality or frequency. The elder may always have had shortness of breath going up the stairs but now must rest three times instead of negotiating the stairs without resting.[9] A change in the degree of disability will be discovered by a careful interviewer.

Table 7–1 Geriatric Review of Systems

General	Weight change	Genitourinary	Incontinence
	Fatigue		Dysuria
	Falls		Nocturia
	Anorexia		Hematuria
	Anemia		Sexual functioning
	Poor nutrition	Musculoskeletal	Morning stiffness
Special Senses	Visual changes		Joint pain
	Cataract		Joint swelling
	Hearing changes		Limitation of
	Imbalance		movement
	Vertigo	Neurology	Memory problems
Mouth and Teeth	Dentures		Headaches
	Denture discomfort		Syncope
	Dry mouth		Gait
Respiratory	Cough		Sensory function
	Hemoptysis		Sleep disorders
	Dyspnea		Transient focal
Cardiovascular	Chest pain on exertion		symptoms
	Orthopnea		Voice changes
	Ankle edema	Psychiatric	Depression
	Claudication		Alcoholism
Gastrointestinal	Dysphagia		Anxiety
	Melena		
	Change in stool caliber		
	Laxative use		
	Constipation		

Trying to confirm the diagnosis of every abnormality may not be in the patient's best interest. The physician-patient relationship may be undermined if it depends solely on discovering reversible disease rather than on optimal management of chronic disorders. The elderly often have multiple chronic illnesses that, although incurable, have aspects that can be modified to enhance function and limit discomfort.[10] Of course, a balance must be struck. The clinician must not be too quick to assume the symptoms are fully explained by the most serious or advanced chronic disease. There may be less serious but treatable conditions that contribute to disability.[9] Blind pessimism is unwarranted.

OVERVIEW OF THE PHYSICAL EXAMINATION

The physical assessment really begins when the clinician first meets the patient and observes how the patient behaves and how well the patient is dressed and groomed. Does the patient seem well-nourished or thin and emaciated? Does the patient move about easily or unsteadily and unbalanced? How easily does the patient arise from a chair to go to the examining table? While taking the history, the clinician should observe the patient for involuntary movement, cranial nerve dysfunctions, and difficult respiration and should listen for fluent speech.

The examination should require as few changes in position as possible. With the patient seated, the head, eyes, ears, nose, throat, neck, heart, lungs, joints, and neurologic examinations follow in turn. The patient is then positioned supine for examination of the abdomen, peripheral pulses, breasts, genitalia, and inguinal regions. The patient can then be turned into the lateral decubitus position for rectal examination. Finally, the patient is brought to a standing position so orthostatic blood pressure and pulse changes can be detected and balance and gait can be tested.

It is important to remember that many elders adapt remarkably well to physical, psychologic, and physiologic incapacities. The labor and energy this requires should not be underestimated: Growing old is hard work!

COMPONENTS OF THE EXAMINATION

Pulse

The measurement of vital signs, temperature, and height and weight has been basic to physical assessment for centuries. The Chinese methods of diagnosis, thousands of years old, include questioning, feeling the pulse, and observing the voice and body.[11] The radial artery is convenient for the determination of the heart rate. When the pulse is irregular, it is further characterizable as regularly irregular or irregularly irregular. A *regularly irregular* pulse may indicate consistently dropped beats, as in the Wenckebach phenomenon, or added beats, as in premature ventricular contractions. An *irregularly irregular* pattern often represents atrial fibrillation but can also be caused by premature ventricular or atrial contractions. Palpation of the carotid pulse with simultaneous auscultation of the heart is helpful in timing murmurs or other sounds emanating from the heart.

Blood Pressure

Blood pressure should be taken both with the patient supine and standing, especially if the patient is taking medication for hypertension. Some fall in the systolic blood pressure is fairly common in elderly persons, particularly those who have chronic disease or are on medication.[12] In one study of orthostatic blood pressure, after one minute of quiet standing, 24% of 494 persons over age 65 sustained a fall of 20 mm Hg or more in systolic blood pressure. Five percent had decreases of 40 mm Hg or more.[13] When elderly patients without risk factors for postural hypotension (such as chronic disease or medication use) were tested, only 8 of 125 persons (6.4%) had a 20 mm Hg or greater fall in systolic blood pressure on standing.[14]

The fall in blood pressure on standing can be exaggerated if the blood volume is low or if the reflex orthostatic mechanisms are impaired due to age or medication. Even mild sodium depletion (serum sodium levels of 137 mEq/L to 142 mEq/L) secondary to diuretics can result in marked postural hypotension in the elderly although no such change occurs in younger subjects.[15]

The balloon of the blood pressure cuff should encircle about two-thirds of the arm's circumference. If the patient is obese, a wide cuff is used, since a smaller cuff may overestimate the blood pressure. Conversely, a frail elder with a thin arm may need a smaller-than-normal cuff, perhaps a pediatric cuff, to avoid a spuriously low reading. Palpation of the cuff pressure at which the radial pulse disappears is a way to check the accuracy of the auscultated systolic blood pressure.

The Korotkoff sounds are listened for with the bell of the stethoscope pressed lightly over the brachial artery. The pressure at which the sounds are first heard is the systolic pressure. The sounds may become muffled before they disappear, and the pressure at the point where the muffling occurs should be recorded between the systolic and diastolic pressures (e.g., 165/88/74 mm Hg). Occasionally patients have an "auscultatory gap" in which the sounds disappear only to reappear again at a lower pressure. If the auscultatory gap is not recognized, the diastolic pressure may be erroneously recorded as higher than its true value or the systolic pressure may be erroneously recorded as lower than its true value.

Atherosclerosis may result in misleading blood pressure readings. The blood pressure reading may vary from one arm to the other because atherosclerosis involvement may be slightly asymmetrical. Stiff peripheral arteries may result in spuriously high readings. Osler used a simple maneuver to detect the presence of atherosclerosis interfering with blood pressure measurement. Osler's maneuver is performed by inflating the blood pressure cuff above systolic pressure and then palpating the radial or brachial artery. If the pulseless artery is palpable, the true intra-arterial blood pressure reading may be lower than the blood pressure obtained by auscultation. Patients whose arteries remained palpable (Osler positive) when the cuff was inflated above systolic pressure had a blood pressure reading taken by auscultatory methods that was 20% higher than the intra-arterial measured pressure.[16] Some subjects had a diastolic cuff reading of 120 or 100 mm Hg and a simultaneous intra-arterial pressure reading of 80 mm Hg. Such patients, with pseudohypertension, might be erroneously diagnosed and treated as hypertensive. Perhaps elderly hypertensive patients are particularly susceptible to the adverse effects of antihypertensive drugs because of this type of overestimation of blood pressure.[16]

Antihypertensive drugs can sometimes be withdrawn from elders without the return of hypertension. For example, of 169 patients withdrawn from therapy in one study, 51 patients had immediate blood pressure increases and medication was reinstituted. Of the 118 remaining patients, 43 (25% of the total group) were still normotensive one year later, 16 required treatment for hypertension, 34 were treated with diuretics for congestive heart failure or angina pectoris, and 12 were lost to follow-up.[17]

This evidence should not deter appropriate treatment of hypertension in older adults. For the age group 60 to 69 at entry, the Hypertension Detection and Follow-up Program showed that control of diastolic blood pressure reduced the incidence of stroke by 45%. Overall mortality was 16% lower at the end of the 5-year period.[18,19] Studies of older subjects demonstrated a reduction in cardiovascular mortality and stroke.[20-24]

Isolated systolic hypertension is defined as a blood pressure of greater than 160 mm Hg systolic while the diastolic blood pressure remains less than 90 mm Hg. Isolated systolic hypertension is quite common and is estimated to be present in 20% of persons over the age of 80 and in about 13% of those aged 70 to 79.[25] Isolated systolic hypertension "disappears" in up to one-third of cases simply as a result of measuring the blood pressure at repeated visits.[26] Although believed by many in the past to represent a "normal" phenomenon for the elderly, sustained isolated systolic hypertension is associated with increased risk of stroke and increased cardiovascular risk, even in the elderly.[18,19,27-30] Reduction of the cardiovascular risk may not be the only benefit of hypertension control. When the systolic blood pressure of patients with multi-infarct dementia was controlled so that the measurement fell between 135 and 150 mm Hg, cognitive improvement was noted.[31]

Low blood pressure is associated with some additional risk in the elderly.[29] It may expose the older person to falling hazard and injury but may only become evident if the patient is examined for orthostatic changes in blood pressure. It should prompt a search for a remedial condition such as overmedication, anemia, or Addison's disease.[32]

Respiration

After assessment of the pulse and blood pressure, the respirations are observed and counted to assess their rate and depth. The clinician should look for use of accessory muscles of respiration and for retraction in the supraclavicular fossae. During the history taking, does the patient have to interrupt speaking to catch his or her breath? The usual rate in adults is about 12 to 18 breaths per minute.

Temperature

It is generally well known that the elderly frequently do not have a normal febrile response to infections. That pneumonia may present without fever, for example, was observed by Osler, who remarked, "in old age, pneumonia may be latent, coming on without chill."[33] Indeed, the elderly are prone to *hypothermia* even from mildly cool ambient temperatures. Body temperatures of less than 95°F may not be readable on most clinical thermometers, and emergency departments are usually equipped with special thermometers that register lower temperatures. Medications that interfere with the thermoregulatory mechanism, such as tranquilizers, antihypertensives, vasodilators, and antidepressants put the elderly patient, who may already have numerous predisposing chronic conditions, at increased risk for hypothermia. Alcohol use may contribute to this risk as well.[34,35]

Height and Weight

Although measurement of weight is standard for every patient encounter, measurement of the height is not. Measurement of height is useful for evaluating the patient's weight by means of a standard weight-height table. Height may be estimated using landmark measurements on the arm and leg.[36] Serial height measurements may be useful. Recording serial height measurements in an aging woman who has a vertebral compression fracture due to osteoporosis may reveal loss of height and kyphosis due to other asymptomatic fractures or bone loss. Therapy might then become more aggressive to prevent further bone loss (e.g., hormonal therapy). Serial height measurements might also increase the patient's awareness of osteoporosis and improve compliance with regimens of calcium, vitamin D, and, if prescribed, hormonal replacement.

Older persons have an increased risk of malnutrition because of inappropriate food intake, social isolation, disability, chronic medical conditions, and medications.[37] Good nutrition underlies adequate functioning and a sense of well-being. Change in the patient's weight is an important parameter to follow in hospitalized or institutionalized patients, who have an increased risk of malnutrition.[38] Loss of subcutaneous fat, muscle wasting, and edema on physical examination may signal chronic malnourishment.[39]

Skin

Assessment of the skin should occur during examination of areas of the body. Changes in skin condition are generally believed to constitute the quintessential mark of aging itself. The elderly generally have less subcutaneous fat, and consequently the skin is thinner, especially on the dorsa of the hands and on the forearms. Elasticity is lost, and the skin turgor is routinely diminished, even in patients who are adequately hydrated. Wrinkling and creasing occur, resulting in crow's feet at the corners of the eyes and lines on the forehead. Older adults often have decreased sweat and sebaceous gland production, so dry skin is a common finding. The tendency toward dryness can be exaggerated by disease (hypothyroidism) or medication (anticholinergics such as antidepressants). Dry skin contributes to conditions such as nummular eczema and "winter itch."

The normal skin changes that occur in aging include the development of hyperpigmented macular lesions called senile freckles or lentigines and also commonly age or liver spots. Cherry hemangiomas, small red or violet growths, are most often seen on the trunk or extremities and are very common. *Seborrheic keratoses* are pigmented lesions with a waxy or greasy surface that have a "stuck on" appearance and generally occur on the trunk and face. Seborrheic keratoses may become secondarily infected. Early lesions could resemble melanoma or other conditions. Skin tags are fleshy soft growths, typically with a pedicle, and are frequently ignored unless injured by clothing or jewelry.

Solar lentigo is a brown, flat lesion that is believed to be related to chronic exposure to sunlight. Solar lentigo is to be distinguished from lentigo maligna, which is an insidious flat lesion with irregular borders and a distinct variegated color that may include flecks of black. It is believed to represent melanoma *in situ;* raised areas may represent invasion into the dermis. Doubt about the nature of any lesion should be resolved by biopsy or excision.

Actinic keratoses occur on sun-exposed areas of the skin. The lesions are usually multiple and scaly, enlarging slowly over many years. Some can develop into squamous cell carcinoma, and a sudden spurt of growth in a senile keratosis should alert the physician to that possibility. A cutaneous horn is a very proliferative hyperkeratotic form of senile keratosis in which the hyperkeratosis resembles a horn. Such lesions can become quite large.

Basal cell carcinoma is the most common cancer of the skin. Fortunately, basal cell carcinomas only rarely metastasize. Most occur on the head and neck, and they may take the form of an ulcer or a nodule. A characteristic feature of the ulcerative type is a firm, rolled border. One 65-year-old woman had such a lesion behind the ear for six months that she ascribed to irritation from her glasses. Squamous cell carcinoma is another common lesion. *Squamous cell carcinoma* has the potential for metastasis, and sometimes regional lymphadenopathy is found. Typically the lesions arise on sun-exposed areas, especially the face, and are hard and fixed. They eventually become erythematous and scaling, initially resembling an actinic keratosis. Unchecked, however, squamous cell carcinoma and basal cell carcinoma, although eminently treatable, may be devastating and disfiguring.

Nummular eczema is particularly seen in the winter and is characterized by coin-shaped areas, resembling ringworm, on the arms and legs that may become secondarily infected. The lesions are intensely pruritic and chronic. The etiology of nummular eczema is unknown, but the low indoor humidity usual in winter dries the skin and intensifies the itch.

Seborrheic dermatitis also affects the elderly. Seborrhea symmetrically involves the scalp, face, and body folds with scaly indistinct macules and papules. These lesions are often greasy and sometimes pruritic. Seborrheic dermatitis is particularly common in persons with Parkinson's disease.

Psoriasis affects all age groups. The characteristic lesions in psoriasis are the scaly patches that typically involve the scalp, elbows, and knees. Psoriasis may also cause pitting of the nails and may be associated with arthritis.

Herpes zoster causes a painful eruption in the distribution of a peripheral nerve. After a primary infection with the virus that causes chickenpox, the virus remains dormant, possibly for decades, until it erupts as "shingles." The pain may precede the rash, causing confusion with other conditions. Herpes zoster involving the first branch of the trigeminal nerve can involve the eye, resulting in corneal scarring. A clue that this is occurring is the presence of vesicles at the tip of the nose. Unfortunately, pain can persist in the involved area even after the lesions have resolved.

Clues to physical abuse of the older adult may come from the examination of the skin. Bruises and welts on the chest, shoulders, back, arms, or legs, perhaps in various stages of healing, could signal a case of abuse. Unusual patterns, such as bruises that are clustered, might reflect the use of an instrument or a hand or even biting. Lacerations and abrasions on the lips, the eyes, or parts of the face may be associated with infection. Hemorrhages beneath the scalp may have resulted from hair pulling. Of course, frail elderly persons are more prone to injuries from falls as well, making detection of real abuse more difficult. In addition, many elderly persons also bruise easily due to capillary fragility or poor nutrition. In any case, the possibility that such abuse is occurring and accounts for some physical findings should be considered when the pattern of injury does not fit the history obtained (see Chapter 4).[40-44]

Decubitus Ulcers

Impaired mobility puts the older adult at risk for the development of decubitus ulcers, or pressure sores. Other risk factors include malnutrition, dehydration, anemia, cardiovascular disease, edema, and urinary or fecal incontinence.[45] A pressure ulcer can develop rapidly (e.g., as a result of lengthy surgery). Constant vigilance is required to prevent pressure ulcers in institutionalized or hospitalized older adults.[46] Recurrent or extensive decubiti in older adults might signal abuse or neglect. Patients with decreased mobility, especially older patients admitted to the hospital or nursing home, should be evaluated for risk of decubiti using a standard assessment tool (Exhibit 7–1).[47] If they are present, treatment should be based on the stage of ulceration, and measures to prevent further development of pressure sores should be instituted.[45]

Hair and Nails

Among the most notable indicators of age are changes in the color and distribution of hair. Hair color becomes gray or whitened. Progressive thinning of all body hair, including hair of the axillae and pubis, occurs with age. The growth of facial hair in elderly women can sometimes be quite distressing, but measures to reduce the problem, such as depilatory agents, can be recommended. Lack of hair on the lower extremities may indicate diminished peripheral circulation but is often a normal finding in the elderly. The nails are frequently affected by *onychomycosis,* a chronic fungal condition of the nail. Thickened, brittle, and crumbling nails are difficult to treat and are a common problem for neglected persons living alone.

Head

The patient is examined in the sitting position starting with the head and working down. The head and skull should be examined for evidence of trauma, especially in cases of delirium or sudden changes in mental status. Besides palpation for tenderness and deformity of the skull, the temporal artery can be examined for

Patient's Name			Evaluator's Name			Date of Assessment
Sensory perception Ability to respond meaningfully to pressure-related discomfort	1. *Completely limited:* Unresponsive (does not moan, flinch, or grasp) to painful stimuli, as a result of diminished level of consciousness or sedation, OR limited ability to feel pain over most of body surface.	2. *Very limited:* Responds only to painful stimuli. Cannot communicate discomfort except by moaning or restlessness, OR has a sensory impairment that limits the ability to feel pain or discomfort over 1/2 of body.	3. *Slightly limited:* Responds to verbal commands but cannot always communicate discomfort or need to be turned, OR has some sensory impairment that limits ability to feel pain or discomfort in 1 or 2 extremities.	4. *No impairment:* Responds to verbal commands. Has no sensory deficit that would limit ability to feel or voice pain or discomfort.		
Moisture Degree to which skin is exposed to moisture	1. *Constantly moist:* Skin is kept moist almost constantly by perspiration, urine, etc. Dampness is detected every time patient is moved or turned.	2. *Moist:* Skin is often but not always moist. Linen must be changed at least once a shift.	3. *Occasionally moist:* Skin is occasionally moist, requiring an extra linen change approximately once a day.	4. *Rarely moist:* Skin is usually dry; linen requires changing only at routine intervals.		
Activity Degree of physical activity	1. *Bedfast:* Confined to bed.	2. *Chairfast:* Ability to walk severely limited or nonexistent. Cannot bear own weight and/or must be assisted into chair or wheelchair.	3. *Walks occasionally:* Walks occasionally during day but for very short distances, with or without assistance. Spends majority of each shift in bed or chair.	4. *Walks frequently:* Walks outside the room at least twice a day and inside room at least once every 2 hours during waking hours.		
Mobility Ability to change and control body position	1. *Completely immobile:* Does not make even slight changes in body or extremity position without assistance.	2. *Very limited:* Makes occasional slight changes in body or extremity position but unable to make frequent or significant changes independently.	3. *Slightly limited:* Makes frequent though slight changes in body or extremity position independently.	4. *No limitations:* Makes major and frequent changes in position without assistance.		

continues

Exhibit 7–1 continued

	1. Very poor:	2. Probably inadequate:	3. Adequate:	4. Excellent:
Nutrition Usual food intake pattern	Never eats a complete meal. Rarely eats more than 1/3 of any food offered. Eats 2 servings or less of protein (meat or dairy products) per day. Takes fluids poorly. Does not take a liquid dietary supplement, OR is NPO[1] and/or maintained on clear liquids or IV[2] for more than 5 days.	Rarely eats a complete meal and generally eats only 1/2 of any food offered. Protein intake includes only 3 servings of meat or dairy products per day. Occasionally will take a dietary supplement, OR receives less than optimum amount of liquid or tube feeding.	Eats over half of most meals. Eats a total of 4 servings of protein (meat, dairy products) each day. Occasionally will refuse a meal, but will usually take a supplement if offered, OR is on a tube feeding or TPN[3] regimen, which probably meets most of nutritional needs.	Eats most of every meal. Never refuses a meal. Usually eats a total of 4 or more servings of meat and dairy products. Occasionally eats between meals. Does not require supplementation.
Friction and shear	1. *Problem:* Requires moderate to maximum assistance in moving. Complete lifting without sliding against sheets is impossible. Frequently slides down in bed or chair, requiring frequent repositioning with maximum assistance. Spasticity, contractures, or agitation leads to almost constant friction.	2. *Potential problem:* Moves feebly or requires minimum assistance. During a move, skin probably slides to some extent against sheets, chair, restraints, or other devices. Maintains relatively good position in chair or bed most of the time but occasionally slides down.	3. *No apparent problem:* Moves in bed and in chair independently and has sufficient muscle strength to lift up completely during move. Maintains good position in bed or chair at all times.	

Total score

[1]NPO: Nothing by mouth.   [2]IV: Intravenously.   [3]TPN: Total parenteral nutrition.

tenderness. Changes in the skull that are characteristic of Paget's disease should be sought, such as frontal bossing or an increase in hat size.

Temporal arteritis (or giant cell arteritis) is a condition in which the temporal arteries become tender and may lose their pulsations. This disorder may present as a headache that is unilateral and classically temporal. There may be dimness of vision. Temporal arteritis is an important condition to recognize because if untreated it can lead to blindness. Fever and an elevated white blood cell count may occur. The sedimentation rate is markedly increased in advanced cases. Symmetrical pain and weakness of shoulders and hips can accompany temporal arteritis (polymyalgia rheumatica).

Eyes

After the cranium is assessed, the eyes are examined. Age-related changes in the eyes include darkening of the skin around the orbits, crow's feet, slower pupillary light reflex (which still, however, ought to be equal bilaterally), decreased tearing, and decreased adaptation to the dark. The older person, perhaps because of diminished pupil size and increased thickness and opacity of the lens, needs more illumination to compensate than someone younger.

The structures surrounding the eye itself are inspected first. *Xanthomas* are fat deposits sometimes seen in the skin near the eyes and may be associated with elevated levels of blood lipids. Loss of the lateral third of the eyebrows, although a classic sign of hypothyroidism, may be a normal finding in some elderly persons. On each eyelid the examiner will find a central, relatively rigid tarsal plate that, in advancing age, may become lax, leading to *ectropion* (eversion of the lids) and exposing the eyes to drying and infection. The margin of the lid may also roll backward toward the eye so that the eyelashes brush against the cornea, causing *entropion.*

The sclera is normally white but is uniformly yellow in patients with jaundice. In elderly persons, the periphery of the sclera may be yellow due to deposits of fat showing through thinned scleral membranes. *Pingueculae* are thin fatty structures that usually lie laterally on the eyeball. They may increase in size with advancing age but are benign and generally cause no problem with vision. The conjunctiva, or lining of the eye, can become inflamed or infected. This is a common eye problem in the elderly, particularly since the elderly are prone to have dry eyes. Dry eyes may predispose the conjunctiva to infection by bacterial or viral agents. Conjunctivitis is associated with a red eye and purulent discharge, but discomfort is minimal. A painful red eye may signal iritis, glaucoma, or an abrasion.

Arcus senilis is a striking finding in the eyes of some older persons. Initially a thin line limited to the upper portion of the eye, it becomes thicker and denser and completely encircles the cornea. While arcus is found with other stigmata in persons with familial hypercholesterolemia, many persons with arcus will have normal cholesterol levels. Arcus senilis is a common finding in persons aged 65 years and older.[48]

The lens of the eye produces new fibers throughout life but none are lost. These accumulate in the center of the lens, increasing its density and contributing to the development of senile cataracts that are generally bilateral. The lens loses its elasticity with advanced age so that the eye is more farsighted (presbyopia). Before ophthalmoscopy, the patient's visual acuity is checked for reading and distance, with and without glasses.

The pupils may react more sluggishly to light but should be equal in size. Many disorders can cause asymmetry of the pupils, including central nervous system lesions and diabetes; drugs can have this effect as well. After iridectomy, the pupil may be irregular. The extraocular muscles are checked for full range of motion: up and down, left and right.

Ophthalmoscopic examination of each eye should begin by focusing on the most anterior structures first and then working back to the retina. A *cataract* may be best visualized by focusing on the lens with an ophthalmoscope. A cataract appears as a black area against the orange reflection from the retina. The precise significance of a cataract depends on how much it interferes with the patient's vision, function, and work.

Increased lens opacity with advancing age allows less light to pass to the retina than at younger ages. The 60-year-old retina receives only a fraction of the amount of light as the 20-year-old retina.[49] Improved lighting may be all that is required to allow an elderly person to read small print, such as that in a telephone directory or the newspaper. Provision of excellent lighting in waiting and examination rooms is essential.

Examination of the retina with an ophthalmoscope requires some practice. The normal fundus reveals the optic disc, the macula, and arteries and veins. Pigment in the retina usually corresponds to skin pigmentation. The normal optic disc is frequently outlined by pigment. In elders with hypertension or arteriosclerosis and sometimes in normal elders, so-called copper-wire changes caused by thickening of the arteriolar walls may be seen. As the vessel walls become more thickened, the vessels appear white or silver. Nicking, or narrowing, of venules by crossing arterioles occurs as the process continues. Exudates, hemorrhages, and cotton-wool spots may also be seen on the retina as a result of hypertension or diabetes.

Macular degeneration is a major cause of visual disability in the elderly. The macula, the region of the retina with sharpest acuity, is affected. Visual acuity is decreased but peripheral vision is preserved. Special studies by an ophthalmologist may be required to establish a diagnosis of macular degeneration.

In *glaucoma,* the intraocular pressure is elevated and there is contraction of the visual field. On ophthalmoscopic examination, the optic cup, which is a depression in the optic nerve as it emerges from the retina, is accentuated. The visual field of the Alzheimer's disease patient is contracted when compared with that of patients who were demented from other causes. This may significantly alter the demented patient's perception of the environment.[50]

Ears

After the practitioner examines the eyes, the otoscope is used to examine the ears. Painless nodules on the pinnae of the ear could be basal cell carcinomas, rheumatoid nodules, or even gouty tophi. Common changes seen with age include increased ear lobe length, hair growth in the canal, and accumulation of cerumen. Loss of hearing that is due to problems with the external ear include impacted cerumen, external otitis, or foreign body. External otitis can be due to allergic reactions to the material in hearing aids.[51] Malignant otitis externa is a Pseudomonas infection that involves the ear canal and presents as granulation tissue at the juncture of bone and cartilage.

The normal tympanic membrane is gray or pink with a light reflex produced by its cone shape. The malleus, which is the first of the three small bones in the inner ear, can be seen indenting the membrane, pointing posteriorly. The tympanic membrane may be thickened in the elderly person (tympanosclerosis), possibly as a result of scarring from prior infections. Effusions occur in relation to eustachian tube dysfunction, as in allergy or upper respiratory tract infection.

Hearing is assessed during the history-taking session but can be grossly gauged by such techniques as whispering words in the patient's ear. Many patients have cerumen as the primary or contributing cause of hearing loss.[52] Hearing loss may, for the sake of simplicity, be divided into conductive loss and sensorineural loss.[53] *Conductive hearing loss* implies interference in the conduct of sound energy into the inner ear. It can be due to foreign bodies, cerumen, abnormalities of the tympanic membrane, otitis media or externa, or involvement of the ossicles with Paget's disease, rheumatoid arthritis, or otosclerosis (in which the stapes become fixed to the oval window of the cochlea).[53]

Sensorineural loss means disease anywhere from the organ of Corti to the brain. The cells within the organ of Corti are not replaced; there is thus a gradual loss as the person ages. The result is high-tone hearing loss because it is hair cells in the basal turn of the organ of Corti, those sensitive to high tone, that are lost. *Presbycusis* is sensorineural hearing loss due to aging of the inner ear.[53] Often both conductive and sensorineural hearing loss are present simultaneously, and the precise nature of the defect requires sophisticated audiometric testing. The ability to hear high-frequency sounds is affected first so that certain consonants and sibilants become unintelligible (for example, *f, s, th, ch,* and *sh*). Understanding speech depends in large measure on the clear perception of these high-frequency consonants rather than low-frequency vowel sounds.

Sensorineural hearing loss can also be due to toxic damage to the hair cells of the organ of Corti from aspirin, aminoglycoside antibiotics, or diuretics; trauma; and a wide variety of disorders ranging from vascular insufficiency (the inner ear is dependent on a single end artery for its blood supply) to central nervous system disease.

The combination of hearing loss and cognitive impairment can lead to social isolation and paranoia and may make mental status testing a real challenge. A case has been made for the routine audiometric testing of both nursing home residents and community-dwelling elderly because self-reporting of hearing problems is not reliable and there is a high prevalence of hearing loss in elderly persons.[54,55]

Three simple clinical tests using a tuning fork may help sort out the type of hearing loss: the Rinne test, the Weber test, and the Schwabach test. To perform the *Rinne test,* the tuning fork is struck and applied to the mastoid prominence behind the ear. When the patient indicates he or she no longer hears the sound, the vibrating fork is immediately put near the external canal. Normally the sound is then heard and the test is said to be positive. Put another way, air conduction is better than bone conduction. A negative test, one in which the patient does not hear the tuning fork when placed near the canal, suggests there is a conduction loss in that ear.

Whether there is indeed a conductive hearing loss can then be confirmed by the *Weber test.* A vibrating tuning fork is placed on the vertex of the head, and the patient is asked if the sound is heard better in one ear. Normally, the sound appears to come from the middle. If a conductive defect is present in one ear, the sound is heard best in that ear (bone conduction makes up for the defect). On the other hand, if deafness in an ear is due to neural problems, that ear will not sense any sound and the sound will only be heard in the contralateral "good" ear.

The *Schwabach test* confirms a diagnosis of sensorineural deafness by comparing the patient's hearing with the examiner's. The vibrating tuning fork is put on the patient's mastoid process. When the sound is no longer heard by the patient, the fork is put on the examiner's mastoid process. If the sound is heard by the examiner, then a sensorineural deficit in the patient is confirmed.

Nose

The otoscope can be used to examine the nasal mucosa and the internal nasal architecture. Nasal patency should be tested by occluding one nostril. Nasal congestion due to vasomotor rhinitis, characterized by postnasal drip, little sneezing, and no eosinophils in a nasal smear, can be particularly disturbing and interfere with sleep.

Rhinophyma of the nose starts as a diffuse redness, followed by papules, pustules, and, later, dilated venules. Excess ingestion of alcohol may be associated. The paranasal sinuses may be palpated for tenderness. Any chronic drainage that does not respond to therapy should be investigated.

The sense of smell decreases with age, and the decrease is often experienced as a loss of taste. The loss of the sense of smell can be significant for nutrition and safety. Many older persons cannot enjoy the pleasant smells of food cooking, smells that stimulate the appetite and make eating enjoyable, and the inability to smell leaking natural gas creates a risk of serious accident. With age, the anterior taste buds, which are sensitive to sweet and salt, deteriorate before the posterior taste buds, which are sensitive to bitter and sour; thus, elderly patients frequently complain that food tastes bitter or sour. When cooking, additional undesirable amounts of salt may be added to food to compensate for the loss of taste. Progressive loss of the senses of smell and taste mean that, for elders, the appearance and consistency of food plays a proportionately greater role in food's appeal.

Mouth and Teeth

Cheilosis, or fissures at the angles of the mouth, may be a sign of poor nutrition and vitamin deficiency. Carcinomatous lesions may occur on the lips, which are highly exposed to sunlight. The oral mucosa may be dry because of diminished sputum production or due to drugs the patient is taking, particularly those with anticholinergic side effects. The oral mucosa should be carefully inspected for lesions by using the tongue blade to move the buccal mucosa away from the teeth. *Leukoplakia* is a white patch or plaque on any of the mucous membranes of the mouth that may appear to be painted on the surface. These patches may be present for years and represent a premalignant condition. Such lesions should be biopsied for definitive diagnosis. Other lesions with a similar appearance are Candida (thrush) and lichen planus. Traumatic injury, in particular from ill-fitting dentures, may damage the oral mucosa, producing erythematous tissue changes. In addition to inspection, a moistened glove may be used to palpate the buccal cavity, including the lips and floor of the mouth, for areas of induration. Palpation is particularly important to evaluate complaints related to the oral region, to assess suspicious areas, and to evaluate persons at risk for oral cancer (e.g., patients with a history of tobacco or alcohol use).

A lesion of the hard palate, with no particular clinical significance except that it be recognized as benign, is the torus palatinus. It must be reiterated, however, that any masses not in the midline are suspect as neoplasms. A slowly growing asymptomatic lesion with a rough surface, irregular margin, and firm consistency should be biopsied, no matter how long it has been there.

Tooth loss and periodontal disease are extremely common in older persons. As many as half of all persons over age 65 are edentulous.[56] Studies show that elderly persons, especially denture wearers, are likely to see their physician more frequently than their dentist.[56,57] For this reason it is particularly important to remove the dentures and inspect the mouth surfaces for areas of irritation and for suspicious lesions. The upper and lower lips are examined, including hidden surfaces. Poorly fitting dentures can have far-reaching consequences, such as malnutrition, and result in numerous problems, such as traumatic ulcers, denture stomatitis, and possibly even cancer.

Any dental malocclusion, as well as abnormal speech sounds, such as slurred *ss*, clicks, or whistles, which signal improperly fitting dentures, should be recognized. The patient may fail to realize that a misfitting has developed.[57] Elderly patients should be encouraged to visit the dentist every year or two so that dentures can be adjusted to account for changing mandibular bone structure.

Elders who retain teeth need to have their oral hygiene assessed. *Dental caries* may appear as soft white, yellow, or brown areas on the tooth. The patient may complain of sensitivity to extremes of temperature. *Periodontal disease*, a major cause of tooth loss, involves inflammation and destruction of the supporting structures of the teeth.[58] Foul breath odor is common with dental infections, retention of food particles in the teeth or dentures, or chronic periodontal disease. It can also result from sinusitis or pulmonary infection.

The examination of the tongue also may be revealing. A sore, red, inflamed tongue may be found in patients with vitamin B_{12} or iron deficiency. Hairy or black tongue is a condition in which it looks as if the tongue is growing short hairs. It is symptomless and appears during treatment with antibiotics that inhibit normal bacteria and permit fungal overgrowth. The tongue may also be observed for fasciculations, which indicate lower motor neuron disease, and for abnormal movements such as tardive dyskinesia.

Neck

The neck presents several important structures for examination: the lymph nodes, the trachea, the thyroid gland, and the carotid arteries. The posterior and anterior cervical lymph node chains as well as the supraclavicular area should be carefully palpated. Virchow's node, enlargement of the lymph node in the left supraclavicular fossa, is a classic sign of metastatic gastrointestinal carcinoma. The trachea should be checked for lateral deviation, and a search made for jugular venous distention, which could be a sign of heart failure. Prominent pulsations above the clavicle may represent kinking of a carotid artery or prominence of the innominate artery.

The carotids should be gently palpated. The pulses should be symmetrical. A bounding or collapsing pulse, in which the upstroke of the pulse wave is very sharp and the downstroke falls rapidly, may be present in a patient with essential hypertension, thyrotoxicosis, or aortic regurgitation or in an extreme emotional state. The carotids may be auscultated using the bell of the stethoscope, listening for bruits that signify turbulent blood flow (and not necessarily hemodynamically significant narrowing). The presence of *bruits* suggests the possibility of atherosclerosis and could be an important finding in a patient with a history of syncope, stroke, or transient ischemic attack. In asymptomatic patients, bruits are probably more indicative of coronary artery disease than of cerebrovascular disease, at least in elderly men.[59-61]

An attempt should be made to palpate the thyroid gland for enlargement from both in front and in back of the patient, even though the gland is generally not easily palpated. If the gland is enlarged, it must be determined whether the gland is diffusely enlarged (goiter) or exhibits discrete nodularity. Sometimes a bruit may be heard over vascular thyroid lesions, and occasionally a thrill is felt. Thyroid disease in the elderly is notorious for subtle presentation. For example, hypothyroidism may manifest solely as depression or mental deterioration. The symptoms of hypothyroidism, which are easily misinterpreted by the older patient or the physician, include dry skin, constipation, sleepiness, lethargy, cold intolerance, and fatigue.[62] Periodic evaluation of serum thyroid-stimulating hormone levels has been suggested in order to detect impending hypothyroidism.[8,63,64]

Hyperthyroidism or thyrotoxicosis may present without the signs and symptoms usually found in younger persons, such as exophthalmos, restlessness, hyperactivity, and tachycardia.[62] Atrial fibrillation occurs in half of elderly hyperthyroid patients but in only 10% of younger patients, whereas ocular changes are less common in the elderly.[65] The term "apathetic thyrotoxicosis" has been used to refer to hyperthyroidism in the elderly with nonspecific signs and symptoms.[66] Results of thyroid function tests may be falsely reassuring unless the triiodothyronine (T_3) value measured by radioimmunoassay is specifically requested. Constipation, weight loss, and anorexia of hyperthyroidism may resemble a gastrointestinal carcinoma.[62] The hyperthyroid state may precipitate heart failure as the presenting illness.[65]

Heart and Lungs

The heart and lungs may be examined next, while the patient is still seated. Cardiovascular disease and morbidity is common in the elderly.[67] In the elderly, angina pectoris may very well present as dyspnea rather than as pain. Other common presentations are palpitations or syncope on exertion.[68] Patients presenting with transient ischemic attack, stroke, or an episode of confusion should have myocardial infarction considered in the differential diagnosis. Even when the pain is typical, an elderly person may ascribe it to other causes, attributing jaw pain to arthritis and epigastric pain to hiatal hernia or "ulcer."[67] Heart disease may also be associated with nonspecific fatigue or weakness.

The palm of the examiner's hand is placed over the apex of the patient's heart to palpate the apex pulsation. Normally the apex pulsation covers an area the size of a half-dollar. If the apex pulsation is not easily palpated, the patient may be asked to lean forward or to move into a left lateral decubitus position. Cardiac hypertrophy as a result of hypertension, for example, produces a small vigorous apical beat. Dilated ventricles, as from mitral regurgitation, cause the apex beat to be lateral to the midclavicular line. The heart size probably remains unchanged in healthy elderly persons.[69]

In auscultating the heart, the examiner should start at the apex using the diaphragm, "inch" across to the left lower sternal border, then to the left second intercostal space, then cross to the right and move down the right sternal border. The first and second heart sounds are listened to first. Simultaneous palpation of the carotid pulse may help identify which sound is the first heart sound. Since the first heart sound is produced by the closure of the mitral and tricuspid valves, it sounds louder than the second heart sound over the mitral and tricuspid areas (the apex of the heart and the right lower sternal border, respectively).

The sequence of auscultation is repeated to listen for murmurs and for silence in systole and diastole. High-pitched clicks and many murmurs will best be heard using the diaphragm of the stethoscope. Lower-pitched sounds, such as gallops and diastolic rumbles arising from the mitral and tricuspid valves, will best be heard with the bell of the stethoscope. *Diastolic murmurs* are always significant and may be caused by mitral stenosis. Aortic or pulmonic regurgitation may also be associated with diastolic murmurs. Mitral stenosis, which is generally due to rheumatic heart disease, may be "silent" in the elderly.[70] Atrial fibrillation, particularly when accompanied by mitral stenosis, is a significant risk factor for stroke.[71]

Systolic murmurs are common in persons over the age of 65.[72,73] Functional flow murmurs from a dilated aortic annulus are short, early systolic murmurs heard at the cardiac base. The second heart sound is normally split, and the carotid upstrokes are normal. The murmur of aortic stenosis is a systolic ejection (diamond-shaped murmur) at the base, classically with diminished carotid upstrokes, sustained apical impulse, and a fourth heart sound. These findings may not be present in the elderly patient, however.[73,74] Mitral regurgitation in the elderly is commonly due to ischemic heart disease and results in a holosystolic murmur.[67] Since systolic murmurs are so prevalent in the elderly, distinguishing benign murmurs from significant murmurs in asymptomatic patients can be difficult.[75]

Abnormalities of the heart rhythm may be poorly tolerated by the elderly, who generally have less reserve capacity than younger persons. Atrial fibrillation, for example, may not be tolerated because early diastolic filling in the elderly heart is considerably diminished.[74] The contribution of the atrial "kick" to ventricular filling, lost in atrial fibrillation, becomes critical to appropriate cardiac output.

Arrhythmias are apparently quite prevalent in otherwise healthy elders, with prognosis and significance probably related to the presence of overt or unrecognized coronary artery disease.[76-80] In one study of 106 elders monitored by electrocardiograph 24 hours a day, one-fourth had multifocal premature ventricular contractions and 4 had ventricular tachycardia. After 18 months of follow-up, recordings showed no difference between the 13 persons who died compared with the group as a whole.[80] In another study, supraventricular tachycardia was present in 28% of 50 patients over the age of 80, who were studied with 24-hour ambulatory electrocardiographic monitoring. Every patient exhibited supraventricular ectopic beats, and 65% of the patients had more than 20 ectopic beats per hour. Premature ventricular contractions were also quite common, occurring in 32% of the patients at a rate of greater than 10 premature beats per hour. In 18% of the patients, the premature contractions were multifocal.[81]

Following the cardiac examination, the lungs are examined by auscultation and percussion. Assessment of respiration began when the patient came into the examining room. The rate and depth of breathing, as well as any use of accessory muscles of respiration, were observed. The aged lung has less elasticity due to loss of elastin and to collagen cross-linking.[82]

While listening over the chest and asking the patient to take a few deep breaths, the physician must be alert for signs of hyperventilation, such as dizziness, especially in the elderly person, to avoid inducing syncope. Normally, only so-called vesicular breath sounds are heard over the chest. Bronchial or tubular breath sounds can be heard over the trachea. If one hears such sounds over the peripheral lung fields, consolidation due to infection, tumor, or other causes is suggested.

Rales are sounds produced by the movement of fluid or exudate in the airways. Small amounts of fluid may be detected as posttussive rales. For posttussive rales to be heard, the patient must expire fully and cough. When he or she inspires with the next breath, fine crackles can be heard. The cough collapses some wet alveoli, which are then heard opening in inspiration. Moist rales or rhonchi are gurgling sounds arising from larger bronchi. Moist breath sounds at the bases in the elderly often do not represent congestive heart failure.[8] Such marginal or atelectatic rales are heard most frequently in aged, debilitated, or bedridden patients or in habitual shallow breathers. These sounds should disappear after the patient takes a few deep breaths. Other adventitious sounds heard in the lungs are friction rubs and wheezes.

The lung fields are percussed for areas of dullness or hyperresonance as a further way to detect any abnormality. An underlying consolidation or effusion will yield dullness or flatness on percussion. In chronic obstructive pulmonary disease, the lungs are often hyperresonant (i.e., the pitch on auscultation is higher than that over the normal lung). A check is then made for tactile fremitus: After the ulnar surfaces of both the examiner's hands are applied to either side of the patient's chest, the patient is asked to speak (say "ninety-nine"). Differences in vibration from one side to another may be significant. Consolidation, as in pneumonia, increases fremitus. Sometimes it is helpful to auscultate the lung fields and simultaneously tap the sternum. Increased transmission of the sound through areas of consolidation is sometimes identified more readily when using this technique rather than simple percussion. The clinician listens over the lung fields and asks the patient to say "E." The "E" will frequently sound like "A" over a pleural effusion (egophony).

Musculoskeletal System

At the time the lungs are auscultated, any kyphosis or scoliosis is noted. Severe kyphosis can interfere with breathing and cardiovascular function. Tenderness over the spinous processes may portend a vertebral fracture. The joints are inspected next, particularly the joints of the hands. Osteoarthritis is common and especially affects the distal interphalangeal joints of the hands as well as the knees. Bony overgrowths at the distal interphalangeal joint are called *Heberden's nodes*. Limitation of external rotation of the hip can be an early sign of osteoarthritic involvement there.[8] Indeed, the range of motion of all the joints should be assessed.

Rheumatoid arthritis in the hands tends to affect the proximal interphalangeal joints. Joint swelling seen in a rheumatoid joint is not bone but rather synovium and soft tissue swelling; it can be felt along the dorsal surface of the involved interphalangeal joint. Progression of the disease produces ulnar deviation in the hands at the metacarpophalangeal joints as well as a tendency for joints to sublux. Morning pain and stiffness may last several hours for the patient with rheumatoid arthritis, whereas the patient with osteoarthritis is relieved from pain after a short period of limbering up the affected joints.

Clubbing of the fingers may indicate an underlying chronic disorder resulting in hypoxia. A normal nail, when viewed from the side, forms an angle with the skin of the nail bed. Clubbing results when the angle is greater than normal and the finger has a "rounded" appearance. Clubbing is seen in chronic lung disorders, carcinoma of the lung, and other disorders associated with chronic hypoxia. The feet may be examined for changes in the joints and for clubbing as well. Frequently, the examination of the foot reveals evidence of diabetes, neglect, or peripheral vascular disease. The examination of the lower extremities may be deferred until the abdominal examination, when the patient will be supine.

Fractures due to osteoporosis are a serious problem for aged women. Ideally *osteoporosis* should be addressed before a woman becomes elderly, for once osteoporosis is established, there is little hope for restoration of bone mass.[83] Osteoporosis may be associated with many conditions, such as hyperparathyroidism, prolonged immobilization, steroid excess, malignancy, and multiple myeloma; the differential diagnosis includes osteomalacia (mineralization defect). Most bone loss, however, is probably due to involutional osteoporosis, either postmenopausal or age related.[84]

After menopause, bone is lost at a rapid rate, although most of the loss occurs in trabecular bone found in the vertebrae and the distal radius. Cortical bone tends to be lost more gradually and at a constant rate as the person ages. The loss of cortical bone may be related to an age-dependent decrease in the absorption of calcium and a consequent increase in the level of parathyroid hormone and increased bone turnover.[85]

As might be expected, since the bone loss in postmenopausal women tends to be in trabecular bone, fractures occur at those sites. Vertebral crush fractures are common, often accompanied by sudden severe pain and tenderness over the spinous process of the involved vertebra. Some fractures are not clinically evident and are seen on roentgenography in an asymptomatic but perhaps kyphotic woman. Loss of height may be a tip-off.

Age-related bone loss, most prominent in cortical bone, as found in the hip, is called senescent or senile osteoporosis. Women with the condition outnumber men because of their smaller initial bone mass, but of course the disproportion is not as great as in the case of hypogonadal or postmenopausal osteoporosis. Senile osteoporosis becomes most troublesome (because of hip fractures) at a more advanced age than postmenopausal osteoporosis. Age-related bone loss occurs in trabecular bone as well, so vertebral fractures may continue to be a problem.[85]

Risk factors for the development of osteoporosis may help guide decisions regarding whom to treat with estrogen and progesterone, since there are few contraindications to the use of calcium and vitamin D. The more risk factors present, the greater the risk for osteoporosis (Table 7–2). Some of the most important risk factors are postmenopausal status (within 20 years after menopause), European (especially northern European) or Asian heredity, premature (or surgical) menopause, and low calcium intake. Excessive ingestion of caffeine or protein has also been implicated.[86] An Osteoporosis Risk Assessment Questionnaire has been devised as a tool to educate women and assess the risk of the disease.[87] Assessment of risk should occur at least once in the perimenopausal period. Unfortunately, plain roentgenograms are not helpful, since at least a third of the bone mass must be lost before osteoporosis is recognized on film.[88] The place of sophisticated techniques to measure bone density may be useful to delineate persons at high risk.[89-94]

Causes of osteopenia other than osteoporosis must be kept in mind when evaluating the patient. The work-up requires the measurement of serum calcium, phosphorous, and alkaline phosphatase levels in addition to thyroid function tests, complete blood cell count, and possibly serum protein electrophoresis, parathy-

Table 7–2 Risk Factors for the Development of Osteoporosis

Postmenopausal (within 20 years after menopause)
White or Asian
Premature menopause
Positive family history
Short stature and small bones
Leanness
Low calcium intake
Inactivity
Nulliparity
Gastric or small-bowel resection
Long-term glucocorticoid therapy
Long-term use of anticonvulsants
Hyperparathyroidism
Thyrotoxicosis
Smoking
Heavy alcohol use

Source: Reprinted by permission of *The New England Journal of Medicine* (1986;314:1683), Copyright © 1986.

---

roid hormone assay, and serum cortisol determination.[84] Osteomalacia, for example, associated with a mineralization defect, may result in an elevated alkaline phosphatase concentration and abnormal serum calcium and phosphorous values. Such findings would be a clue that a disorder other than involutional osteoporosis is present.

Paget's disease of bone frequently is asymptomatic, diagnosed when its characteristic "mosaic" pattern is seen on a roentgenogram obtained for unrelated reasons. Simultaneously, excess bone resorption and deposition occur in a disorganized manner. Severe bone deformity or bony swelling can result. The disorder is more common in men. Pagetic bone can be painful. Frequently the skull is involved, although Paget's disease can be limited to any single bone. Involvement of the cranium can result in cranial nerve compression and deafness. High-output cardiac decompensation can occur because of arteriovenous fistulas in affected bones. A small percentage of affected bones may undergo malignant degeneration. The classic patient with Paget's disease of bone has a large skull and prominent frontal bones. Therefore, although Paget's disease is often asymptomatic, with only an elevated alkaline phosphatase level to mark its presence, it can result in bone pain, deformities, deafness, cardiac decompensation, neurologic deficits, and fractures. The high blood flow in pagetoid bone occasionally produces a bruit heard on auscultation of the skull.

Abdomen

The patient is placed supine so that the abdomen, breasts, peripheral pulses, genitalia, and the rectum may be examined. It is important to make the older patient as comfortable for this part of the examination as possible. A pillow can be used or the head of the examining table elevated slightly to support the patient's head and upper back; a perfectly flat position is uncomfortable for some older adults.

The physician begins the examination of the abdomen with inspection, noting any distention or scars from previous surgery. The physician should listen to the abdomen before proceeding with palpation to avoid inducing peristaltic activity. Partial bowel obstruction produces "rushing" sounds, and when obstruction is complete, the sounds may become tinkling or very high pitched. Ileus produced by obstruction or from other causes, such as pneumonia or appendicitis, may result in absence of bowel sounds. Abdominal wall rigidity is not as common a sign of peritoneal irritation among the elderly as among younger patients.

Constipation may produce a mass of feces that can easily be palpated and mistaken for a tumor. Conversely, a silent abdominal mass may be the only sign of a gastrointestinal carcinoma. Tortuosity or aneurysm of the abdominal aorta may also be felt as a pulsatile mass in the abdomen. An abdominal aortic aneurysm may have lateral as well as anteroposterior pulsation; this distinguishes it from a mass in front of the aorta, which merely transmits the pulsations to the examining hand. In thin persons, it may be normal to feel the aortic pulsation and may be quite alarming to the unsuspecting examiner. An abdominal ultrasound is a noninvasive way to evaluate the patient for the possibility of an aneurysm. Leaking aneurysm or mesenteric ischemia should be considered in diagnosing the cause of abdominal pain in older adults.

In addition to palpating and percussing the liver to estimate its size, the mid-lower abdomen is palpated to check for bladder distention. A finding of distention may be important in the evaluation of incontinence or as a sign of urinary retention from prostatic hypertrophy. Urinary retention may be the cause of otherwise unexplainable confusion.

With the patient still supine, the peripheral pulses in the feet are checked. The femoral arteries may be palpated in the groin and auscultated for bruits. Bruits heard in the femoral arteries are evidence of diffuse atherosclerotic disease. While examining the area of the groin, the physician can check for lymph node swelling. The feet and lower legs can be examined for skin changes and skin breakdown. Diabetics are at increased risk for foot ulcers and infection. Decubiti and heel sores are common, particularly in patients who are bedfast. The legs are examined for evidence of arterial insufficiency, namely, laterally placed ulcers, loss of the skin appendages, and poor circulation in the toes. Venous insufficiency may be signalled by pigmented, medially placed ulcers.

Breasts

Palpation and examination of the breasts should not be neglected. Ideally this examination is done both while the patient is sitting and again while the patient is supine during the abdominal examination. A search is made for nipple retraction, skin changes, and masses, which, because of loss of connective tissue and adipose, are often more easily appreciated in the elderly woman. Retraction of the nipple secondary to age-related changes can be everted with gentle pressure around the nipple. Retraction due to an underlying growth, however, cannot be everted by such gentle pressure. The nipples are palpated so as to express any discharge present. All four quadrants of both breasts are examined, including the axillary tail, and a careful inspection is made for any asymmetry. The skin under large, pendulous breasts is examined for maceration due to perspiration.

The male breasts are not exempt from disease and should also be examined. Gynecomastia (breast enlargement) in an elderly male can result from a variety of causes, including bronchiogenic carcinoma, thyroid disease, testicular tumors, drugs (such as spironolactone), liver cirrhosis, and other types of cancer.

Genitourinary System

The genitalia in both men and women may be examined in conjunction with the rectal examination. This part of the examination may be deferred but never neglected.

The male genitalia should be examined for suspicious lesions, discharge, and testicular masses. The glans of the penis in an uncircumsized man is checked by retracting the foreskin. The prostate is palpated during the rectal examination. The prostate is frequently enlarged in elderly men but should feel soft and nonnodular. The two lobes of the prostate can usually be distinguished by the median furrow between them. Since lobes of the prostate not palpable by the examining finger may enlarge and cause obstruction, a normal-sized gland on physical examination does not rule out urinary obstruction from prostatic enlargement. Do not neglect the evaluation of the prostate in the work-up of back pain.

The female genitalia should, at a minimum, be inspected for lesions of the skin, although a bimanual and speculum pelvic examination, which is often neglected, is mandatory if urinary incontinence is a problem or if the patient is due for a Papanicolaou smear.[95,96] Note is made of any cystocele, rectocele, or uterine prolapse that may occur as the pelvic musculature becomes lax with age.

After menopause, the estrogen responsive tissues of the genitalia and the lower urinary tract atrophy. This leads to dryness of the vagina, shrinkage of the vagina and its surrounding structures, altered bacterial resistance, and weakened uterine ligaments. Urinary incontinence and infections may result. Postmenopausal changes in the vagina cause itching, burning, and dyspareunia (painful inter-course), which are symptoms most elderly women are reluctant to spontaneously volunteer. The context of the pelvic examination, however, is a natural one in which to broach such subjects in a straightforward and supportive manner. Vaginal atrophy may also be associated with bleeding, but it should be emphasized that all postmenopausal bleeding must raise suspicions of uterine carcinoma until this possibility can be ruled out. Additionally, palpable ovaries are never normal in an elderly woman.

Rectal examination may be performed after the patient is helped into the lateral decubitus position (alternatively, the patient may be asked to bend over the exam-ination table). The examiner should tell the patient what to expect and when. The anus is inspected for tears, irritation, and external hemorrhoids, and the tone of the anal sphincter, which may diminish with age, is noted. A gloved finger is used to make a sweep of the entire rectum, being sure to take in its entire circumference. The patient is asked to strain, as at stool, to bring down any lesions just outside the reach of the examining finger. A stool sample to test for occult blood is obtained.

Older adults may not want to bring *urinary incontinence* to the attention of their doctor, preferring instead to make adjustments on their own, such as decreasing fluid intake and using absorbent napkins. The physician, in addition to performing a neurologic examination that includes testing for perineal sensation and sacral re-flexes and a pelvic examination (in the case of women) or a prostate examination (in the case of men), should examine the abdomen for grossly distended bladder and look for leaking of urine in the supine and standing position.[97] Fecal inconti-nence is a serious problem among the institutionalized elderly and is a significant risk factor for formation of decubiti.[98]

Sexual functioning in late life was formerly a taboo subject, yet older adults in good health may continue sexual expression and intimacy. Potentially treatable problems such as impotence in men or diminished vaginal lubrication in women can significantly diminish quality of life and should be addressed. Problems with sexual functioning may be at the root of depression or poor adherence to thera-peutic regimens. Education regarding sexually transmitted diseases, including AIDS, continues to be important for older adults.[99]

Nervous System

The neurologic examination is performed after bringing the patient to a sitting position. It consists of six components: a test of intellectual function, a test of the cranial nerves, a motor examination, a sensory examination, a test of reflexes, and an examination of cerebellar function. Testing mental status is discussed at length in Chapter 2. The importance of the mental status examination should be empha-sized again. Unless in an advanced stage, patients with Alzheimer's disease appear neurologically normal to an examiner who neglects to test cognitive functioning specifically.

Age-related changes in the nervous system include decreased vibratory sensation (especially in the legs), less brisk deep tendon reflexes, and decreased ability to gaze upward.[100] The Achilles reflex is frequently unobtainable. The so-called pathologic reflexes, such as the grasp, palmomental, glabellar, and snout reflexes, are characteristic of release of cortical inhibition but are fairly common in normal elderly persons. Concomitant presence of these release signs may signal arteriosclerotic changes in the brain or dementia.[101] Demented patients with pathologic reflexes may have more functional impairment and poorer prognosis, but the release signs may also be present in patients without dementia.[102,103]

Sensation may be tested by evaluation of the patient's ability to feel a soft cotton-tipped applicator, sharp pinprick, and vibrating tuning fork. Such examination is often quite subjective, and sometimes deficits are not reproducible. Impaired mental status or aphasia may make sensory examination more difficult, prone to error, or even impossible. More complex sensory integration is examined by asking the patient to identify common objects placed in his or her hands, such as a coin, comb, or paper clip (stereognosis). Position sense (proprioception) is examined by asking the patient to identify the direction in which the toes or fingers are displaced by the examiner. Elderly patients asked to stand with their feet together and eyes closed (Romberg test) may have some difficulty complying, perhaps due to impaired proprioception.

Motor tone is frequently increased in elderly persons. Passive movement of the patient's limb by the examiner may commonly demonstrate gegenhalten, or involuntary rigidity, which should not be mistaken for lack of cooperation. Strength is decreased, as is muscle mass, especially in the small muscles of the hands. Coarse senile tremors may involve the head as well as the hands, may improve after alcohol use, and may worsen with stress or fatigue.

Gait and Balance

Falling is an example of a geriatric problem with multiple contributing causes and serious consequences. The response to any unexplained fall by an elderly person should be a careful consideration of the circumstances of the fall and a thorough search for underlying physical illness. The risk of falling increases with advancing age, and simple diagnostic evaluation may identify persons at increased risk.[104–106] The patient can be observed as he or she is requested to sit and rise from a chair, walk and turn around, and bend down to pick up an object off the floor.[107] Does the patient rise from a chair in a single movement? Is the patient steady in walking and turning without grasping for support, using smooth, continuous movement? Does the patient seem sure of him- or herself when bending? Observe the patient climbing and descending a flight of stairs, if possible.[108] It is a good policy to test balance and gait in a standard way (Exhibit 7–2) for patients with neurologic disorders and to assess the effect of medications that might interfere with balance.[109,110]

Driving

Asking the older patient about driving habits is a good introduction to discussing the level of functioning. Indeed, concern about driving may be what has prompted the evaluation. Inquire about changes in driving habits the older patient has made to accommodate diminished vision or hearing (e.g., restricting driving to daylight hours or non-rush-hour traffic or avoiding high-speed roadways). Medications affect the ability to drive, and both the number and type of medications have been linked to "near misses" on the road.[111,112] Remind the patient about the hazards of drinking and driving. Occasionally it is necessary to document in writing to the patient that it is no longer safe for him or her to drive[113]; laws on reporting vary from state to state.[112] The clinical assessment should focus on range of motion of the neck, upper extremities, and lower back; visual acuity and visual fields; hearing; and the individual's medication regimen and risk of functional impairment.[114–116]

LABORATORY ASSESSMENT

In many respects, the laboratory assessment of the older patient is the same as in general medicine. Certain changes, however, such as changes in hematologic values and in renal function, deserve mention. Standard medical textbooks can be consulted for appropriate laboratory and radiographic evaluation methods for particular medical problems, such as congestive heart failure or anemia. Tempering the evaluation of abnormalities in the elder is the recognition that frail homeostatic mechanisms may be upset not only by "diseases" but also by iatrogenic factors.

Important as it is to be aware of the normal changes that occur with age, it is also important to be aware of stable characteristics and values. Anemia, for example, is not a concomitant feature of aging. In the United States, iron deficiency is rare and is found most commonly in infants. Low hemoglobin or hematocrit values in the elderly need to be addressed.

Five particularly important areas are discussed below: hematologic values, renal function, thyroid disorders, glucose intolerance, and cholesterol.

Exhibit 7–2 Tinetti Balance and Gait Evaluation

BALANCE
Instructions: Seat the subject in a hard armless chair. Test the following maneuvers. Select one number that best describes the subject's performance in each text, and add up the scores at the end.

1. Sitting balance
   Leans or slides in chair   = 0
   Steady, safe   = 1 _____

2. Arising
   Unstable without help   = 0
   Able but uses arms to help   = 1
   Able without use of arms   = 2 _____

3. Attempt to arise
   Unable without help   = 0
   Able but requires more than one attempt   = 1
   Able to arise with one attempt   = 2 _____

4. Immediate standing balance (first 5 seconds)
   Unsteady (staggers, moves feet, marked trunk sway)   = 0
   Steady but uses walker or cane or grabs other objects for support   = 1
   Steady without walker, cane, or other support   = 2 _____

5. Standing balance
   Unsteady   = 0
   Steady but wide stance (medial heels more than 4 inches apart)
     or uses cane, walker, or other support   = 1
   Narrow stance without support   = 2 _____

6. Nudging (With subject's feet as close together as possible, push lightly
     on the sternum with palm of hand three times.)
   Begins to fall   = 0
   Staggers and grabs, but catches self   = 1
   Steady   = 2 _____

7. Eyes closed (at same position as in No. 6)
   Unsteady   = 0
   Steady   = 1 _____

8. Turning 360 degrees
   Discontinuous steps   = 0
   Continuous steps   = 1 _____
   Unsteady (grabs and staggers)   = 0
   Steady   = 1 _____

---

continues

Exhibit 7–2 continued

9. Sitting down
    Unsafe (misjudges distance, falls into chair)   = 0
    Uses arms or lacks smooth motion   = 1
    Safe, smooth motion   = 2 ____

GAIT

Instructions: The subject stands with the examiner, and then walks down hallway or across room, first at the usual pace and then back at a rapid but safe pace, using a cane or walker if accustomed to one.

10. Initiation of gait (immediately after being told to go)
    Any hesitancy or several attempts to start   = 0
    No hesitancy   = 1 ____

11. Step length and height
    Right swing foot:
      Fails to pass left stance foot with step   = 0
      Passes left stance foot   = 1 ____
      Fails to clear floor completely with step   = 0
      Completely clears floor   = 1 ____
    Left swing foot:
      Fails to pass right stance foot with step   = 0
      Passes right stance foot   = 1 ____
      Fails to clear floor completely with step   = 0
      Completely clears floor   = 1 ____

12. Step symmetry
    Right and left step length unequal   = 0
    Right and left step equal   = 1 ____

13. Step continuity
    Stopping or discontinuity between steps   = 0
    Steps appear continuous   = 1 ____

14. Path (Observe excursion of either left or right foot over about 10 feet of the course.)
    Marked deviation   = 0
    Milk to moderate deviation or uses walking aid   = 1
    Walks straight without aid   = 2 ____

15. Trunk
    Marked sway or uses walking aid   = 0
    No sway but flexion of knees or back or spreads arms out while walking = 1
    No sway, flexion, use of arms, or use of walking aid   = 2 ____

continues

Exhibit 7–2 continued

16. Walking stance	
Heels apart	= 0
Heels almost touch while walking	= 1 _____

Balance score: _____ /16   Gait score: _____ /12

Total score: _____ /28

Source: Adapted with permission from Tinetti M, Performance-oriented assessment of mobility problems in elderly patients, *Journal of the American Geriatrics Society* (1986;34:119–126), as cited in *Patient Care* (1994;28:10–32).

Hematologic Values

Studies of hematologic values in healthy old persons reveal that there is no significant change with healthy aging.[117,118] Zauber and Zauber[117] studied the hematologic parameters of elderly persons over age 84 who had no cancer, no chronic hematologic disorder, no chronic inflammatory conditions such as rheumatoid arthritis, no congestive heart failure or symptomatic chronic lung disease, no history of gastric resection, and no medication use known to affect the bone marrow. In addition, the patients had stable weight, a bilirubin value less than 1.5 mg/dL, a creatinine value less than 1.5 mg/dL, and a calcium value less than 10.5 mg/dL. In this select group of elderly subjects, the hematocrit and mean corpuscular volume (MCV) were not significantly different from a group of younger healthy controls aged 30 to 50. The elderly men had a hematocrit of 0.438 ± 0.33 and an MCV of $91.3 \ \mu m^3 \pm 5.4 \ \mu m^3$; the women had a hematocrit of 0.407 ± 0.29 and an MCV of $90.5 \ \mu m^3 \pm 4.1 \ \mu m^3$.[117]

Iron deficiency may be assessed by sampling the bone marrow, but measurement of the serum ferritin concentration is a far less invasive method. The serum iron value and the MCV are probably not as helpful for assessment of iron stores. The ferritin level, which rises with advanced age and in acute inflammatory conditions, is low in iron-deficient patients (i.e., less than 12 ng/mL).[119]

Low serum iron and increased total iron-binding capacity (TIBC) suggest iron deficiency, while low serum iron in the face of normal TIBC suggests anemia of chronic disease. Patterson and colleagues[120] found that a ferritin level of 45 ng/mL was 78% sensitive and 89% specific for the diagnosis of iron deficiency compared with the "gold standard" of a bone marrow examination. Also, the ratio of the serum iron to the TIBC, when equal to or less than 11%, was quite specific for iron deficiency, although neither measurement was helpful by itself. The MCV was low in only 14 of 66 patients (21%) with documented iron deficiency by bone marrow examination.[120]

The extent of the work-up of anemia in an elderly patient may be abbreviated because the patient's general medical condition does not warrant an aggressive approach. On the other hand, most patients with evidence of anemia and iron deficiency require a work-up for gastrointestinal blood loss, which is the common cause of anemia and iron deficiency in the elderly. Negative stool guaiac tests do not rule out gastrointestinal blood loss, since such bleeding may be intermittent.

Patients with macrocytosis and anemia should be evaluated for low vitamin B_{12} or folate levels or for pernicious anemia. Larson and coworkers,[121] in the evaluation of dementia, found that a patient with a normal complete blood cell count had a very small chance of having a low vitamin B_{12} level. Macrocytosis may be an early sign of such a deficiency.[122] In the elderly, however, a low vitamin B_{12} level may not represent a true deficiency, since most patients with low levels of vitamin B_{12} had normal Schilling test results and normal values of urinary methylmalonic acid.[123,124] Transport mechanisms may be altered in older adults.[125] Still, case reports occur of dramatic improvement with therapy after documented low levels of vitamin B_{12}.[126,127]

The erythrocyte sedimentation rate (ESR) is slightly elevated with age and is somewhat higher in women. The upper limit of normal for men under 50 is 15 mm/hr; in men over 50, the upper limit is 20 mm/hr. The corresponding values for women are 20 mm/hr and 30 mm/hr respectively.[128] The ESR is usually elevated in patients with temporal arteritis or polymyalgia rheumatica and parallels the activity of disease process in these conditions as well as rheumatoid arthritis.[129] Severe anemia can elevate the ESR as well.

Antinuclear antibodies and rheumatoid factor are commonly detected in elderly persons but may not indicate the presence of disease, particularly when present in low titer.

Renal Function

Renal function changes with age in the absence of disease have been well documented and are generally well known. The glomerular filtration rate (GFR) falls with age, so that elderly men had a GFR of 80 mL/min per 1.73 m^2 of body surface area, while the younger cohort had a normal GFR of 120 mL/min.[130] A nomogram for creatinine clearance according to age is available.[131] In addition, a formula can be used in estimating the GFR from the patient's age, weight in kilograms, and the serum creatinine value:

$$\frac{(140 - \text{age}) \times \text{weight in kilograms}}{72 \times \text{serum creatinine}}$$

For the estimation of GFR in women, the result of the calculation is multiplied by 0.85.[132] Some caveats are in order when using the serum creatinine value to evaluate renal function. First, the serum creatinine value can only be used to estimate renal function in a steady state. In other words, if the renal function is changing rapidly, such as in an acutely ill patient receiving gentamicin, the creatinine value will not accurately reflect the GFR or creatinine clearance at that moment. Second, in the elderly, the creatinine value may be lower for any given GFR, reflecting the decreased muscle mass commonly found in older patients. Third, the creatinine value is not linearly related to the GFR. Instead, the relationship is an exponential one. When the creatinine value is low, small changes in the serum creatinine level represent large changes in the GFR. So, for example, a change in the serum creatinine level from 1.3 to 1.9 mg/dL may represent a much larger drop in GFR (perhaps a fall of 50%) than a change of 6.2 to 6.8 mg/dL.[133] Changes in renal function as well as a relative increase in body fat with age are critical factors to consider in prescribing for the elderly, since these changes are intimately related to the distribution and elimination of drugs in the body.

The blood urea nitrogen (BUN) value is also frequently used as an indication of kidney function. Many factors other than kidney function can affect the BUN value, however, including the patient's protein intake and liver function and the presence of any gastrointestinal blood. The ratio of the BUN value to the serum creatinine level can be used as a guide in estimating the specific contribution of kidney function to the elevated BUN value. As a general rule, the ratio of BUN to serum creatinine is approximately 10:1. If the BUN value is raised out of proportion to the serum creatinine level, the elevation may be secondary to dehydration or gastrointestinal blood loss or may be the antianabolic effect of tetracycline in a patient with underlying renal disease.[133]

Thyroid Function

Unsuspected thyroid disorder may result in unexplained disability or delirium.[134,135] The level of thyroid-stimulating hormone (TSH) shows a gradual increase with advancing age, particularly in women. The prevalence of an elevated TSH value is around 2% to 7% in most studies.[63,136,137] Many elders have diminished thyroid reserve, that is, an elevated TSH value but a normal thyroxine (T4) value. Patients with mildly elevated TSH, normal T4, and high titers to antimicrosomal antibodies tend eventually to develop clinically overt hypothyroidism at as great a rate as 5% to 8% per year.[64,138,139] Such patients may benefit from prophylactic therapy with thyroid hormone.[138,140]

Hyperthyroidism may not be as common in the elderly as hypothyroidism, but if the diagnosis is suspect, a normal serum T4 value and free thyroxine index should not dissuade the physician from seeking further evidence, since some patients have only an elevated triiodothyronine (T3) value. It has been recommended that all elderly patients, especially those entering the hospital or those who exhibit depression or "failure to thrive," should have samples drawn for TSH and T_4 determination.[63,141] A potential problem is that interpretation of thyroid function tests is complicated by concurrent disease, so that some ill elderly patients have a decreased T_3 or an elevated T_4 yet are euthyroid.[142–144]

Glucose Intolerance

Since glucose intolerance increases with age, using standard blood sugar values for the diagnosis of diabetes mellitus would label a high number of elderly persons "diabetic."[145,146] There is increasing person to person variability in glucose tolerance with advancing age.[147,148] Since the fasting blood sugar (FBS) level rises at a rate of about 2 mg/dL per decade and the two-hour postprandial level rises at 8 to 20 mg/dL per decade after age 35, a 40-year-old woman with an FBS of 90 mg/dL and a two-hour postprandial glucose value of 130 mg/dL could "normally" have, at age 80, an FBS of 98 mg/dL and a two-hour postprandial glucose level of 190 to 210 mg/dL.[146] A nomogram to estimate the age-ranked percentile of a blood sugar measurement has been published for interpreting results of the oral glucose tolerance test.[149]

Cholesterol

Total cholesterol increases with age, reaching a plateau at approximately age 60 in men and 70 in women.[150] Reduction in cholesterol levels, especially LDL, reduces the risk of subsequent angina and myocardial infarction, effects that take five to ten years to accrue.[151] The implication is that vigorous treatment is justified in a person aged 65 years with 20 or more years of life ahead but not in persons with end-stage conditions or among the old old (see Chapter 8). The overall quality of life and functional status must be considered in deciding how aggressively to treat hypercholesterolemia.

CONCLUSION

The physical examination of the older patient is not markedly different from the physical examination of any adult. The focus on factors contributing to functional loss, the frequent barriers to communication present in the elderly, and the difficulty of many elders in obtaining adequate access to medical care (because of their values or lack of transportation) distinguish the examination of older adults. The physical examination is complementary to functional, social, economic, and values assessment. Evaluation of these other domains is often the key to the solution of the multifaceted problems of living experienced by older adults.

REFERENCES

1. Ham RJ. Functional assessment of the elderly patient. In: Reichel W, ed. *Clinical Aspects of Aging.* 3rd ed. Baltimore, Md: Williams & Wilkins, 1989:26–40.

2. Fried L, Storer DJ, King DE, Lodder F. Diagnosis of illness presentation in the elderly. *J Am Geriatr Soc.* 1991;39:117–123.

3. Galazka SS. Preoperative evaluation of the elderly surgical patient. *J Fam Pract.* 1988; 27:622–632.

4. Goldman L. Cardiac risks and complications of noncardiac surgery. *Ann Intern Med.* 1983; 98:504–513.

5. Keeler EB, Solomon DH, Beck JC, et al. Effect of patient age on duration of medical encounters with physicians. *Med Care.* 1982;20:1101–1108.

6. Cadieux RJ, Kales JD, Zimmerman L. Comprehensive assessment of the elderly patient. *Am Fam Physician.* 1985;31:105–111.

7. Weed L. *Medical Records, Medical Education, and Patient Care.* Cleveland, Ohio: Case Western Reserve Press, 1970.

8. Ham RJ. *Geriatrics I.* American Academy of Family Physicians home study self assessment monograph 89. Kansas City, Mo: American Academy of Family Physicians, 1986.

9. Besdine RW. The educational utility of comprehensive functional assessment in the elderly. *J Am Geriatr Soc.* 1983;31:651–656.

10. Williams ME, Hadler NM. Illness as the focus of geriatric medicine. *N Engl J Med.* 1983;308:1357–1360.

11. Lyons AS, Petrucelli RJ. *Medicine: An Illustrated History.* New York, NY: Harry N. Abrams Inc, 1978.

12. Mader SL. Aging and postural hypotension: an update. *J Am Geriatr Soc.* 1989;37:129–137.

13. Caird FI, Andrews GR, Kennedy RD. Effect of posture on blood pressure in the elderly. *Br Heart J.* 1973;35:527–530.

14. Mader SL, Josephson KR, Rubenstein LZ. Low prevalence of postural hypotension among community-dwelling elderly. *JAMA.* 1987;258:1511–1514.

15. Shannon RP, Wei JY, Rosa RM, et al. The effect of age and sodium depletion on cardiovascular response to orthostasis. *Hypertension.* 1986;5:438–443.

16. Messerli FH, Ventura HO, Amodeo C. Osler's maneuver and pseudohypertension. *N Engl J Med.* 1985;312:1548–1551.

17. Hansen AG, Jensen H, Laugesen LP, et al. Withdrawal of antihypertensive drugs in the elderly. *Acta Med Scand.* 1983;676(suppl):178–185.

18. Hypertension Detection and Follow-Up Program Cooperative Group. Five-year findings of the Hypertension Detection and Follow-Up Program, I: reduction in mortality of persons with high blood pressure, including mild hypertension. *JAMA.* 1979;242:2562–2571.

19. Hypertension Detection and Follow-Up Program Cooperative Group. Five-year findings of the Hypertension Detection and Follow-Up Program, II: mortality by race, sex, and age. *JAMA.* 1979; 242:2572–2577.

20. Amery A, Birkenhager W, Brixko P, et al. Mortality and morbidity results from the European Working Party on High Blood Pressure in the Elderly Trial. *Lancet.* 1985;1:1349–1354.

21. National Heart Foundation of Australia. Treatment of mild hypertension in the elderly: report by the Management Committee. *Med J Aust.* 1981;2:398–402.

22. Veterans Administration Cooperative Study Group on Antihypertensive Agents. Effects of treatment on morbidity in hypertension. *JAMA.* 1970;213:1143–1152.

23. Dahlof B, Lindholm LH, Hansson L, et al. Morbidity and mortality in the Swedish trial in old persons with hypertension (STOP-hypertension). *Lancet.* 1991;338:1281–1285.

24. MRC Working Party. Medical Research Council trial of treatment of hypertension in older adults. *Br Med J.* 1992;304:405–412.

25. Hulley SB, Feigal D, Ireland C, et al. Systolic Hypertension in the Elderly Program (SHEP): the first three months. *J Am Geriatr Soc.* 1986;34:101–105.

26. Gifford RW. Isolated systolic hypertension in the elderly. *JAMA.* 1982;247:781–785.

27. Kannel WB. Implications of Framingham study data for treatment of hypertension: impact of other risk factors. In: Laragh JH, Buhler FR, Seldin DW, eds: *Frontiers in Hypertension Research.* New York, NY: Springer-Verlag, 1981:17–21.

28. Shekelle RB, Ostfeld AM, Klawans HL. Hypertension and risk of stroke in an elderly population. *Stroke.* 1974;5:71–75.

29. Applegate WB, Rutan GH. Advances in the management of hypertension in older persons. *J Am Geriatr Soc.* 1992;40:1164–1174.

30. SHEP Cooperative Research Group. Prevention of stroke by antihypertensive drug treatment in older persons with isolated systolic hypertension. *JAMA.* 1991;265:3255–3264.

31. Meyer JS, Judd BW, Tawakina T, et al. Improved cognition after control of risk factors for multi-infarct dementia. *JAMA.* 1986;256:2203–2209.

32. Morley JE, Solomon DH. Major issues in geriatrics over the last five years. *J Am Geriatr Soc.* 1994;42:218–225.

33. Berk SL, Smith JK. Infectious diseases in the elderly. *Med Clin North Am.* 1983;67:273–293.

34. Subcommittee on Health and Long-term Care. *Hypothermia: A Preventable Tragedy: A Cold Weather Guide for the Elderly.* Washington, DC: US Government Printing Office, 1981.

35. Reuler JB. Hypothermia: pathophysiology, clinical settings, and management. *Ann Intern Med.* 1978;89:519–527.

36. Haboubi NY, Hudson PR, Pathy MS. Measurement of height in the elderly. *J Am Geriatr Soc.* 1990;38:1008–1010.

37. The Nutrition Screening Initiative. *Report of Nutrition Screening: Toward a Common View.* Washington, DC: The Nutrition Screening Initiative, 1991.

38. Dwyer JT, Gallo JJ, Reichel W. Assessing nutritional status in elderly patients. *Am Fam Physician.* 1993;47:613–620.

39. Detsky AS, Smalley PS, Chang J. Is this patient malnourished? *JAMA.* 1994;271:54–58.

40. O'Malley TA, Everitt DE, O'Malley HC, et al. Identifying and preventing family-mediated abuse and neglect of elderly persons. *Ann Intern Med.* 1983;98:998–1005.

41. American Medical Association, Council on Scientific Affairs. Elder abuse and neglect. *JAMA.* 1987;257:966–971.

42. Kimsey LR, Tarbox AR, Bragg DF. Abuse of the elderly—the hidden agenda, I: the caretakers and the categories of abuse. *J Am Geriatr Soc.* 1981;29:465–472.

43. Rathbone-McCuan E, Goodstein RK. Elder abuse: clinical considerations. *Psychiatr Ann.* 1985;15:331–339.

44. Taler G, Ansello EF. Elder abuse. *Am Fam Physician.* 1985;32:107–114.

45. Allman RM. Pressure ulcers among the elderly. *N Engl J Med.* 1989;320:850–853.

46. Brandeis GH, Morris JN, Nash DJ, Lipsitz LA. The epidemiology and natural history of pressure ulcers in elderly nursing home residents. *JAMA.* 1990;264:2905–2909.

47. *Pressure Ulcers in Adults.* Clinical practice guidelines. Rockville, Md: US Department of Health and Human Services, Public Health Service, Agency for Health Care Policy and Research, 1992.

48. Macaraeg PVJ, Lasagna L, Snyder B. Arcus not so senilis. *Ann Intern Med.* 1968;68:345–354.

49. Weale RA. Retinal illumination and age. *Trans Illum Eng Soc.* 1961;26:95.

50. Steffes R, Thralow J. Visual field limitation in the patient with dementia of the Alzheimer's type. *J Am Geriatr Soc.* 1987;35:198–204.

51. Ruben RJ, Kruger B. Hearing loss in the elderly. In: Katzman R, Terry RD, eds. *The Neurology of Aging.* Philadelphia, Pa: FA Davis, 1983:123–148.

52. Goldberg EM. *Helping the Aged: A Field Experiment in Social Work.* London, Allen & Unwin, 1970. Cited in Mader S. Hearing impairment in elderly persons. *J Am Geriatr Soc.* 1984;32:548–553.

53. Mader S. Hearing impairment in elderly persons. *J Am Geriatr Soc.* 1984;32:548–553.

54. Corbin S, Reed M, Nobbs H, et al. Hearing assessment in homes for the aged. *J Am Geriatr Soc.* 1984;32:396–400.

55. Gillhome-Herbst K, Humphrey C. Hearing impairment and mental state in the elderly living at home. *Br Med J.* 1980;281:903–905.

56. National Center for Health Statistics. *Edentulous Persons: United States—1971.* Data from National Health Survey, series 10, No 89. Hyattsville, Md: Department of Health, Education, and Welfare, 1974. Cited in Gordon SR, Jahnigen DW. Oral assessment of the edentulous elderly patient. *J Am Geriatr Soc.* 1983;31:797–801.

57. Gordon SR, Jahnigen DW. Oral assessment of the edentulous elderly patient. *J Am Geriatr Soc.* 1983;31:797–801.

58. Gordon SR, Jahnigen DW. Oral assessment of the dentulous elderly patient. *J Am Geriatr Soc.* 1986;34:276–281.

59. Chambers BR, Norris JW. Outcome in patients with asymptomatic neck bruits. *N Engl J Med.* 1986;315:860–865.

60. Feussner JR, Matchar DB. When and how to study the carotid arteries. *Ann Intern Med.* 1988;109:805–818.

61. Health and Public Policy Committee, American College of Physicians. Diagnostic evaluation of the carotid arteries. *Ann Intern Med.* 1988;109:835–837.

62. Hurley JR. Thyroid disease in the elderly. *Med Clin North Am.* 1983;67:497–516.

63. Livingston EH, Hershman JM, Sawin CT, et al. Prevalence of thyroid disease and abnormal thyroid tests in older hospitalized and ambulatory persons. *J Am Geriatr Soc.* 1987;35:109–114.

64. Cooper DS. Subclinical hypothyroidism. *JAMA.* 1987;258:246–247.

65. Morrow LB. How thyroid disease presents in the elderly. *Geriatrics.* 1978;33:42–45.

66. Thomas FB, Mazzaferri EL, Skillman TG. Apathetic thyrotoxicosis: a distinctive clinical and laboratory entity. *Ann Intern Med.* 1970;72:679.

67. Wei JY, Gersh BJ. Heart disease in the elderly. *Curr Probl Cardiol.* 1987;12:1–65.

68. *Heart Failure: Evaluation and Care of Patients with Left-Ventricular Failure.* Clinical practice guidelines. Rockville, Md: US Department of Health and Human Services, Public Health Service, Agency for Health Care Policy and Research, 1994.

69. Potter JF, Elahi D, Tobin JD, et al. The effect of age on the cardiothoracic ratio of man. *J Am Geriatr Soc.* 1982;30:404–409.

70. Selzer A, Cohn K. Natural history of mitral stenosis in review. *Circulation.* 1972;45:878–887.

71. Wolf PA, Abbott RD, Kannel WB. Atrial fibrillation: A major contributor to stroke in the elderly. *Arch Intern Med.* 1987;147:1561–1564.

72. Wei JY. Heart disease in the elderly. *Cardiovasc Med.* 1984;9:971–982.

73. Roberts WC, Perloff JK, Costantino T. Severe valvular aortic stenosis in patients over 65 years of age. *Am J Cardiol.* 1971;27:497–506.

74. Thompson ME, Shaver JA. Aortic stenosis in the elderly. *Geriatrics.* 1983;10:50–65.

75. Gerstenblith G, Frederiksen J, Yin FCP, et al. Echocardiographic assessment of a normal adult aging population. *Circulation.* 1977;56:273–278.

76. Heger JJ. Cardiac arrhythmias in the elderly. *Cardiovasc Clin.* 1981;12:145–159.

77. Fleg JL, Kennedy HL. Cardiac arrhythmias in a healthy elderly population: detection by 24-hour ambulatory electrocardiography. *Chest.* 1982;81:302–307.

78. Martin A, Benbow LJ, Butrous GS, et al. Five-year follow-up of 101 elderly subjects by means of long-term ambulatory cardiac monitoring. *Eur Heart J.* 1984;5:592–596.

79. Dreifus LS. Cardiac arrhythmias in the elderly: clinical aspects. *Cardiol Clin.* 1986;4:273–283.

80. Camm AJ, Evans KE, Ward DE, et al. The rhythm of the heart in active elderly subjects. *Am Heart J.* 1980;99:598–603.

81. Kantelip JP, Sage E, Duchene-Marullaz P. Findings on ambulatory electrocardiographic monitoring in subjects older than 80 years. *Am J Cardiol.* 1986;57:398–401.

82. Boucek RJ, Noble NL, Marks A. Age and fibrous proteins of the human lungs. *Gerontologia.* 1961;5:150–156.

83. Riggs BL, Melton LJ. The prevention and treatment of osteoporosis. *N Engl J Med.* 1992; 327:620–627.

84. Raisz LG. Osteoporosis. *J Am Geriatr Soc.* 1982;30:127–138.

85. Riggs BL, Melton LJ. Involutional osteoporosis. *N Engl J Med.* 1986;314:1676–1686.

86. Chestnut CH. An appraisal of the role of estrogens in the treatment of postmenopausal osteoporosis. *J Am Geriatr Soc.* 1984;32:604–608.

87. Larson KA, Shannon SC. Decreasing the incidence of osteoporosis-related injuries through diet and exercise. *Public Health Rep.* 1984;99:609–613.

88. Consensus Conference. Osteoporosis. *JAMA.* 1984;252:799–802.

89. Cummings SR, Black D. Should perimenopausal women be screened for osteoporosis? *Ann Intern Med.* 1986;104:817–823.

90. Ott S. Should women get screening bone mass measurements? *Ann Intern Med.* 1986; 104:874–876.

91. Hall FM, Davis MA, Baran DT. Bone mineral screening for osteoporosis. *N Engl J Med.* 1987;316:212–214.

92. Johnston CC, Slemenda CW, Melton LJ. Clinical use of bone densitometry. *N Engl J Med.* 1991;324:1105–1109.

93. Tosteson ANA, Rosenthal DI, Melton LJ, Weinstein MC. Cost effectiveness of screening perimenopausal white women for osteoporosis: bone densitometry and hormone replacement therapy. *Ann Intern Med.* 1990;113:594–603.

94. Cummings SR, Browner WS, Grady D, Ettinger B. Should prescription of postmenopausal hormone therapy be based on the results of bone densitometry? *Ann Intern Med.* 1990;113:565–566.

95. Mandelblatt J, Gopaul I, Wistreich M. Gynecological care of elderly women: another look at Papanicolaou smear testing. *JAMA.* 1986;256:367–371.

96. Riesenberg DE. The Papanicolaou smear in elderly women. *JAMA.* 1986;256:393.

97. Vernon MS. Urinary incontinence in the elderly. *Prim Care.* 1989;16:515–528.

98. Madoff RD, Williams JG, Caushaj PF. Fecal incontinence. *N Engl J Med.* 1992;326:1002–1007.

99. Catania JA. Older Americans and AIDS: transmission risks and primary prevention research needs. *Gerontologist.* 1989;29:373–381.

100. Katzman R, Terry RD. *The Neurology of Aging.* Philadelphia, Pa: FA Davis, 1983.

101. Thomas RJ. Blinking and the release reflexes: are they clinically useful? *J Am Geriatr Soc.* 1994;42:609–613.

102. Molloy DW, Clarnette RM, McIlroy WE, et al. Clinical significance of primitive reflexes in Alzheimer's disease. *J Am Geriatr Soc.* 1991;39:1160–1163.

103. Hodges JR. Neurological aspects of dementia and normal aging. In: Huppert FA, Brayne C, O'Connor DW, eds. *Dementia and Normal Aging.* Cambridge: Cambridge University Press, 1994:118–129.

104. Nevitt MC, Cummings SR, Kidd S, Black D. Risk factors for recurrent nonsyncopal falls: a prospective study. *JAMA.* 1989;261:2663–2668.

105. Studenski S, Duncan PW, Chandler J, et al. Predicting falls: the role of mobility and nonphysical factors. *J Am Geriatr Soc.* 1994;42:297–302.

106. Tinetti ME, Speechley M, Ginter SF. Risk factors for falls among elderly persons living in the community. *N Engl J Med.* 1987;319:1701–1705.

107. Tinetti ME, Speechley M. Prevention of falls among the elderly. *N Engl J Med.* 1989;320:1055–1059.

108. Tinetti M. Performance-oriented assessment of mobility problems in elderly patients. *J Am Geriatr Soc.* 1986;34:119–126.

109. Beck JC, Freedman ML, Warshaw GA. Geriatric assessment: focus on function. *Patient Care.* 1994;28:10–32.

110. O'Brien K. Getting around: a simple office workup to assess patient function. *Geriatrics.* 1994;49:38–42.

111. Lillie SM. Evaluation for driving. In: Yoshikawa TT, Cobbs EL, Brummel-Smith K, eds. *Ambulatory Geriatric Care.* St. Louis, Mo: Mosby, 1993:131–141.

112. Metzner JL, Dentino AN, Godard SL, et al. Impairment in driving and psychiatric illness. *J Neuropsychiatry.* 1993;5:211–220.

113. Carr DB. Assessing older drivers for physical and cognitive impairment. *Geriatrics.* 1993;48:46–51.

114. Canadian Medical Association. Physicians' Guide to Driver Examination. 5th ed. *Can Med Assoc J.* 1991;15 (July suppl):1–64.

115. Reuben DB, Silliman RA, Traines M. The aging driver: medicine, policy, and ethics. *J Am Geriatr Soc.* 1988;36:1135–1142.

116. Underwood M. The older driver: clinical assessment and injury prevention. *Arch Intern Med.* 1992;152:735–740.

117. Zauber NP, Zauber AG. Hematologic data of healthy very old people. *JAMA.* 1987;257: 2181–2184.

118. Timiras ML, Brownstein H. Prevalence of anemia and correlation of hemoglobin with age in a geriatric screening clinic population. *J Am Geriatr Soc.* 1987;35:639–643.

119. Rubenstein E, Federman DD, eds. Normal laboratory values. *Scientific American Medicine.* New York, NY: Scientific American Inc, 1987.

120. Patterson C, Turpie ID, Benger AM. Assessment of iron stores in anemic geriatric patients. *J Am Geriatr Soc.* 1985;33:764–767.

121. Larson ER, Reifler BV, Sumi SM, et al. Diagnostic tests in the evaluation of dementia: a prospective study of 200 elderly outpatients. *Arch Intern Med.* 1986;146:1917–1922.

122. Carmel R. Macrocytosis, mild anemia, and delay in the diagnosis of pernicious anemia. *Arch Intern Med.* 1979;139:47–50.

123. Grinblat J, Marcus DL, Hernandez F, et al. Folate and vitamin B_{12} levels in an urban elderly population with chronic diseases: assessment of two laboratory folate assays: microbiologic and radioassay. *J Am Geriatr Soc.* 1986;34:627–632.

124. Matchar DB, Feussner JR, Watson DJ, et al. Significance of low serum vitamin B_{12} levels in the elderly. *J Am Geriatr Soc.* 1986;34:680–681. Abstract.

125. Marcus DL, Shadick N, Crantz J. Low serum B_{12} levels in a hematologically normal elderly population. *J Am Geriatr Soc.* 1987;35:635–638.

126. Gross JS, Weintraub NT, Neufeld RR, et al. Pernicious anemia in the demented patient without anemia or macrocytosis: a case for early recognition. *J Am Geriatr Soc.* 1986;34:612–614.

127. Wieland RG. Vitamin B_{12} deficiency in the nonanemic elderly. *J Am Geriatr Soc.* 1986;34:690.

128. Bottinger LE, Svedberg CA. Normal erythrocyte sedimentation rate and age. *Br Med J.* 1967;2:85–87.

129. Sox HC, Liang MH. The erythrocyte sedimentation rate: guidelines for rational use. *Ann Intern Med.* 1986;104:515–523.

130. Davies DF, Shock NW. Age changes in glomerular filtration rate, effective renal plasma flow, and tubular excretory capacity in adult males. *J Clin Invest.* 1950;29:496–507.

131. Rowe JW, Andres R, Tobin JD, et al. Age-adjusted normal standards for creatinine clearance in man. *Ann Intern Med.* 1976;84:567–569.

132. Cockroft DW, Gault MH. Prediction of creatinine clearance from serum creatinine. *Nephron.* 1976;16:31–41.

133. Rose BD. *Pathophysiology of Renal Disease.* New York, NY: McGraw-Hill Book Co, 1981.

134. Rae P, Farrar J, Beckett G, Toft A. Assessment of thyroid status in elderly people. *Br Med J.* 1993;307:177–180.

135. Bemben DA, Hamm RM, Morgan L, et al. Thyroid disease in the elderly, II: predictability of subclinical hypothyroidism. *J Fam Pract.* 1994;38:583–588.

136. Tunbridge WMG, Evered DC, Hall R, et al. The spectrum of thyroid disease in a community: the Whickham Survey. *Clin Endocrinol.* 1977;7:481–493.

137. Sawin CT, Chopra D, Azizi F, et al. The aging thyroid: increased prevalence of elevated serum thyrotropin levels in the elderly. *JAMA.* 1979;242:247–250.

138. Rosenthal MJ, Hunt WC, Garry PJ, et al. Thyroid failure in the elderly: microsomal antibodies as discriminant for therapy. *JAMA.* 1987;258:209–213.

139. Nystrom E, Bengtsson C, Lindstedt G, et al. Screening for thyroid disease. *Lancet.* 1981; 2:927–928.

140. Griffin JE. Hypothyroidism in the elderly. *Am J Med Sci.* 1990;299:334–345.

141. Bahemuka M, Hodkinson HM. Screening for hypothyroidism in elderly inpatients. *Br Med J.* 1975;1:601–603.

142. Blum M. Thyroid function and disease in the elderly. *Hosp Pract.* October 1981:105–116.

143. Burrows AW, Shakespear RA, Hesch RD, et al. Thyroid hormones in the elderly sick: T4 euthyroidism. *Br Med J.* 1975;2:437–439.

144. Helfand M, Crapo LM. Screening for thyroid disease. *Ann Intern Med.* 1990;112:840–849.

145. Bennett PH. Diabetes in the elderly: diagnosis and epidemiology. *Geriatrics.* 1984;39:37–41.

146. Lipson LG. Diabetes in the elderly: diagnosis, pathogenesis, and therapy. *Am J Med.* 1986; 80(suppl 5A):10–21.

147. Shinokata H. Age as an independent determinant of glucose tolerance. *Diabetes.* 1991; 40:44–51.

148. Busby MJ, Bellantoni MF, Tobin JD, et al. Glucose tolerance in women: the effect of age, body composition, and sex hormones. *J Am Geriatr Soc.* 1992;40:497–502.

149. Elahi D, Clark B, Andres R. Glucose tolerance, insulin sensitivity and age. In: Armbracht HJ, Coe RM, Wongsurawat N, eds. *Endocrine Function and Aging.* New York, NY: Springer-Verlag, 1990:48–63.

150. Kronmal RA, Cain KC, Ye Z, Omenn GS. Total cholesterol levels and mortality risk as a function of age. *Arch Intern Med.* 1993;153:1065–1073.

151. Verdery R, Busby-Whitehead J. Lipid abnormalities in the elderly. In: Reichel W, ed. *Clinical Aspects of Aging.* 4th ed. Baltimore, Md: Williams & Wilkins, 1995.

8

Health Maintenance and Disability Prevention

The concept of health maintenance takes on new meaning for the elderly, in whom chronic conditions such as arthritis and diabetes are common. While primary prevention of most chronic conditions currently remains out of reach, it is often still possible to limit the disability of chronic illness and enhance the quality of life. The domains of multidimensional geriatric assessment lay out a framework for targeting preventive strategies tailored to the older patient. The aspects of mental state, functional status, social situation, values history, and medical considerations act as a *focus* of preventive activities and as a *guide* for highlighting preventive activities that are appropriate for the individual patient. An individualized plan for health promotion and disability prevention should be informed by multidimensional assessment.

As Eubie Blake, the jazz composer and pianist, observed on his 100th birthday, "These docs, they always ask you how you live so long. I tell 'em, if I'd known I was gonna live this long, I'd have taken better care of myself."[1] Health maintenance and disability prevention for the old begins with appropriate decisions concerning diet and lifestyle made in the early and middle years of life. For older persons approaching the limit of natural life expectancy, the goal of prevention becomes preservation of functional capacity and not simply prolonging life.[2-4] Approaches to prevention of cancer, cardiovascular disease, cerebrovascular disease, and the infections preventable through immunization are complemented by a focus on prevention of the problems specific to old age.[5] "Geriatric" problems, including incontinence, falls, functional impairment, and polypharmacy, may not easily fit into a disease model of illness.

The elderly are a distinctly heterogeneous group. Older persons in good health, frail elders with functional disability living at home, and elderly residents of institutions each require a unique level of appropriate health promotion and disease prevention activities.[5] This heterogeneity must be considered in recommending a strategy for prevention of disability and preservation of health.[6] Although many disorders of the elderly are chronic and not curable, early detection and treatment of problems that interfere with functioning is a reasonable goal.[7] Some interventions may actually be *more* efficacious with advancing age (Table 8–1).[8]

Kennie[2,3,9] and others[10,11] have suggested that primary care practitioners practice "opportunistic case finding"—use the problem-oriented patient visit to carry out a search for unreported illnesses. In pediatric practice, case finding is routine. When a child is seen for an acute illness, a few moments are spent evaluating development, giving anticipatory guidance, and checking for compliance with vaccination schedules. Current reimbursement structures do not encourage this practice in adult medicine; however, the process may be facilitated through consideration of components of the multidimensional assessment in a "prevention-oriented medical record."[12] Opportunistic case finding integrates the traditional medical care delivery system with a process of continual review and search for unreported problems of health or function.[2,3,9,11]

Prevention is sometimes categorized as primary, secondary, or tertiary. *Primary* prevention involves forestalling the development of disease (e.g., flu vaccination to prevent development of influenza). *Secondary* prevention involves early detection and treatment of disease during an asymptomatic phase (e.g., detection of hypertension). *Tertiary* prevention is directed toward avoidance of negative consequences among persons with the disease (e.g., preventing complications of diabetes through meticulous control of blood sugar). Preventive measures may also be categorized as universal, selective, or indicated.[13] *Universal* measures are desirable for the entire group of elderly persons (e.g., intake of an adequate diet). *Selective* measures are warranted when the individual belongs to a group with a higher than average risk of disease (e.g., intensive examinations of persons with a family history of colorectal cancer). *Indicated* measures apply to persons who have a higher than average risk of disease based on history or examination (e.g., control of hypertension).[13]

Although health care professionals can counsel the patient regarding the pros and cons of specific screening procedures and behaviors, the patient ultimately must accept responsibility for decisions about personal behavior affecting health.[14] The patient must believe that a particular condition would have an adverse effect on personal comfort and independence unless detected at an early stage. Familiarity with a disease through the experience of friends or as a result of educational material may enhance compliance with screening procedures.

Table 8–1 Preventive Services That Have Improved or Diminished Effectiveness in the Old Old (age 80 years and older)

Preventive Service	Improved Effectiveness	Diminished Effectiveness
Historical		
Accidents		
Falls prevention; particularly with a history of previous falls	X	
Motor vehicle		X
Mobility/ADL/IADL assessment	X	
Nutrition (undernutrition) screening or counseling	X	
Podiatry care	X	
Polypharmacy identification	X	
Dementia screening	X	
Urinary incontinence identification	X	
Physical examination		
Blood pressure		X
Cancer screening		
Breast		X
Cervical		X
Hearing screening	X	
Visual acuity screening	X	
Laboratory		
Cholesterol		X
Interventions		
Advance directives counseling	X	
Vaccinations		
Influenza immunization	X	

ADL denotes activities of daily living; *IADL* denotes instrumental activities of daily living.

Source: Reprinted with permission from Zazove P, Mehr DR, Ruffin MT, Klinkman MS, Peggs JF, Davies TC. A Criterion-Based Review of Preventive Health Care in the Elderly, *The Journal of Family Practice* (1992;34[3]:320–347), Copyright © 1992, Appleton & Lange.

These issues and beliefs should be explored in formulating the health maintenance plan.

Recommendations of the U.S. Preventive Services Task Force regarding the scheduling of periodic health examinations for persons aged 65 years and older are shown in Exhibit 8–1. Assessment activities could be performed at annual checkups or during intermittent visits for unrelated problems (opportunistic case finding). Health maintenance and disability prevention measures should be tai-

Exhibit 8–1 The US Preventive Services Task Force Guidelines for Persons Aged 65 Years and Older

Schedule: Every Year[1]

Screening

History
Prior symptoms of transient ischemic attack
Dietary intake
Physical activity
Tobacco/alcohol/drug use
Functional status at home

Physical Exam
Height and weight
Blood pressure
Visual acuity
Hearing and hearing aids
Clinical breast exam[2]
HIGH-RISK GROUPS
  Auscultation for carotid bruits (HR1)
  Complete skin exam (HR2)
  Complete oral cavity exam (HR3)
  Palpation for thyroid nodules (HR4)

Laboratory/Diagnostic Procedures
Nonfasting total blood cholesterol
Dipstick urinalysis
Mammogram[3]
Thyroid function tests[4]
HIGH-RISK GROUPS
  Fasting plasma glucose (HR5)
  Tuberculin skin test (PPD) (HR6)
  Electrocardiogram (HR7)
  Papanicolaou smear[5] (HR8)
  Fecal occult blood/sigmoidoscopy (HR9)
  Fecal occult blood/colonoscopy (HR10)

Counseling

Diet and Exercise
Fat (especially saturated fat), cholesterol, complex carbohydrates, fiber, sodium, calcium[4]
Caloric balance
Selection of exercise program

Substance Use
Tobacco cessation

Alcohol and other drugs:
Limiting alcohol consumption
Driving/other dangerous activities while under the influence
Treatment for abuse

Injury Prevention
Prevention of falls
Safety belts
Smoke detector
Smoking near bedding or upholstery
Hot water heater temperature
Safety helmets
HIGH-RISK GROUPS
  Prevention of childhood injuries (HR12)

Dental Health
Regular dental visits, tooth brushing, flossing

Other Primary Preventive Measures
Glaucoma testing by eye specialist
HIGH-RISK GROUPS
  Discussion of estrogen replacement therapy (HR13)
  Discussion of aspirin therapy (HR14)
  Skin protection from ultraviolet light (HR15)

Immunizations
Tetanus-diphtheria (Td) booster[6]
Influenza vaccine[7]
Pneumococcal vaccine
HIGH-RISK GROUPS
  Hepatitis B vaccine (HR16)

Remain Alert For:
Depressive symptoms
Suicide risk factors (HR11)
Abnormal bereavement
Changes in cognitive function
Medications that increase risk of falls
Signs of physical abuse or neglect
Malignant skin lesions
Peripheral arterial disease
Tooth decay, gingivitis, loose teeth

continues

Exhibit 8–1 continued

Leading Causes of Death:

Heart disease

Cerebrovascular disease

Obstructive lung disease

Pneumonia/influenza

Lung cancer

Colorectal cancer

This list of preventive services is not exhaustive. It reflects only those topics reviewed by the U.S. Preventive Services Task Force. Clinicians may wish to add other preventive services after considering the patient's medical history and other individual circumstances.

[1]The recommended schedule applies only to the periodic visit itself. The frequency of the individual preventive services listed in this table is left to clinical discretion, except as indicated in other footnotes.

[2]Annually for women until age 75, unless pathology detected.

[3]Every 1–2 years for women until age 75, unless pathology detected.

[4]For women.

[5]Every 1–3 years.

[6]Every 10 years.

[7]Annually.

HR1: Persons with risk factors for cerebrovascular or cardiovascular disease (e.g., hypertension, smoking, CAD, atrial fibrillation, diabetes) or those with neurologic symptoms (e.g., transient ischemic attacks) or a history of cerebrovascular disease.

HR2: Persons with a family or personal history of skin cancer, or clinical evidence of precursor lesions (e.g., dysplastic nevi, certain congenital nevi), or those with increased occupational or recreational exposure to sunlight.

HR3: Persons with exposure to tobacco or excessive amounts of alcohol, or those with suspicious symptoms or lesions detected through self-examination.

HR4: Persons with a history of upper-body irradiation.

HR5: The markedly obese, persons with a family history of diabetes, or women with a history of gestational diabetes.

HR6: Household members of persons with tuberculosis or others at risk for close contact with the disease (e.g., staff of tuberculosis clinics, shelters for the homeless, nursing homes, substance abuse treatment facilities, dialysis units, correctional institutions); recent immigrants or refugees from countries in which tuberculosis is common (e.g., Asia, Africa, Central and South America, Pacific Islands); migrant workers, residents of nursing homes, correctional institutions, or homeless shelters; or persons with certain underlying medical disorders (e.g., HIV infection).

HR7: Men with two or more cardiac risk factors (high blood cholesterol, hypertension, cigarette smoking, diabetes mellitus, family history of CAD); men who would endanger public safety were they to experience sudden cardiac events (e.g., commercial airline pilots); or sedentary or high-risk males planning to begin a vigorous exercise program.

HR8: Women who have not had previous documented screening in which smears have been consistently negative.

HR9: Persons who have first-degree relatives with colorectal cancer; a personal history of endometrial, ovarian, or breast cancer; or a previous diagnosis of inflammatory bowel disease, adenomatous polyps, or colorectal cancer.

continues

Exhibit 8–1 continued

HR10: Persons with a family history of familial polyposis coli or cancer family syndrome.

HR11: Recent divorce, separation, unemployment, depression, alcohol or other drug abuse, serious medical illnesses, living alone, or recent bereavement.

HR12: Persons with children in the home or automobile.

HR13: Women at increased risk for osteoporosis (e.g., Caucasian, low bone mineral content, bilateral oophorectomy before menopause or early menopause, slender build) and who are without known contraindications (e.g., history of undiagnosed vaginal bleeding, active liver disease, thromboembolic disorders, hormone dependent cancer).

HR14: Men who have risk factors for myocardial infarction (e.g., high blood cholesterol, smoking, diabetes mellitus, family history of early-onset CAD) and who lack a history of gastrointestinal or other bleeding problems, or other risk factors for bleeding or cerebral hemorrhage.

HR15: Persons with increased exposure to sunlight.

HR16: Homosexually active men, intravenous drug users, recipients of some blood products, or persons in health-related jobs with frequent exposure to blood or blood products.

Source: Reprinted from *Guide to Clinical Preventive Services: An Assessment of the Effectiveness of 169 Interventions* by the US Preventive Services Task Force, Williams & Wilkins, 1989.

---

lored to the circumstances and values of the individual patient and can be spread out over several visits. Although substantial evidence for the efficacy of some measures is lacking, "low effort" interventions, such as counseling to wear seat belts, are still worthwhile.[8,15]

The reader is advised to consider the detailed rationale for preventive measures outlined in several sources that are revised periodically: the Canadian Task Force on the Periodic Health Examination,[16–18] the series of articles by Frame,[19–22] the Report of the U.S. Preventive Services Task Force,[23] the review of preventive health services by Sox,[24] the Institute of Medicine report entitled *The Second Fifty Years: Promoting Health and Preventing Disability,*[6] and the reviews of Woolf, Kamerow, and colleagues,[25,26] Murphy and Coletta,[26a] and Klinkman, Zazove, and colleagues.[8,15] Only the latter four sources are entirely devoted to the special needs of the elderly; the last source separately considers recommendations for persons aged 80 years and older.

In the summary that follows, cancer, cardiovascular and cerebrovascular disease, and immunizations are considered first. The latter part of the chapter deals with "geriatric" problems that may be amenable to early detection and preventive strategies. It must be emphasized that tension and controversy exist regarding preventive measures, especially as they pertain to older adults. Recommendations should be informed by research involving the specified conditions occurring in patients with characteristics similar to those of our own patients, but the relevant information may not be available.

CANCER

Cervical Cancer

Beyond its function as a screening test for the detection of asymptomatic cancer of the uterine cervix, the Pap smear serves as the focal point for all the periodic health examinations women receive. The procedure affords an opportunity to examine the vagina and vulva for lesions and to broach issues related to sexuality. Younger women take health maintenance visits for granted, but older women may not consider that such examinations apply, since reproductive concerns seem far in the past. Older women are likely to be cared for by an internist or family physician, not a gynecologist, and may not specifically request a gynecologic examination. The primary care physician will have to remember to recommend pelvic and breast examination.

There appears to be general agreement that after age 65[8,15,23] (or at least after age 70)[21] Pap smear testing is no longer necessary. If an elderly woman has had repeated Pap smear testing, an upper age limit for the exam makes sense; however, many women in the current older cohort have not had Pap smears at regular intervals.[27,28] Mandelblatt and colleagues offered a Pap smear to 1,542 women aged 65 and older and found that 53 assented.[27] For 25% of this group, this was the first Pap smear, and only 26% gave a history of routine Pap smears. In addition to detecting cervical carcinoma, other gynecologic problems were uncovered, including breast cancer. Among 320 older women offered a Pap smear in primary care, 24% reported never having had one, and only 24% gave a history of adequate screening.[29] No women who were asked by their primary care provider refused to have a Pap smear, and 75% assented when asked by someone other than the primary care provider. As the current cohort of women ages, more older women will have undergone screening with the Pap smear. Since many of the current cohort of elderly women have never had cervical screening, the Pap smear remains important.

Breast Cancer

During examination of the breasts, it is prudent to instruct the patient in the proper technique for breast self-examination. Most authorities recommend that all women, regardless of age, be instructed in breast self-examination,[5,21] though agreement is not unanimous.[23] Mammography combined with professional breast examination appears to be effective in reducing mortality from breast carcinoma.[21,23] The American Cancer Society urged monthly breast self-examination, as well as physician examination every 3 years, between the ages of 20 and 40, followed by annual examinations thereafter.[30] In addition, mammography was recommended once between the ages of 35 and 40, every 2 years between the ages of

40 and 50, and annually thereafter. Women with a strong family history of breast cancer require closer monitoring. Frame[21] recommended annual mammography after age 50 years; indeed, five times as many cancers were detected among women aged 50 and older compared to younger women.[31] After age 75,[8,23] or at least after age 85,[32] the value of breast cancer screening is uncertain.

Ovarian and Endometrial Cancer

Screening for ovarian and endometrial cancer is not specifically recommended.[8,16,17,21,23,30,33] Pelvic examinations during general physical examination of women should include bimanual examination.[30,34] Endometrial biopsy should be considered for women at increased risk for endometrial cancer or in whom hormonal replacement therapy is contemplated. Older women should be taught to report postmenopausal bleeding, which may be a harbinger of endometrial cancer.

Colorectal Cancer

Screening for colorectal carcinoma may involve examination of the stool for occult blood, digital rectal examination, and flexible sigmoidoscopy. The examination of the stool for occult blood is noninvasive and relatively acceptable to patients. In the fifth decade of life, a positive test for occult blood was estimated to have a 27% predictive value for cancer; after age 70, the predictive value of a positive test was 52%.[35] In a nursing home, Mangla and coworkers[36] studied the value of annual stool tests for occult blood. Of 450 chronically ill patients, 21 (4.7%) were stool positive for occult blood. After extensive work-up, 3 cancers of the gastrointestinal tract were found. The other positive tests resulted in a diagnosis of 5 cases of duodenal ulcer and 7 cases of diverticulosis. The stool test for occult blood is not specific for colon cancer, and although it is generally acceptable to patients, positive tests require an invasive search for etiology that may not be warranted for debilitated older patients.

Persons screened with stool for occult blood showed reduction in colon cancer mortality at follow-up.[37] The six-slide stool specimen study for occult blood was recommended by the American Cancer Society yearly after age 50,[30] by Frame every 2 years between the ages of 40 and 50 and annually thereafter,[21] and by the Canadian Task Force on the Periodic Health Examination annually starting at age 46.[16] Updated recommendations do not include testing but do not suggest stopping screening that is in place.[38] The U.S. Preventive Services Task Force suggested that screening be offered to persons aged 50 and older.[23] Most colon cancers will be out of reach of the examining finger, but the rectal examination is the only time that some patients will have the stool sampled for occult blood.

Screening for colon cancer with flexible sigmoidoscopy can detect presymptomatic lesions, reduce mortality in those with cancer, and diagnose cancers at an earlier stage.[39,40] A shift toward more right-sided colon carcinoma could limit the effectiveness of the test.[41] The discomfort of flexible sigmoidoscopy reduces patient compliance with the procedure except for patients who are symptomatic (and hence no longer primarily concerned with screening) or highly motivated by a family history of colon cancer. Genetic markers may someday allow screening to be directed toward high-risk patients.[42] The number of persons eligible for screening is enormous, given recommendations that patients submit to the procedure every 3 to 5 years.[30] Screening at longer intervals may be efficacious; persons who had undergone flexible sigmoidoscopy over a 10-year follow-up interval had one-third the risk of fatal colon cancer when compared to persons not screened.[40]

CARDIOVASCULAR AND CEREBROVASCULAR DISEASE

Risk factors for cardiovascular and cerebrovascular disease are similar; they include hypertension, elevated blood cholesterol, and glucose intolerance.[43] Atrial fibrillation may be a particular risk factor for cerebrovascular disease among older adults.[44] Behavioral factors such as smoking, consumption of alcohol, dietary fat, and sedentary lifestyle play a role in the development of these disorders. Exercise has a number of beneficial effects, such as maintenance of function,[45] increased strength and fitness,[46] and sharpened memory and cognitive function.[47] Older adults should be advised to maintain an appropriate level of exercise.

Blood Pressure

Blood pressure should be measured at every health care visit employing the method described in Chapter 7. Elevated blood pressure should be confirmed on three separate occasions.[48] Hypertension is diagnosed if blood pressure is consistently above 140/90.[49] Isolated systolic hypertension appears to be associated with increased risk for adverse effects even among the very old.[50,51] Treatment should be individualized, considering concomitant risk factors for cardiovascular disease, medical conditions, and the risks of treatment.[52]

Auscultation of the Carotid Arteries

Auscultation of the carotid arteries is not recommended for asymptomatic individuals, since carotid endarterectomy is only effective for symptomatic and sig-

nificant stenosis of the carotid arteries.[53] If symptoms suggestive of transient ischemic attack are present, the arteries should be evaluated.[54]

Cholesterol

Although the relationship of serum cholesterol to risk of coronary artery disease
may not be as strong in advanced age, intervention may still have an important effect, since cardiovascular events and angina are more common (high population
attributable risk).[55–58] At least among persons aged 70 years and older, hypercholesterolemia may not be as important a risk factor for cardiovascular mortality or
morbidity.[58a] A healthy 60-year-old may have 20 or more years of life ahead, but
cholesterol screening is probably unwarranted in patients with a poor prognosis or
poor quality of life.[8] This is an example of an area in which we need more information to guide practice in the care of older adults.

INFECTIOUS DISEASE

Influenza Vaccine

Influenza vaccine is recommended yearly in the fall for older adults.[23,59] Older
persons with concurrent chronic heart, lung, or metabolic diseases, especially
those residing in nursing homes, are at increased risk compared with the general
population during influenza epidemics. Caregivers of such persons should probably be immunized as well. Not all eligible elders receive the vaccine—physicians
forget to offer it or elders refuse it. Some older persons refuse the vaccine because
they fear an adverse reaction or heard about neighbors or friends who "took sick"
after receiving the vaccine. Asking specifically about such notions may dispel
myths about the vaccine and enhance acceptance.

Pneumococcal Vaccine

Pneumococcal vaccine is recommended at least once for all older adults,[23,60] despite a dearth of evidence for the vaccine's efficacy in trials involving older
adults.[61] Pneumococcal pneumonia and sepsis are significant causes of illness,
while the vaccine is well tolerated.

Tetanus Vaccine

Older adults are at higher risk for tetanus than young adults.[62] Tetanus vaccination every 10 years is recommended by several authorities.[8,16,20,23] Unvaccinated
persons need to receive the three-dose primary series. Immunization of adults with

acellular pertussis vaccine combined with tetanus vaccination may become a standard in the future.[63]

GERIATRIC-ORIENTED SCREENING AND DISABILITY PREVENTION

Functional Impairment

Functional status is predictive of important outcomes such as mortality and hospitalization and can yield clues about mental status and depression (see Chapter 3). It is reasonable to ask older adults about changes in driving habits and ability to shop, do housework, and use the telephone. The family may relate that the patient is having difficulty taking medications appropriately. Concerns that arise in these circumstances should prompt evaluation for dementia, delirium, psychiatric disorders, substance abuse, and medication effects to forestall further decline. Older adults should be encouraged to adopt an appropriate exercise regimen, and steps should be taken to avoid acute losses in functional capacity as a result of bedrest in the hospital.[64,65]

Hearing Impairment

Hearing loss increases with age and is a potentially remedial condition associated with collateral effects, such as poor communication with caregivers, isolation, paranoia, and functional decline.[66] Hearing loss may simulate cognitive impairment. Simple methods to assess auditory function should be applied (e.g., clearing the ear canal of wax). Audiometry is widely available in most office practices and periodic screening would be reasonable.

Visual Impairment

Visual loss is associated with numerous collateral effects as well, including increased propensity for falls, confusion, and accidents.[5] Screening for visual impairment by questioning the patient about changes in vision may be supplemented by asking the patient to read from the newspaper or the Snellen eye chart. Glaucoma is characterized by increased intraocular pressure, cupping and pallor of the optic disc, and characteristic visual field defects. Glaucoma is more common in older people than in younger people and is the leading cause of blindness among African Americans.[67] Ocular hypertension is found in about 25% of older adults, and although it does not necessarily develop into glaucoma, persons over the age of 65 should be periodically screened by an eye specialist.[23] Persons with risk factors for glaucoma, such as diabetes, hypertension, severe myopia, chronic therapy with corticosteroids, or a family history of glaucoma should be screened by an optometrist or ophthalmologist.

Alcohol Abuse

The prevalence of alcohol abuse in older adults is said to be about 5%[68-70] but may be considerably higher among medical patients.[69] Numerous factors, including common stereotypes of alcoholics and the aged, conspire to make alcoholism difficult to detect in older persons.[69,71,72] Evaluation for alcohol use problems should accompany evaluation of older persons with functional impairment, seizures, falls, cognitive impairment, depression, anxiety, insomnia, and adverse reactions to prescribed medications.[71,73] Comorbid psychiatric conditions such as depression and alcoholism may put the older adult at increased risk for suicide.[74,75]

Among the brief measures of alcohol abuse are the 4-item CAGE,[76,77] the 10-item AUDIT,[78-80] and the 24-item MAST-G.[81,82]

The CAGE can be committed to memory:

1. Ever felt the need to *cut down* on your drinking?
2. Ever felt *annoyed* by criticism of your drinking?
3. Ever felt *guilty* about drinking?
4. Ever take a morning drink *(eye-opener)?*

Two affirmative answers to the CAGE questions are said to be suggestive of alcoholism.[76,77] The AUDIT (Exhibit 8–2) was developed under the auspices of the World Health Organization (*AUDIT* is an acronym for the Alcohol Use Disorder Identification Test). Each item is rated on a 4-point scale; with a cutoff point of 8, the test was 92% sensitive and 93% specific.[79] Unlike the CAGE, the AUDIT includes items about amount consumed and problems related to alcohol consumption.

Polypharmacy

While abuse of illicit substances is uncommon among older persons, misuse of prescription medications such as hypnotics may be a significant problem.[83] The use of psychoactive drugs increases with advancing age,[84-92] despite increased hazard of cognitive impairment,[93] physical dependency,[94] and injury.[95] Use of several drugs multiplies the risk for adverse reactions, and additional drugs may be prescribed in an effort to control symptoms that arise.[96] A not too infrequent dilemma is the older patient who has been receiving anticonvulsants, thyroid replacement,

Exhibit 8–2 Alcohol Use Disorder Identification Test (AUDIT)

AUDIT is a brief structured interview, developed by the World Health Organization, which can be incorporated into a medical history. It contains questions about recent alcohol consumption, dependence symptoms, and alcohol-related problems.

Begin the AUDIT by saying: "Now I am going to ask you some questions about your use of alcoholic beverages *during the past year.*" Explain what is meant by alcoholic beverages (i.e., beer, wine, liquor [vodka, whiskey, brandy, etc.]).

Record the score for each question in the box on the right side of the question [ ].

1. How often do you have a drink containing alcohol?
   ☐ Never (0) [ ]
   ☐ Monthly or less (1)
   ☐ 2 to 4 times a month (2)
   ☐ 2 to 3 times a week (3)
   ☐ 4 or more times a week (4)

2. How many drinks containing alcohol do you have on a typical day when you are drinking?
   ☐ None (0) [ ]
   ☐ 1 or 2 (1)
   ☐ 3 or 4 (2)
   ☐ 5 or 6 (3)
   ☐ 7 or 9 (4)
   ☐ 10 or more (5)

3. How often do you have six or more drinks on one occasion?
   ☐ Never (0) [ ]
   ☐ Less than monthly (1)
   ☐ Monthly (2)
   ☐ Weekly (3)
   ☐ Daily or almost daily (4)

4. How often during the last year have you found that you were unable to stop drinking once you had started?
   ☐ Never (0) [ ]
   ☐ Less than monthly (1)
   ☐ Monthly (2)
   ☐ Weekly (3)
   ☐ Daily or almost daily (4)

5. How often during the last year have you failed to do what was normally expected from you because of drinking?
   ☐ Never (0) [ ]
   ☐ Less than monthly (1)
   ☐ Monthly (2)
   ☐ Weekly (3)
   ☐ Daily or almost daily (4)

continues

Exhibit 8–2 continued

6. How often during the last year have you needed a first drink in the morning to get yourself going after a heavy drinking session?
   ☐ Never   (0)   [ ]
   ☐ Less than monthly   (1)
   ☐ Monthly   (2)
   ☐ Weekly   (3)
   ☐ Daily or almost daily   (4)

7. How often during the last year have you had a feeling of guilt or remorse after drinking?
   ☐ Never   (0)   [ ]
   ☐ Less than monthly   (1)
   ☐ Monthly   (2)
   ☐ Weekly   (3)
   ☐ Daily or almost daily   (4)

8. How often during the last year have you been unable to remember what happened the night before because you had been drinking?
   ☐ Never   (0)   [ ]
   ☐ Less than monthly   (1)
   ☐ Monthly   (2)
   ☐ Weekly   (3)
   ☐ Daily or almost daily   (4)

9. Have you or someone else been injured as the result of your drinking?
   ☐ Never   (0)   [ ]
   ☐ Less than monthly   (1)
   ☐ Monthly   (2)
   ☐ Weekly   (3)
   ☐ Daily or almost daily   (4)

10. Has a relative, friend, or a doctor or other health worker been concerned about your drinking or suggested you cut down?
   ☐ Never   (0)   [ ]
   ☐ Less than monthly   (1)
   ☐ Monthly   (2)
   ☐ Weekly   (3)
   ☐ Daily or almost daily   (4)

Record the total of the specific items.   [ ]

A score of 8 or greater may indicate the need for a more in-depth assessment.

Source: Developed by the World Health Organization, AMETHYST Project, 1987.

digoxin, or psychotropic medications for decades, and the original rationale or justification for the use of these medications is not known. The review of *all* medicines the patient is taking, including over-the-counter medications, should be part of virtually every contact with the patient. Ask the patient to bring in all currently used medicines in a brown bag and ask an assistant to list the drugs and how they are taken. We can anticipate a trend in which physicians will prescribe psychotropic medications with greater caution.

Smoking

Cigarette smoking is a well-documented major cause of chronic disability and death. Even for elderly persons, cessation of smoking can be beneficial. In a study of 2,674 persons aged 65 to 74, when compared to nonsmokers and ex-smokers, older smokers had a 52% increased mortality secondary to cardiovascular disease. Persons who stopped smoking reduced their mortality rate to the rate of nonsmokers in 1 to 5 years.[97]

Falls

Among the elderly, accidents and falls are major causes of disability. Safety hazards (poor lighting, frayed wires, ashtrays near the bed, slippery floors and rugs), host factors (poor eyesight, unsteadiness, osteoporosis), and recent environmental changes (new residence, recent alterations in familiar surroundings) all conspire to make the elderly prone to falls. Elderly pedestrians may not be aware of the significant hazard traffic poses at intersections.[5] A history of falls and medical conditions associated with impairment in sensory or motor functioning will put an older adult at increased risk for falling. Avoidance of sedative drugs and gentle exercises that increase strength and function are suggested for patients at risk for falling.

Cognitive Impairment

Evaluation of cognitive status would seem prudent (1) in the face of functional decline, (2) when behavioral changes occur, (3) to monitor the effects of medication, and (4) at the time of hospital or nursing home admission. If the physician recognizes cognitive changes during the history and physical examination, or if the family reports problems related to behavior or mental functioning, assessment of cognitive status is warranted.

Given the high rate of dementia among the oldest old and the potential for adverse effects on independence, persons over the age of 75 years might be tested at least once using a standard mental status examination.[8] Currently there is no effective intervention that delays the onset or changes the trajectory of the common forms of dementia, namely Alzheimer's dementia and vascular dementia, so that any benefit of finding "early" cases must be balanced against the anxiety and depression engendered in the patient and family and the uncertainty of diagnosis.[98,99] Mild cognitive impairment accompanied by depressive symptoms may presage the onset of dementia.[100–102] Finding incipient cases of dementia will be critical if potential new pharmacologic strategies for prevention and treatment, such as use of THA,[103] aspirin,[104] or nonsteroidal anti-inflammatory drugs,[105] are to be effectively employed. Recognition of cognitive impairment provides an opportunity to prevent complications arising from coexisting medical or psychiatric conditions.[106] Early diagnosis also affords the opportunity for discussions about advance directives and driving,[8,107] although such discussions are best considered universal interventions for older persons.

Depression

Clinicians should be alert for signs and symptoms that might stem from depression.[23] Psychiatric disorders, including depression, are not detectable during an asymptomatic phase because the presence of symptoms is the only way to make a diagnosis.[108] At the same time, symptoms that do not reach the threshold for diagnosis appear to create a risk of development of depression.[109–113] Visits in primary care settings provide opportunities to prevent mental disorders or their sequelae.[106,114–116] Older adults who have chronic pain,[117,118] a newly diagnosed medical illness,[119] stroke,[120–122] functional dependence,[123] cancer,[124] insomnia,[125] or who have experienced significant life events such as bereavement[126] or institutionalization[127,128] should be carefully assessed for development of depression. Caregivers,[129,130] persons who live alone,[131,132] women, and persons with less than a high school education[133] may also be considered to be at higher than average risk for depression.

Diagnosis of depression in the elderly is complicated by coexisting medical diseases whose symptoms overlap those of depression,[134–136] the tendency of the elderly to deny dysphoria,[137] and anxiety symptoms in depressed patients that deflect attention away from the true diagnosis.[138] Physicians should not be afraid to ask about suicidal ideation among older persons with symptoms that may be attributable to depression, especially among older adults who express helplessness or hopelessness about their circumstances.[139–142]

Thyroid Disorders

Treatment of hypothyroidism may be associated with improvement in cognitive function even among older persons without dementia.[143] Because of the subtle ways that hypothyroidism can present in the elderly, either with few symptoms or with symptoms ascribed to aging,[144,145] screening elderly persons with TSH (thyroid-stimulating hormone) may be warranted every 2 or 3 years, at least in older women.[146-148]

Advance Directives

Despite progressive legal developments that permit and encourage advance directives, older adults typically do not make use of advance directives, assuming that family members will be consulted and can make appropriate decisions in the event of critical illness and loss of decision-making capacity. Even studies specifically designed to increase the use of advance directives have generally met with limited success, with some exceptions.[149,150] Although the primary care setting would be an excellent one for ongoing discussions regarding patient wishes in the event of terminal or irreversible illness, few older persons broach the subject with their doctors. The American College of Physicians recommended that any decisions made should become part of the medical record.[151]

Advance directives are expected to extend patient autonomy, relieve patient anxiety about unwanted treatment, reduce family arguments regarding treatment decisions, and increase physician confidence in treatment decisions.[152] Disadvantages of Living Wills include ambiguity, application only to terminal illness, and emphasis only on less aggressive treatment.[153] Instructional directives can be specific but therefore are limiting when implemented. Instructions are also subject to interpretation at a later date, when circumstances unforeseen by the patient might have arisen.[154] Other problems with advance directives are that no one wants to think seriously about death, advance directives may not be "portable" in a mobile society, ideas of "quality of life" change with age, and no document is able to define all situations. Therapeutic advances and the patient's prognosis can change between execution of the directive and its implementation,[155] the patient may change his or her mind,[156] or the directive may not even be followed.[157] Designation of a proxy is not without difficulty, since the proxy may not be available when decisions are made or may not have discussed preferences with the patient (see Chapter 5).

Anticipatory Guidance

Anticipatory guidance regarding physical and psychological changes that occur with aging and in the midst of bereavement or occupational changes may help the older adult who is dealing with these issues. The older adult may need information about the physical changes related to sexual functioning, menopause,[158] and

AIDS.[159] Expectations and prior coping in times of stress will determine how well the older person deals with stresses occurring at a time of life when social and economic resources may be more strained. Surveillance should be increased, and contacts with the primary care professional provide excellent opportunities for discussion of reactions to stressful events, especially depression, functional decline, or relocation.

SCREENING IN NURSING HOMES

Richardson provided a review of the application of recommendations for health maintenance and disability prevention to nursing home patients.[160] Certain of the conditions described above are especially prevalent among older adults who live in nursing homes, namely, hearing and visual impairment, tendency to fall, dementia, depression, hypothyroidism, and polypharmacy. In addition, tuberculin skin testing is appropriate for all new patients admitted to a nursing home.[23] Planning for acute illness with the patient and family through the use of advance directives should be addressed.

Older adults in nursing homes should have excellent access to medical and social evaluations; few newly detected abnormalities may be noted on physical examination or laboratory investigation performed purely for screening purposes. Here we focus on nursing home patients for whom tests are performed solely as a means of screening, not as a way to monitor some pre-existing condition. For example, determination of serum electrolyte values in a patient on a diuretic and digoxin would not be considered a screening test and might need to be performed at frequent intervals dictated by clinical judgment.

Domoto and associates found that only 0.7% of abnormal annual screening laboratory tests led to further evaluation and that only 0.1% had a significant effect on the patient's management.[161] In a mixed group of institutionalized and ambulatory patients, a review of 100 patient records by Wolf-Klein and associates revealed that of 756 new laboratory abnormalities in 15,000 tests, only 12 affected the treatment plan.[162] Levinstein and associates found only 0.8% of the tests done for screening purposes resulted in the discovery of an unknown abnormality that was believed to benefit the patient.[163] Any benefit derived from annual laboratory testing could be captured by checking serum electrolyte values, blood urea nitrogen, creatinine, and glucose levels and performing a complete blood cell count, thyroxine test, and urinalysis. Routine chest roentgenograms and electrocardiograms were not helpful.[163]

Irvine and associates demonstrated a fair number of new problems and old problems requiring a change in regimen.[164] Annual history and physical examinations were performed in a nursing home by internists who were not responsible for the patients' care but were employed specifically for the study. In addition to the history and physical examination, a bedside pelvic and rectal examination was done, and a stool specimen was tested for occult blood. A new problem was found in 21% of patients. The most common new problems identified in 732 examinations were hypothyroidism (1.9%), heme-positive stool (1.4%), poor dentition (1.2%), prostatic nodules (1%), breast mass (1%), and rashes or benign skin conditions (1.2%). In 39% of cases, an old problem required re-evaluation by laboratory studies or alteration in the treatment regimen. Among the more common problems were peripheral edema (3.7%), anemia (3.3%), thyroid function abnormality (2.6%), dementia (2.6%), diabetes mellitus (2.3%), depression (1.9%), hearing loss (1.8%), hypertension (1.6%), and chronic lung disease (1.4%). The investigators then asked the nine primary care physicians to estimate the value of 149 findings in 96 randomly selected charts. Five findings (3.4%) were believed to be of major importance, and 40 findings (26.8%) were of "intermediate importance." Although the authors found that annual physical examinations in the nursing home yielded a finding in 51% of all examinations, they concluded that the value of the annual physical examination in nursing homes was limited because the findings were generally not clinically significant.[164] Perhaps outcome measures such as functional status or mortality would be more objective measures of the value of such screening.

The negative results of these studies apply primarily to laboratory studies; pessimism may not be warranted in the case of geriatric-oriented preventive measures. Even among nursing home patients, substantial heterogeneity can be expected, and the value of screening procedures must be evaluated on an individual basis that considers functional status, mental status, and prognosis.[160] The importance of avoiding polypharmacy by careful review of medications and judicious use of measurement of serum drug levels cannot be overemphasized. As a practical matter, good medical care of nursing home residents would prescribe periodic review of the medical problem list and medications at 6- to 12-month intervals.

CONCLUSION

The most reasonable approach to screening for unrecognized problems in the elderly is to incorporate some screening activities within the context of routine, episodic patient encounters. The elderly will have well-established habits or disease processes, and the task of screening becomes one of detecting conditions that could potentially disrupt or interfere with function. Persons in good health at age 65 can expect to remain functionally independent for 10 years or more,[165] so health maintenance and promotion activities remain important in late life.

No scheme for health maintenance and promotion will be useful to the patient unless it is carried out by the physician. Physicians frequently recommend screening procedures in general terms but may fail to follow through when they see the patient. The health maintenance and disability prevention protocol should be adapted to the particular practice and negotiated with the patient. Setting goals for preventive care, keeping a health maintenance record of health promotion protocols in the patient's chart, asking the nurse to clip a reminder to the chart when a test is due, and having a nurse or physician assistant actually perform screening procedures will foster compliance with health maintenance schedules.[166-170] Computers may facilitate reminders and scheduling in the future.[171] Preventive guidelines and protocols tailored to local conditions will become routinely implemented for the young-old, the middle-old, and the old-old.

REFERENCES

1. Sampson A, Sampson S, eds. *The Oxford Book of Ages.* New York, NY: Oxford University Press, 1985.

2. Kennie DC. Good health care for the elderly. *JAMA.* 1983;249:770–773.

3. Kennie DC. Health maintenance of the elderly. *J Am Geriatr Soc.* 1984;32:316–323.

4. Fried LP, Bush TL. Morbidity as a focus of preventive health care in the elderly. *Epidemiol Rev.* 1988;10:48–64.

5. Stults BM. Preventive health care for the elderly. *West J Med.* 1984;141:832–845.

6. Institute of Medicine. *The Second Fifty Years: Promoting Health and Preventing Disability.* Washington, DC: National Academy Press, 1992.

7. Rubenstein LZ, Josephson KR, Nichol-Seamons M, et al. Comprehensive health screening of well elderly adults: an analysis of a community program. *J Gerontol.* 1986;41:342–352.

8. Zazove P, Mehr DR, Ruffin MT, Klinkman MS, Peggs JF, Davies TC. A criterion-based review of preventive health care in the elderly, II: a geriatric health maintenance program. *J Fam Pract.* 1992;34:320–347.

9. Kennie DC. *Preventive Care for Elderly People.* New York, NY: Cambridge University Press, 1993.

10. US Public Health Service. Implementing preventive care. *Am Fam Physician.* 1994; 50:103–108.

11. Spitzer WO, Mann KV. The public's health is too important to be left to public health workers: a commentary on *Guide to Clinical Preventive Services. Ann Intern Med.* 1989;111:939–942.

12. Sloane P. A prevention oriented medical record. *J Fam Pract.* 1979;9:89–96.

13. Gordon R. An operational classification of disease prevention. *Public Health Rep.* 1983; 98:107–109.

14. Becker MH. *The Health Belief Model and Personal Health Behavior.* Thorofare, NJ: Charles B. Slack, Inc, 1974.

15. Klinkman MS, Zazove P, Mehr DR, Ruffin MT. A criterion-based review of preventive health care in the elderly, I: theoretical framework and development of criteria. *J Fam Pract.* 1992; 34:205–224.

16. Canadian Task Force on the Periodic Health Examination. The periodic health examination. *Can Med Assoc J.* 1979;121:1193–1254.

17. Canadian Task Force on the Periodic Health Examination. The periodic health examination: 1984 update. *Can Med Assoc J.* 1984;130:4–11.

18. Goldbloom R, Battista RN, Haggerty J. The periodic health examination, I: introduction. *Can Med Assoc J.* 1989;141:205–207.

19. Frame PS. A critical review of adult health maintenance, I: prevention of atherosclerotic disease. *J Fam Pract.* 1986;22:341–346.

20. Frame PS. A critical review of adult health maintenance, II: prevention of infectious diseases. *J Fam Pract.* 1986;22:417–422.

21. Frame PS. A critical review of adult health maintenance, III: prevention of cancer. *J Fam Pract.* 1986;22:511–520.

22. Frame PS. A critical review of adult health maintenance, IV: prevention of metabolic, behavioral, and miscellaneous conditions. *J Fam Pract.* 1986;23:29–39.

23. US Preventive Services Task Force. *Guide to Clinical Preventive Services: An Assessment of the Effectiveness of 169 Interventions.* Baltimore, Md: Williams & Wilkins, 1989.

24. Sox HC. Preventive health services in adults. *N Engl J Med.* 1994;330:1589–1595.

25. Woolf SH, Kamerow DB, Lawrence RS, Medalie JH, Estes EH. The periodic health examination of older adults: the recommendations of the U.S. Preventive Services Task Force, I: counseling, immunizations, and chemoprophylaxis. *J Am Geriat Soc.* 1990;38:817–823.

26. Woolf SH, Kamerow DB, Lawrence RS, Medalie JH, Estes EH. The periodic health examination of older adults: the recommendations of the U.S. Preventive Services Task Force, II: screening tests. *J Am Geriatr Soc.* 1990;38:933–942.

26a. Murphy JB, Coletta E. Health maintenance and prevention for older persons. In: Reichel W, ed. *Clinical Aspects of Aging.* 4th ed. Baltimore, Md: Williams & Wilkins, 1995:31–40.

27. Mandelblatt J, Gopaul I, Wistreich M. Gynecological care of elderly women: another look at Papanicolaou smear testing. *JAMA.* 1986;256:367–371.

28. Celentano DD, Shapiro S, Weisman CS. Cancer preventive screening behavior among elderly women. *Prev Med.* 1982;11:454–463.

29. Weintraub NT, Violi E, Freedman ML. Cervical cancer screening in women aged 65 and over. *J Am Geriatr Soc.* 1987;35:870–875.

30. American Cancer Society. Guidelines for the cancer-related checkup: recommendations and rationale. *Cancer.* 1980;30:194–240.

31. Kerlikowske K, Grady D, Barclay J, Sickles EA, Eaton A, Ernster V. Positive predictive value of screening mammography by age and family history of breast cancer. *JAMA.* 1993;270:2444–2450.

32. American Geriatrics Society Clinical Practice Committee. Screening for breast cancer in elderly women. *J Am Geriatr Soc.* 1989;37:883–884.

33. Canadian Task Force on the Periodic Health Examination. The periodic health examination, II: 1987 update. *Can Med Assoc J.* 1987;139:128–135.

34. Oboler SK, LaForce FM. The periodic physical examination in asymptomatic adults. *Ann Intern Med.* 1989;110:214–226.

35. Winawer SJ, Andrews M, Flehinger B, et al. Progress report on controlled trial of fecal occult blood testing for the detection of colorectal neoplasia. *Cancer.* 1980;45:2959–2964.

36. Mangla JC, Pereira M, Murphy J. Diagnosis of occult gastrointestinal lesions by stool guaiac testing in a geriatric hospital. *J Am Geriatr Soc.* 1981;29:473–475.

37. Ahlquist DA, Wieand HS, Moertel CG, et al. Accuracy of fecal occult blood screening for colorectal neoplasia: a prospective study using hemoccult and hemoquant tests. *JAMA.* 1993;269:1262–1267.

38. Canadian Task Force on the Periodic Health Examination. The periodic health examination, II: 1989 update. *Can Med Assoc J.* 1989;141:209–216.

39. Dales LG, Friedman GD, Collen MF. Evaluating periodic multiphasic health checkups: a controlled trial. *J Chronic Dis.* 1979;32:385–404.

40. Selby JV, Friedman GD, Quesenberry CP, et al. A case-control study of screening sigmoidoscopy and mortality from colorectal cancer. *N Engl J Med.* 1992;326:653–657.

41. Greene FL. Distribution of colorectal neoplasms. *Am Surg.* 1983;49:62–65.

42. Ransohoff DF, Lang CA. Sigmoidoscopic screening in the 1990s. *JAMA.* 1993; 269: 1278–1281.

43. Nolan KA, Blass JP. Preventing cognitive decline. *Clin Geriatr Med.* 1992;8:19–34.

44. Woo J, Lau E, Kay R. Elderly subjects aged 70 years and above have different risk factors for ischemic and hemorrhagic strokes compared to younger subjects. *J Am Geriatr Soc.* 1992;40:124–129.

45. Simonsick EM, Lafferty ME, Phillips CL, et al. Risk due to inactivity in physically capable older adults. *Am J Public Health.* 1993;83:1443–1450.

46. Morey MC, Cowper PA, Feussner JR, et al. Evaluation of a supervised exercise program in a geriatric population. *J Am Geriatr Soc.* 1989;37:348–354.

47. Stones MJ, Dawe D. Acute exercise facilitates semantically cued memory in nursing home residents. *J Am Geriatr Soc.* 1993;41:531–534.

48. Joint National Committee. The 1988 Report of the Joint National Committee on Detection, Evaluation, and Treatment of High Blood Pressure. *Arch Intern Med.* 1988;148:1023–1038.

49. Working Group on Management of Patients with Hypertension and High Blood Cholesterol. National Education Programs Working Group Report on the Management of Patients with Hypertension and High Blood Cholesterol. *Ann Intern Med.* 1991;114:224–237.

50. SHEP Cooperative Research Group. Prevention of stroke by antihypertensive drug treatment for older persons with isolated systolic hypertension. *JAMA.* 1991;265:3255–3264.

51. Applegate WB, Rutan GH. Advances in the management of hypertension in older persons. *J Am Geriatr Soc.* 1992;40:1164–1174.

52. Alderman MH. Blood pressure management: individualized treatment based on absolute risk and the potential for benefit. *Ann Intern Med.* 1993;119:329–335.

53. North American Symptomatic Carotid Endarterectomy Trial Collaborators. Beneficial effect of carotid endarterectomy in symptomatic patients with high-grade stenosis. *N Engl J Med.* 1991; 325:445–453.

54. Sauve JS, Laupacis A, Ostbye T, Feagan B, Sackett DL. Does this patient have a clinically important carotid bruit? *JAMA.* 1993;270:2843–2845.

55. National Cholesterol Education Program. *Second Report of the Expert Panel on Detection, Evaluation, and Treatment of High Blood Cholesterol in Adults.* Washington, DC: National Institutes of Health, National Heart, Lung, and Blood Institute, 1993.

56. Lipid Research Clinics Program. The Lipid Research Clinics Primary Prevention Trial results, II: the relationship of reduction in incidence of coronary heart disease to cholesterol lowering. *JAMA.* 1984;251:365–374.

57. Lipid Research Clinics Program. The Lipid Research Clinics Primary Prevention Trial results, I: reduction in incidence of coronary heart disease. *JAMA.* 1984;251:351–364.

58. Anderson KM, Castelli WF, Levy D. Cholesterol and mortality: 30 years of follow-up from the Framingham study. *JAMA.* 1987;257:2176–2180.

58a. Krumholz HM, Seeman TE, Merrill SS, et al. Lack of association between cholesterol and coronary heart disease mortality and morbidity and all-cause mortality in persons older than 70 years. *JAMA.* 1994;272:1335–1340.

59. Nichol KL, Margolis KL, Wuorenma J, van Sternberg T. The efficacy and cost effectiveness of vaccination against influenza among elderly persons living in the community. *N Engl J Med.* 1994;331:778–784.

60. Butler JC, Breiman RF, Campbell JF, Lipman HB, Broome CV, Facklam RR. Pneumococcal polysaccharide vaccine efficacy: an evaluation of current recommendations. *JAMA.* 1993;270:1826–1831.

61. Canadian Task Force on the Periodic Health Examination. Periodic health examination, 1991 update, II: administration of pneumococcal vaccine. *Can Med Assoc J.* 1991;144:665–671.

62. Richardson JP, Knight AL. The prevention of tetanus in the elderly. *Arch Intern Med.* 1991;151:1712–1717.

63. Edwards KM, Decker MD, Graham BS, Mezzatesta J, Scott J, Hackell J. Adult immunization with acellular pertussis vaccine. *JAMA.* 1993;269:53–56.

64. Buchner DM, Wagner EH. Preventing frail health. *Clin Geriatr Med.* 1992;8:1–17.

65. Creditor MC. Hazards of hospitalization of the elderly. *Ann Intern Med.* 1993;118:219–223.

66. Bess FH, Lichtenstein MJ, Logan SA, et al. Hearing impairment as a determinant of function in the elderly. *J Am Geriatr Soc.* 1989;37:123–128.

67. Leske MC. The epidemiology of open angle glaucoma: a review. *Am J Epidemiol.* 1983;118:166–191.

68. Brody JA. Aging and alcohol abuse. *J Am Geriatr Soc.* 1982;30:123–126.

69. Curtis JR, Geller G, Stokes EJ, Levine DM, Moore RD. Characteristics, diagnosis, and treatment of alcoholism in elderly patients. *J Am Geriatr Soc.* 1989;37:310–316.

70. Widner S, Zeichner A. Alcohol abuse in the elderly: review of epidemiology, research, and treatment. *Clin Gerontol.* 1991;11:3–18.

71. Thibault JM, Maly RC. Recognition and treatment of substance abuse in the elderly. *Prim Care.* 1993;20:155–165.

72. Graham K. Identifying and measuring alcohol abuse among the elderly: serious problems with existing instrumentation. *J Stud Alcohol.* 1986;47:322–326.

73. Wattis JP. Alcohol problems in the elderly. *J Am Geriatr Soc.* 1981;29:131–134.

74. Cook BL, Winokur G, Garvey MJ, Beach V. Depression and previous alcoholism in the elderly. *Br J Psychiatry.* 1991;158:72–75.

75. Osgood NJ. The alcohol-suicide connection in late life. *Postgrad Med.* 1987;81:379–384.

76. Mayfield DG, McLeod G, Hall P. The CAGE questionnaire: validation of a new alcoholism screening instrument. *Am J Psychiatry.* 1974;131:1121–1123.

77. Ewing JA. Detecting alcoholism: the CAGE questionnaire. *JAMA.* 1984;252:1905–1907.

78. US Department of Health and Human Services. Screening and brief intervention. In: *Eighth Special Report to the U.S. Congress on Alcohol and Health from the Secretary of Health and Human Services, September 1993*. Washington, DC: US Department of Health and Human Services, Public Health Service, National Institutes of Health, National Institute on Alcohol Abuse and Alcoholism, 1993:297–317.

79. Babor TF, Grant M. From clinical research to secondary prevention: international collaboration in the development of the Alcohol Use Disorders Identification Test (AUDIT). *Alcohol Health Res World.* 1989;13:371–374.

80. Fleming MF, Barry KL. The alcohol use disorders identification test (AUDIT) in a college sample. *Int J Addict.* 1991;26:1173–1185.

81. Blow FC, Brower KJ, Schulenberg JE, Demo-Dananberg LM, Young JS, Beresford TP. The Michigan Alcoholism Screening Test-Geriatric Version (MAST-G): a new elderly-specific screening instrument. *Alcohol Clin Exper Res.* 1992;16:372.

82. Beresford TP. Alcoholism in the elderly. *Int Rev Psychiatry.* 1993;5:477–483.

83. Gottheil E, Druley KA, Skoloda TE, eds. *The Combined Problems of Alcoholism, Drug Addiction, and Aging.* Springfield, Ill: Charles C Thomas, 1985.

84. Campbell AJ, McCosh L, Reinken J. Drugs taken by a population based sample of subjects 65 years and over in New Zealand. *NZ Med J.* 1983;96:378–380.

85. Desai TH, Rajput AH, Desai HB. Use and misuse of drugs in the elderly. *Prog Neuropsychopharmacol Biol Psychiatry.* 1990;14:779–784.

86. Finch J. Prescription drug abuse. *Prim Care.* 1993;20:231–239.

87. Law R, Chalmers C. Medications and elderly people: a general practice survey. *Br Med J.* 1976;1:565–568.

88. Thompson TL, Moran MG, Nies AS. Psychotropic drug use in the elderly. Part I. *N Engl J Med.* 1983;308:134–138.

89. Thompson TL, Moran MG, Nies AS. Psychotropic drug use in the elderly. Part II. *N Engl J Med.* 1983;308:194–199.

90. Williams P. Factors influencing the duration of treatment with psychotropic drugs in general practice: a survival analysis approach. *Psychol Med.* 1983;13:623–633.

91. Rosholm JU, Hansen LJ, Hallas J, Gram LF. Neuroleptic drug utilization in out-patients: a prescription database study. *Br J Clin Pharmacol.* 1993;36:579–583.

92. Takala J, Ryynanen OP, Lehtovirta E, Turakka H. The relationship between mental health and drug use. *Acta Psychiatr Scand.* 1993;88:256–258.

93. Larson EB, Kukull WA, Buchner D, Reifler BV. Adverse drug reactions associated with global cognitive impairment in elderly persons. *Ann Intern Med.* 1987;107:169–173.

94. O'Connor RD. Benzodiazepine dependence: a treatment perspective and an advocacy for control. In: Cooper JR, Czechowicz DJ, Molinari SP, Petersen RC, eds. *Impact of Prescription Drug Diversion Control Systems on Medical Practice and Patient Care.* NIDA research monograph 131. Rockville, Md: Department of Health and Human Services, 1993:266–269. DHHS Publication No. 93-3507 (NIH).

95. Ray WA, Griffin MR, Schaffner W, Baugh DK, Melton LJ. Psychotropic drug use and the risk of hip fracture. *N Engl J Med.* 1987;316:363–369.

96. Montamat SC, Cusack B. Overcoming problems with polypharmacy and drug misuse in the elderly. *Clin Geriatr Med.* 1992;8:143–158.

97. Jajich CL, Ostfeld AM, Freeman DH. Smoking and coronary heart disease mortality in the elderly. *JAMA.* 1984;252:2831–2834.

98. Cooper B, Bickel H. Population screening and the early detection of dementing disorders in old age: a review. *Psychol Med.* 1984;14:81–95.

99. Jones TV, Williams ME. Are mental status questionnaires of clinical value in everyday office practice? An opposing view. *J Fam Pract.* 1990;30:197–200.

100. Reding M, Haycox J, Blass J. Depression in patients referred to a dementia clinic: a three-year prospective study. *Arch Neurol.* 1985;42:894–896.

101. Rabins PV, Merchant A, Nestadt G. Criteria for diagnosing reversible dementia caused by depression: validation by 2-year follow-up. *Br J Psychiatry.* 1984;144:488–492.

102. Emery VO, Oxman TE. Update on the dementia spectrum of depression. *Am J Psychiatry.* 1992;149:305–317.

103. Farlow M, Gracon SI, Hershey LA, Lewis KW, Sadowsky CH, Dolan-Ureno J. A controlled trial of Tacrine in Alzheimer's disease. *JAMA.* 1992;268:2523–2529.

104. Meyer JS, Rogers RL, McClintic K, Mortel KF, Lotfi J. Randomized clinical trial of daily aspirin therapy in multi-infarct dementia: a pilot study. *J Am Geriatr Soc.* 1989;37:549–555.

105. Breitner JCS, Gau BA, Welsh KA, et al. Inverse association of anti-inflammatory treatments and Alzheimer's disease: initial results of a co-twin control study. *Neurology.* 1994;44:227–232.

106. Rabins PV. Prevention of mental disorders in the elderly: current perspectives and future prospects. *J Am Geriatr Soc.* 1992;40:727–733.

107. Warshaw G. Are mental status questionnaires of clinical value in everyday office practice? An affirmative view. *J Fam Pract.* 1990;30:194–197.

108. Ford DE. Principles of screening applied to psychiatric disorders. *Gen Hosp Psychiatry.* 1988;10:177–188.

109. Broadhead WE, Blazer DG, George LK, Tse CK. Depression, disability days, and days lost from work in a prospective epidemiologic survey. *JAMA.* 1990;264:2524–2528.

110. Wells KB, Stewart A, Hays RD, et al. The functioning and well-being of depressed patients: results from the Medical Outcomes Study. *JAMA.* 1989;262:914–919.

111. Johnson J, Weissman MM, Klerman GL. Service utilization and social morbidity associated with depressive symptoms in the community. *JAMA.* 1992;267:1478–1483.

112. Fava GA, Kellner R. Prodromal symptoms in affective disorders. *Am J Psychiatry.* 1991;148:823–830.

113. Horwath E, Johnson J, Klerman GL, Weissman MM. Depressive symptoms as relative and attributable risk factors for first-onset major depression. *Arch Gen Psychiatry.* 1992;49:817–823.

114. Rose G. Mental disorder and the strategies of prevention. *Psychol Med.* 1993;23:553–555.

115. Sartorius N, Henderson AS. The neglect of prevention in psychiatry. *Aust NZ J Psychiatry.* 1992;5:548–553.

116. Institute of Medicine. *Reducing Risks for Mental Disorders: Frontiers for Preventive Intervention Research.* Washington, DC: National Academy Press, 1994.

117. Blumer D, Heilbronn M. Chronic pain as a variant of depressive disease: the pain-prone disorder. *J Nerv Ment Dis.* 1982;170:381–414.

118. Parmelee PA, Katz IR, Lawton MP. The relation of pain to depression among the elderly. *J Gerontol.* 1991;46:15–21.

119. Cadoret RJ, Widmer RB. The development of depressive symptoms in elderly following the onset of severe physical illness. *J Fam Pract.* 1988;27:71–76.

120. Morris PLP, Robinson RG, Raphael B. Prevalence and course of post-stroke depression in hospitalized patients. *Int J Psychiatry Med.* 1990;20:327–342.

121. Schubert DSP, Taylor C, Lee S, Mentari A, Tamaklo W. Physical consequences of depression in the stroke patient. *Gen Hosp Psychiatry.* 1992;14:69–76.

122. Stern RA, Bachman DL. Depressive symptoms following stroke. *Am J Psychiatry.* 1991;148:351–356.

123. Turner RJ, Beiser M. Major depression and depressive symptomatology among the physically disabled: assessing the role of chronic stress. *J Nerv Ment Dis.* 1990;178:343–350.

124. Endicott J. Measurement of depression in patients with cancer. *Cancer.* 1984;53:2243–2249.

125. Ford DE, Kamerow DB. Epidemiologic study of sleep disturbances and psychiatric disorders: an opportunity for prevention? *JAMA.* 1989;262:1479–1484.

126. Harlow SD, Goldberg EL, Comstock GW. A longitudinal study of risk factors for depressive symptomatology in elderly widowed and married women. *Am J Epidemiol.* 1991;134:526–538.

127. Ames D. Depressive disorders among elderly people in long-term institutional care. *Aust NZ J Psychiatry.* 1993;27:379–391.

128. Rovner BW, German PS, Brant LJ, Clark R, Burton L, Folstein MF. Depression and mortality in nursing homes. *JAMA.* 1991;266:215–216.

129. Gallo JJ, Franch MS, Reichel W. Dementing illness: the patient, caregiver, and community. *Am Fam Physician.* 1991;43:1669–1675.

130. Gallo JJ. The effect of social support on depression in caregivers of the elderly. *J Fam Pract.* 1990;30:430–436.

131. Murrell SA, Himmelfarb S, Wright K. Prevalence of depression and its correlates in older adults. *Am J Epidemiol.* 1983;117:173–185.

132. Kaplan GA, Roberts RE, Camacho TC, Coyne JC. Psychosocial predictors of depression: prospective evidence from the Human Population Laboratory Studies. *Am J Epidemiol.* 1987;125:206–220.

133. Gallo JJ, Royall DR, Anthony JC. Risk factors for the onset of major depression in middle age and late life. *Soc Psychiatry Psychiatr Epidemiol.* 1993;28:101–108.

134. Cohen-Cole SA, Stoudemire A. Major depression and physical illness: special considerations in diagnosis and biologic treatment. *Psychiatr Clin North Am.* 1987;10:1–17.

135. Finch EJL, Ramsay R, Katona CLE. Depression and physical illness in the elderly. *Clin Geriatr Med.* 1992;8:275–287.

136. Lopez-Ibor JJ. Masked depressions. *Br J Psychiatry.* 1972;120:245–258.

137. Gallo JJ, Anthony JC, Muthen BO. Age differences in the symptoms of depression: a latent trait analysis. *J Gerontol Psychol Sci.* 1994;49:251–264.

138. Maser JD, Cloninger CR, eds. *Comorbidity of Mood and Anxiety Disorders.* Washington, DC: American Psychiatric Press, 1990.

139. Canadian Task Force on the Periodic Health Examination. Periodic health examination, 1990 update, II: early detection of depression and prevention of suicide. *Can Med Assoc J.* 1990;142:1233–1240.

140. McNamee JE, Offord DR. Prevention of suicide. *Can Med Assoc J.* 1990;142:1223–1230.

141. Abramson LY, Metalsky GI, Alloy LB. Hopelessness depression: a theory based subtype of depression. *Psychol Rev.* 1989;96:358–372.

142. Beck AT, Steer RA, Beck JS, Newman CF. Hopelessness, depression, suicidal ideation, and clinical diagnosis of depression. *Suicide Life Threat Behav.* 1993;23:139–145.

143. Osterweil D, Syndulko K, Cohen SN, et al. Cognitive function in non-demented older adults with hypothyroidism. *J Am Geriatr Soc.* 1992;40:325–335.

144. Bemben DA, Hamm RM, Morgan L, Winn P, Davis A, Barton E. Thyroid disease in the elderly, II: predictability of subclinical hypothyroidism. *J Fam Pract.* 1994;38:583–588.

145. Bemben DA, Winn P, Hamm RM, Morgan L, Davis A, Barton E. Thyroid disease in the elderly, I: prevalence of undiagnosed hypothyroidism. *J Fam Pract.* 1994;38:577–582.

146. Livingston EH, Hershman JM, Sawin CT, et al. Prevalence of thyroid disease and abnormal thyroid tests in older hospitalized and ambulatory persons. *J Am Geriatr Soc.* 1987;35:109–114.

147. Cooper DS. Subclinical hypothyroidism. *JAMA.* 1987;258:246–247.

148. Helfand M, Crapo LM. Screening for thyroid disease. *Ann Intern Med.* 1990;112:840–849.

149. Spears R, Drinka PJ, Voeks SK. Obtaining a durable power of attorney for health care from nursing home residents. *J Fam Pract.* 1993;36:409–413.

150. Rubin SM, Strull WM, Fialkow MF, Weiss SJ, Lo B. Increasing completion of the durable power of attorney for health care: a randomized, controlled trial. *JAMA.* 1994;271:209–212.

151. American College of Physicians. American College of Physicians Ethics Manual, II: the physician and society; research; life-sustaining treatment; other issues. *Ann Intern Med.* 1989;111:327–335.

152. Davidson KW, Hackler C, Caradine DR, et al. Physicians' attitudes on advance directives. *JAMA.* 1989;262:2415–2419.

153. Steinbrook A. Decision making for incompetent patients by designated proxy. *N Engl J Med.* 1984;310:1598–1601.

154. Schneiderman LJ, Arras JD. Counseling patients to counsel physicians on future care in the event of patient incompetence. *Ann Intern Med.* 1985;102:693–698.

155. Buchanan A, Brock DW. Deciding for others. *Milbank Q.* 1986;64(suppl 2):17–94.

156. Danis M, Garrett J, Harris R, Patrick DL. Stability of choices about life-sustaining treatments. *Ann Intern Med.* 1994;120:567–573.

157. Danis M, Southerland LI, Garrett JM, et al. A prospective study of advance directives for life-sustaining care. *N Engl J Med.* 1991;324:882–888.

158. Greendale GA, Judd HL. The menopause: health implications and clinical management. *J Am Geriatr Soc.* 1993;41:426–436.

159. Riley MW, Ory MG, Zablotsky D, eds. *AIDS in an Aging Society: What We Need To Know.* New York, NY: Springer Publishing Co, 1989.

160. Richardson JP. Health promotion for the nursing home patient. *J Am Board Fam Pract.* 1992;5:127–136.

161. Domoto K, Ben R, Wei JY, et al. Yield of routine annual laboratory screening in the institutionalized elderly. *Am J Public Health.* 1985;75:243–245.

162. Wolf-Klein GP, Holt T, Silverstone FA, et al. Efficacy of routine annual studies in the care of elderly patients. *J Am Geriatr Soc.* 1985;33:325–329.

163. Levinstein MR, Ouslander JG, Rubenstein LZ, et al. Yield of routine annual laboratory tests in a skilled nursing home population. *JAMA.* 1987;258:1909–1915.

164. Irvine PW, Carlson K, Adcock M, et al. The value of annual medical examinations in the nursing home. *J Am Geriatr Soc.* 1984;32:540–545.

165. Katz S, Branch LG, Branson MH, et al. Active life expectancy. *N Engl J Med.* 1983;309:1218–1224.

166. Davidson RA, Fletcher SW, Retchin S, et al. A nurse-initiated reminder system for the periodic health examination: implementation and evaluation. *Arch Intern Med.* 1984;144:2167–2170.

167. Frame PS. Periodic health screening in a rural private practice. *J Fam Pract.* 1979;9:57–64.

168. Madlon-Kay DJ. Improving the periodic health examination: use of a screening flow chart for patients and physicians. *J Fam Pract.* 1987;25:470–473.

169. Mandel IG, Franks P, Dickinson JC. Screening guidelines in a family medicine program: a five-year experience. *J Fam Pract.* 1982;14:901–907.

170. Dietrich AJ, Woodruff CB, Carney PA. Changing office routines to enhance preventive care: the preventive GAPS approach. *Arch Fam Med.* 1994;3:176–183.

171. Hogg W. The role of computers in preventive medicine in a rural family practice. *Can Med Assoc J.* 1990;143:33–37.

9

Geriatric Assessment Programs: The Deaconess ElderCare Model

John R. Delfs, Laura Stanley, and Joan Yesner

This chapter reviews selected applications of geriatric assessment, then describes both the inpatient and outpatient geriatric assessment programs of Deaconess ElderCare developed at the New England Deaconess Hospital in Boston, Massachusetts. The Deaconess ElderCare Service, an inpatient early intervention and care coordination service, and the Deaconess ElderCare Geriatric Assessment Center, an outpatient consultation program, demonstrate how inpatient and outpatient geriatric assessment programs, based on the principles of interdisciplinary team process, can be configured and operationalized.

RATIONALE FOR COMPREHENSIVE, TEAM-BASED GERIATRIC ASSESSMENT

The rationale for use of geriatric assessment in a complex situation is that it provides knowledge of the patient's medical condition, functional status, social

The authors thank others who have contributed to developing Deaconess ElderCare, including ElderCare team members Alice Leslie; Ellen Danto-Nocton, MD; Naomi E. Zack, MS, RN,C; Brian Merrick, LICSW; Wilfred S. McCalla, Jr; Thomas T. Perls, MD, MPH; and Edwin Sharrow; as well as other Deaconess Hospital colleagues important in the early development process, including Mary Dunphy, LICSW, MBA; Suzanne Holloran, EdD, RN; Judith Miller, MEd, RN; and Janet O'Day, RN, MSN, MPH.

situation, and personal values and thereby improves decision making and care planning. Actions evolving out of an assessment may include further diagnostic evaluation; treatment for disease states; prevention, reversal, or stabilization of functional loss; and addressing psychosocial issues for the older adult and his or her family. Geriatric assessment should facilitate the overall coordination of care and promote access to health care services that are medically necessary, cost effective, and geographically feasible.

The rationale for the use of a team is that team efforts usually result in more comprehensive data gathering and improved intervention strategies. In the Deaconess ElderCare programs, we have found that each member of the team brings perspectives, process techniques, and sets of professional tools that are in important ways unique. The physician, for instance, typically lends a medical perspective and identifies the interrelationship between disease states, potential and existing, and functional disability and social concerns. The nurse practitioner performs a comprehensive assessment of functional status (identifying baseline as well as current changes), which provides a global picture of the impact of disease and the potential for functional gains. The social worker focuses on emotional and relationship issues and often is a critical force in promoting the team process in role negotiation and in synthesis of perspectives. In addition, the social worker often plays a crucial role in helping the team address emotional and social role issues that begin to be played out in the midst of assessing and managing complex and challenging patient and family crises.

These varying perspectives and approaches, when merged into an interdisciplinary process, tend to result in a comprehensive assessment that is more accurate than an assessment of similar intensity accomplished by one or even two professionals in a similar setting. The strengths of a team are most apparent when a treatment or management dilemma is confronted, as the problem-solving capabilities of a team of professionals working together surpass the sum of the individual capabilities. Finally, implementation of any plan of action is enhanced by the availability of individual team members to communicate successfully with a spectrum of other professionals. This improves the likelihood that essential information will be transferred and that other professional and family caregivers will follow through with recommended courses of action.

APPLICATIONS OF GERIATRIC ASSESSMENT

When older patients require hospitalization, they are at particular risk of iatrogenesis, loss of function, and prolonged hospital stays. Persons over the age of 75 comprise only about 5% of the population but account for approximately one-quarter of all hospital days.[1] This has translated into a disproportionate utilization of health care resources in the context of a pressing need for cost containment.

Despite nearly two decades of studying various options for improving the care and containing the costs of care for complex hospitalized older adults, health care experts are still unclear as to the best approach. There is agreement in the literature, however, that comprehensive geriatric assessment should have an important place in the care of complex older patients.[2,3] In addition, recent meta-analysis of controlled trials of comprehensive geriatric assessment suggests that programs linking this methodology with effective ongoing patient management extend survival and improve function in older persons.[4,5]

Geriatric Evaluation and Treatment Units

The utilization of dedicated units for inpatient geriatric assessment to manage the care of complex hospitalized older adults has been shown to result in improved function, decreased risk of nursing home placement, and lower mortality.[6,7] Nevertheless, the establishment and maintenance of geriatric evaluation units may not be practical for many hospitals, which place patients according to medical or surgical needs, thereby precluding a dedicated unit approach.

Geriatric Outpatient Assessment Programs

Geriatric outpatient assessment can be efficacious in the proper setting. One randomized, controlled trial of outpatient assessment and management over a one-year period showed a significant reduction in the amount of time spent in hospitals and nursing homes.[8] On the other hand, a randomized trial of consultative geriatric assessment for ambulatory older adults in a health maintenance organization failed to show significant benefit.[9] The difference between these two studies appears to be that the successful program directly managed the primary care of older adults whereas the second study involved an outpatient specialty clinic approach with less follow-up and less control in care management.

The National Institutes of Health Consensus Development Conference supported the use of multidisciplinary geriatric assessment but noted that inpatient specialty geriatric evaluation units were the model most clearly demonstrating positive outcomes.[3] The conference identified areas for future research: (1) use of randomized trials of geriatric assessment on quality of life and cost-effectiveness, (2) development of methodologies for targeting appropriate patients, and (3) development of methodologies for addressing coordinated implementation of the care plan.

Consultative Inpatient Geriatric Assessment

The approach to geriatric assessment and management most generalizable to hospital settings throughout the nation is consultative and multidisciplinary in nature. Such an approach would facilitate an attending physician's access to a multidisciplinary evaluation to clarify complex diagnostic and management issues without disrupting the ongoing doctor-patient relationship, nor requiring the type of capital and operating expenditures associated with a dedicated unit. Early studies of inpatient consultative geriatric assessment, however, have usually failed to demonstrate a significant effect on length of stay,[10] functional status, or other measures of outcome.[11,12] Cohen and Feussner[13] suggested that strategies for implementing treatment for care needs identified in the geriatric assessment process were important for ensuring any impact. A number of groups have emphasized the importance of identifying older adults who are at high risk for complications and loss of function and who tend to require use of more resources, both in the community and in the hospital.[14–21] Winograd and colleagues[22] demonstrated that a rapid clinical screening process using specific geriatric criteria could be effective in identifying older adults likely to have longer hospital stays, a higher rate of mortality, and a high rate of nursing home placement.

Recent studies suggest that inpatient geriatric assessment and management can have a significant impact. Hogan and Fox,[23] selecting older adults using a scale of functional impairment, showed in a prospective controlled trial of inpatient geriatric consultation an impact on mortality and function as well as a trend toward decreased institutional care.

One problem in studies of geriatric assessment and management may be sample size. In a meta-analysis of geriatric evaluation and management by Rubenstein and colleagues[4] in 1991, a 39% reduction in mortality was shown following the incorporation of inpatient geriatric consultation services, and a similar decrease occurred after the introduction of inpatient geriatric evaluation and management units. The authors suggested that several factors affect the success of programs utilizing geriatric assessment: the quality of the assessment, the degree to which high-risk older patients are targeted, the capacity to provide direct care and rehabilitation, and the capacity to provide continuity of care or case management.

THE DEACONESS ELDERCARE MODEL

The Deaconess ElderCare model, whether applied in an inpatient or outpatient setting, uses a systematic approach that includes (1) selection of appropriate patients; (2) data collection through historical review and team-based patient evaluation; and (3) an interdisciplinary process for synthesis of the assessment, development of care plans, and introduction of strategies for implementation.

The Deaconess ElderCare Service, described in detail later, is an inpatient geriatric assessment and care coordination service that targets high-risk older adults and intervenes early in the course of the hospital stay. This service combines an initial and ongoing geriatric assessment as a basis for interdisciplinary coordination of care during the hospitalization and postdischarge follow-up in the community.

The Deaconess ElderCare Geriatric Assessment Center, described in detail as the final section of this chapter, is an outpatient consultation program that carries out an interdisciplinary geriatric assessment and uses the assessment to coordinate the extended diagnostic evaluation, recommendations for care planning, and strategies for coordination of care in the community.

Both the inpatient and outpatient services of Deaconess ElderCare focus on supporting primary physicians and other providers in care of high-risk older adults. The goals of the clinical services of Deaconess ElderCare are listed in Table 9–1. The Deaconess ElderCare methodological approach to provision of patient care services through the geriatric assessment process contains six essential components, which are enumerated in Table 9–2. These components will be considered in the following discussion.

Targeting of Appropriate Patients for Geriatric Assessment

As noted earlier, a series of reports have emphasized the importance of targeting patients for geriatric evaluation and management. The Deaconess ElderCare inpatient service has developed a process for targeting and intervening early in the hospital course of appropriate older adults. A specific targeting methodology has not been applied to the outpatient program, although efforts are made to educate physician and community providers about patients appropriate for referral.

Table 9–1 Goals of the Deaconess ElderCare Model

1. Provide comprehensive geriatric assessments of medical issues, social issues, and functional status of high-risk older adults.
2. Promote appropriate access to and use of diagnostic and treatment modalities and services.
3. Encourage and support patient and family in self-advocacy.
4. Facilitate coordinated and efficacious care.
5. Preserve and promote function and personal dignity of the older adult.

Table 9–2 The Deaconess ElderCare Approach

---

1. Targeting of appropriate older adults for early assessment and intervention.
2. Interdisciplinary approach with a core team of physician geriatrician, gerontological nurse practitioner, and gerontological social worker.
3. Development and use of an extended team of other professionals to facilitate diagnosis, treatment, and coordination of care.
4. Patient-centered focus in evaluation and care.
5. Implementation of recommendations through collaboration with primary care providers.
6. Active ElderCare team participation in the coordination of care.

Interdisciplinary Approach

The interdisciplinary team approach is essential for the synthesis of complex sets of information collected from and about an older adult. The traditional "multidisciplinary" approach encourages communication between a group of professionals from different disciplines but may fall short of an integration of effort sufficient to respond successfully to the complex challenges in the management of functionally challenged older adults. The interdisciplinary process fosters communication, negotiation, and a continuing evolution of perspectives and professional roles. Additionally, this process works to reverse the fragmentation of assessment and services that is all too often the rule in the management of care of complex older adults.

The literature on interdisciplinary teamwork in education contains descriptions of its relationship to teamwork in geriatric health care.[24] This literature may be useful for understanding the dynamics involved in development of an interdisciplinary team. For instance, it is important that members of a developing interdisciplinary team be prepared for conflict due to professional identity issues, terminology and jargon, power relationships, and role boundaries, especially during the initial months of team formation. Once the team moves beyond the initial stage, the resulting professional empowerment, clinical efficacy, and close collegiality will constitute more than adequate compensation for the investment in time and energy necessary to get to the next stage. The team's struggles with its own development prepare its members for the conflicts experienced by caregivers and family members. In other words, the team itself models a systems approach for family members and caregivers.

Core ElderCare Team

The Deaconess ElderCare approach to interdisciplinary team functioning involves the use of a professional triad or core team of physician geriatrician, gerontological nurse practitioner, and gerontological social worker. Based on the data available to the team, decisions are made about the specific approach to the older adult and family. While the evaluation protocol defines the standard roles for each team member, the specifics of each situation demand flexibility so that the team's responses fit the particular circumstances and needs of the older adult. Typically, each member of the team is involved in gathering data about and evaluating the older adult and establishing rapport with the older adult, the family, and other caregivers.

In the second phase of the team process, a team meeting is held to share relevant data collected by each discipline, develop a consensus on a set of "care issues," and formulate an initial set of recommendations. In essence, team members strive to understand and communicate a picture of the older adult that is as accurate and balanced as possible. If accurate and balanced perceptions of the current situation and of needs and priorities come to be shared by the older adult, the family, and involved caregivers, the likelihood that interventions will result in desired outcomes is greatly increased.

It is vitally important to communicate with and bring into the process as many persons involved in the day-to-day care and support of the older adult as possible, including the spouse (or significant others), other family members, other informal caregivers, and professional caregivers.

Extended Geriatric Team

A number of professionals with whom an ElderCare team works on a day-to-day basis are considered to be part of an extended team. These professionals include a geropsychiatrist, nutritionist, a pharmacist, rehabilitation specialists, and nurse clinicians. Their role is to evaluate appropriate older adults, round with the core team formally or informally, and attend family conferences to facilitate resolution of diagnostic, treatment, and care-coordination issues. The availability of an extended team of professionals allows priority scheduling for consultations, testing, or other interventions. The members of this team participate in a range of activities related to the functioning of the ElderCare Service and ElderCare Geriatric Assessment Center, including program development; older adult, family, and caregiver education; and continuing professional education. The most frequently accessed members of Deaconess ElderCare's extended team are listed in Table 9–3.

Patient-Centered Focus

A patient-centered care approach results in a specific analysis and articulation of issues that are of most importance to the older adult and respect the individual's sense of dignity.

Table 9–3 Deaconess ElderCare Extended Team Members

Geriatric psychiatrist	Clinical pharmacist
Neuropsychologist	Continuing care nurse
Physical therapist	Placement coordinator
Occupational therapist	Audiologist
Speech therapist	Ophthalmologist
Clinical nutritionist	Behavioral medicine consultant
Clinical nurse specialists	Utilization review nurse
• Complex skin tissue specialist	Hospital lawyer
• Enterostomal nurse clinician	Hospital volunteer

Collaboration with Primary Care Providers

The foremost challenge in the application of geriatric assessment is the translation of the recommendations into a realistic and acceptable plan of care. The Deaconess ElderCare model emphasizes the implementation of care recommendations through a collaboration with primary care providers that includes their involvement in determining the most effective approach to diagnosis and treatment. Communication with primary care clinicians is facilitated through letters, facsimile transmissions, telephone calls, and face-to-face conversations regarding day-to-day issues. The communication network typically includes the attending physician, nursing staff, house staff, and significant family providers as well as other professionals in the institutional or home care setting. The experience of the ElderCare Service has demonstrated that effective communication leads to acceptance and implementation of the majority of recommendations made by the geriatric assessment team.

Care Coordination

A final cornerstone of the successful application of geriatric assessment is the implementation of recommendations. Care coordination is the procedural vehicle by means of which the ElderCare Service fosters such implementation. The care coordination carried out by the ElderCare team ranges from consultation to case management through the interdisciplinary team's collaboration with primary care providers. Care is coordinated through a continuum inclusive of the hospital, the community, and rehabilitation or long-term care settings. Team members make home and institutional visits and follow-up telephone calls and engage in indirect follow-up through communication with the entire spectrum of caregivers in the community.

INPATIENT GERIATRIC ASSESSMENT AND CARE COORDINATION: THE DEACONESS ELDERCARE SERVICE

The Deaconess ElderCare Service is an early-intervention consultative service for high-risk hospitalized older adults.

Patient Selection (Targeting)

Patients age 65 and older who are at high risk for complicated hospital stays and possible poor outcomes are identified through a daily screening of admission hospital records using a methodology developed at Deaconess Hospital. The risk assessment focuses particularly on cognitive and behavioral dysfunction, social risk factors, gait disorders or falls, incontinence, communication dysfunction, skin compromise, and polypharmacy. Patients are selected directly through screening by ElderCare staff or secondarily by staff screening after a consult request from a physician, nurse, or social worker.

Formalization of the Consultation

The admitting physician of a patient meeting the screening criteria is notified of the availability of the ElderCare team. If the attending physician, in response to this information, requests a consult from the Deaconess ElderCare Service, the house officers, the nurse manager on the patient's care unit, the primary nurse, and the department of Social Services and Continuing Care are immediately notified.

The Geriatric Assessment

In a brief team conference, an evaluation and communication strategy is agreed upon. Any of the three core ElderCare Service team members may initiate the assessment, parts of which may occur simultaneously. The initial evaluation notes in the chart address the reason for admission; the history of the patient's present illnesses; the patient's past medical history, including all chronic and active disease processes with an impact on the patient's health and functional status; laboratory data; medications; the family history; the social history, including support systems; the patient's economic status; the patient's values history; and issues of advanced planning for medical and other decision making. At this time, there is also an attempt to gain permission to speak with the family and other caregivers. The physical examination extends to functional and cognitive assessments.

Generation of a Care Plan

Following the initial evaluation by each team member, the ElderCare team meets, exchanges information, defines "care issues," and debates and agrees upon initial recommendations. A team member may contact the physician or other chief caregiver directly by telephone to resolve uncertainties about specific issues or approaches so that issues and recommendations are more likely to include all relevant data and to be acceptable to the treatment decision-maker. The team completes a word-processed report and places it in the patient's chart. This ElderCare initial report includes specific recommendations for diagnostic evaluation, referrals to the extended ElderCare team, and specific nursing and therapeutic considerations. Medication modifications are often made to take into account the patient's age, physiological condition, and cognitive status. Finally, the report contains a list of relevant persons in the care and life of the older adult, along with telephone numbers or other information for contacting them. The list includes family members, friends, home care workers, visiting nurses, and other community providers.

Communication with Care Providers

ElderCare team members also communicate recommendations directly to the appropriate care providers, whether this be by telephone call or during an impromptu meeting at the nursing station. In such discussions, the interdisciplinary nature of the recommendations of the ElderCare team is emphasized and the continuing active role of each team member is identified. On occasion, members of the Deaconess ElderCare Service will determine the need to make a home visit to assess the environment in relation to safety, available resources, and future management of care.

Deaconess ElderCare Service Participation in Hospital Care

There is a daily interdisciplinary re-evaluation to assess medical status, nursing care needs, social issues, and discharge planning needs. ElderCare rounds include a discussion of diagnosis and treatment, drug monitoring, functional preservation issues, status of family and other system relationships, adjustment to hospitalization, and options for care at discharge. Older adults followed by the ElderCare team are seen on a daily basis by at least one team member, and their progress is reported in team rounds. The daily ElderCare note in the chart addresses current care issues, responses to treatment modalities, new recommendations, and the status of discharge planning.

Discharge Planning

The Deaconess ElderCare Service is responsible for discharge planning. Discharge planning is typically not part of most geriatric hospital consultation models, but it is vital to the concept of ongoing care coordination. The team social worker and nurse practitioner take over continuing care and social work responsibilities. The proposed plan is initially discussed with the attending physician, house staff, and primary nurse, and a determination is made as to which clinicians should communicate the recommendations to the older adult and family. The ElderCare team may coordinate an interdisciplinary family meeting to review options and resources for care upon discharge. While the social worker on the team is responsible for the final production of the discharge document, each member of the ElderCare team contributes to the plan. The resulting discharge document is sent to the primary or attending physician, to community caregivers such as the local visiting nurse association, or to the extended care facility.

Postdischarge Care Coordination

The social worker and nurse practitioner of the ElderCare Service conduct telephone follow-up after discharge and in this way maintain close communication regarding the care plan and status of the older adult. An ElderCare team member also may make a home visit within a short time following discharge. As community care coordinators are seen to be reliable, direct ElderCare involvement tapers, but the service continues to be a resource for the older adult and caregivers. If a person is readmitted, the ElderCare team, with the agreement of the attending physician, immediately becomes involved again in the person's care.

OUTPATIENT ASSESSMENT AND CARE COORDINATION: THE DEACONESS ELDERCARE GERIATRIC ASSESSMENT CENTER

The Deaconess ElderCare Geriatric Assessment Center applies the principles of interdisciplinary team assessment and care coordination to the outpatient setting.

Referral and Intake

Unlike the Deaconess ElderCare inpatient service, the outpatient service does not have a specific targeting methodology for early intervention. Most referrals occur when a change or even a crisis in care has occurred. Community education about the outpatient service includes seminars to which various sets of community care providers, such as medical staffs, visiting nurses, and care coordinators, are invited. Also, written materials, including brochures and letters of explanation, describe the situations in which geriatric assessment might be of benefit in a patient's evaluation and care.

Referrals to the Geriatric Assessment Center are divided fairly equally between those made by physicians and those made by family members concerned about deterioration in an aging relative. The initial intake done by the Geriatric Assessment Center coordinator or secretary is the beginning of the intervention. This initial telephone interview gathers demographic information, explains the assessment process, and identifies issues that may need to be explored during the assessment.

Preliminary Data

Introductory materials are sent to the inquiring older adult and family. These materials include a patient self-assessment form that asks for standard information on reasons for referral, recent and past medical history, medications, and functional status. Release of information forms are included so that medical records may be requested in writing or over the telephone.

Assessment Process

The assessment by the ElderCare team takes place in an initial 2-hour session with the older adult and family members. This initial session is followed by an interim period of additional consultation, testing, and data collection. A summary meeting of 1 hour with the older adult, family members, and other significant caregivers follows in 2 to 4 weeks.

Interdisciplinary Team Evaluation

As in the inpatient program, an assessment by the physician, nurse practitioner, and social worker forms the basis for the outpatient consultative service. Standard role responsibilities include these: the nurse practitioner evaluates baseline and current functional status, including mental status; the physician performs most elements of the classical medical history and physical examination; and the social worker focuses on psychosocial issues (e.g., values, family relationships, and coping mechanisms) and service coordination issues. Each clinician's evaluation is facilitated by use of specifically designed data collection forms.

The 2-hour session starts with a 5-minute introduction. It is during this initial several minutes that the session's schedule is explained and initial expectations are explored. Next, the social worker leaves with the older adult and carries out a psychosocial interview, while the nurse practitioner and physician stay with the family and take the medical and functional history. Then there is a brief team meeting during which initial data exchange occurs. After this, the social worker and nurse exchange places. The nurse begins the functional evaluation, including formal mental status testing, and may begin the physical examination, while the social worker meets with the family. The physician, with the records to that point, dictates the historical aspects of the case. Next, the physician trades places with the nurse practitioner and completes the physical examination and any parts of the functional evaluation not yet done. The nurse practitioner joins the social worker and they continue to discuss the case with the family.

The 2-hour session ends with a brief reassembling of the team and the older adult and family, which allows an interim explanation of the progress of the assessment and a discussion of what further consultations, testing, or information gathering should occur before the summary conference. Major diagnostic and therapeutic impressions, unless immediately critical to the older adult's care, are not typically broached at this point, as the team has not yet discussed these with the older adult's primary care professionals.

Initial Evaluation Report

Following the evaluation session, the ElderCare team meets and formulates initial care issues and interim recommendations. The physician then dictates a letter to the referring and/or primary care physician outlining the findings and conveying the initial set of care issues and interim recommendations formulated by the team. The interim recommendations may concern specific medication changes (additions, deletions, or dosage modifications), past historical data required for a more complete picture, testing needed prior to diagnosis or treatment formulation, or services needed to be put into place without further delay to expedite management of specific social or medical crises.

Interim Facilitation of Work-up

Following the initial evaluation session, the ElderCare team, including the clinical coordinator or secretary, will work with the referring or primary care physician and others in the system to implement the interim recommendations. For instance, appointments for geriatric psychiatry evaluation, physical or occupational therapy evaluation, nutritional assessment, neuropsychological testing, neuroimaging, or blood chemistry evaluation are arranged by the ElderCare team in conjunction with the primary care physician.

Summary Conference

The geriatric assessment process ends with a review of the accumulated data and a discussion of recommendations in a summary conference. This meeting is typically held 2 to 4 weeks after the initial evaluation session. The older adult is encouraged to include as many family members as possible. Other care providers, including case workers, visiting nurses, or particularly close friends, may also attend. Prior to the summary meeting, the assessment team meets to review the data, craft the final recommendations, and develop a strategy for the meeting that is tailored to the situation.

In the initial part of the summary meeting, the agenda of the meeting is reviewed, the older adult and family give an update regarding events since the previous session, and questions that may have emanated from the initial letter are addressed. Following this, the physician presents the specific diagnostic findings and associated recommendations. Questions and discussion usually ensue. The nurse practitioner then delineates the impact of the identified problems on functioning, and the social worker reviews relevant psychosocial issues and focuses the discussion on care planning. An important goal of the meeting is to maintain a balance between responding to specific questions and areas of concern and ensuring that the older person and family understand the specific actions that are being recommended. A central theme continues to be the facilitation of communication and follow-up with the primary care provider and the services and resources in the community. A dictated report of the summary conference clarifies the final care issues and recommendations and serves as a conclusion to the initial report. The older adult and family are offered a copy of the final report (as they were a copy of the initial evaluation letter) and are encouraged to use the report to facilitate continuing communication with the primary care provider.

As part of the plan worked out with the physician, older adult, and family, geriatric assessment team members may offer follow-up for monitoring of specific medical conditions, family therapy, or further assistance with service coordination or strategies for behavior management. In addition, an appointment at the Geriatric Assessment Center may be set 2 to 4 months in the future for follow-up of overall physical and social functioning.

CONCLUSION

The Deaconess ElderCare model, implemented in the inpatient setting (Deaconess ElderCare Service) and the outpatient setting (Deaconess ElderCare Geriatric Assessment Center), represents one approach to the application of principles of geriatric assessment in the interdisciplinary team setting. The interdisciplinary team process offers an integrated approach to evaluating the complex needs of older adults and provides a context for effective coordination of care directed toward maximizing function and enhancing overall quality of life.

REFERENCES

1. Densen PM. *Tracing the elderly through the health care system: An update.* Agency for Health Care Policy and Research monograph. Washington, DC: US Department of Health and Human Services, Public Health Service, Agency for Health Care Policy and Research, 1991.

2. Almy TP. Comprehensive functional assessment for elderly patients: position paper by Health and Public Policy Committee, American College of Physicians. *Ann Intern Med.* 1988;109:70–72.

3. Solomon D. National Institutes of Health Consensus Development Conference statement: geriatric assessment methods for clinical decision-making. *J Am Geriatr Soc.* 1988;36:342–347.

4. Rubenstein LZ, Stuck AE, Siu AL, Wieland, DW. Impacts of geriatric evaluation and management programs on defined outcomes: overview of the evidence. *J Am Geriatr Soc.* 1991;39S:8S–16S.

5. Stuck AE, Siu AL, Wieland GD, Adams J, Rubenstein LZ. Comprehensive geriatric assessment: a meta-analysis of controlled trials. *Lancet.* 1993;342:1032–1036.

6. Rubenstein LZ, Josephson KR, Wieland GD, et al. Effectiveness of a geriatric evaluation unit (GEU): a randomized clinical trial. *N Engl J Med.* 1984;31:1664–1670.

7. Applegate WB, Miller ST, Graney MJ, Elam JT, Burns R, Akins DE. A randomized, controlled trial of a geriatric assessment unit in a community rehabilitation hospital. *N Engl J Med.* 1990; 322:1572–1578.

8. Williams ME, Williams TF, Zimmer JG, Hall WJ, Podgorski CA. How does the team approach to outpatient geriatric evaluation compare with traditional care: a report of a randomized controlled trial. *J Am Geriatr Soc.* 1987;35:1071–1078.

9. Epstein AM, Hall JA, Fretwell M, Feldstein M, et al. Consultative geriatric assessment for ambulatory patients: a randomized trial in a health maintenance organization. *JAMA.* 1990;263:538–544.

10. Allen CM, Becker PM, McVey LJ, Saltz CC, Feussner JR, Cohen HJ. A randomized, controlled clinical trial of a geriatric consultation team. *JAMA.* 1986;255:2617–2621.

11. Gayton D, Wood-Dauphinee S, de Lorimer M, Tousignant P, Hanley J. Trial of a geriatric consultation team in an acute care hospital. *J Am Geriatr Soc.* 1987;35:726–736.

12. McVey LJ, Becker PM, Saltz CC, Feussner JR, Cohen HJ. Effect of a geriatric consultation team on functional status of elderly hospitalized patients: a randomized, controlled clinical trial. *Ann Intern Med.* 1989;110:79–83.

13. Cohen HJ, Feussner JR. Comprehensive geriatric assessment: mission not yet accomplished. *J Gerontol.* 1989;44:M175–M177.

14. Fethke CC, Smith IM, Johnson N. Risk factors affecting readmission of the elderly into the health care system. *Med Care.* 1986;24:429–437.

15. Glass R, Weiner M. Seeking a social disposition for the medical patient: CAAST, a simple and objective clinical index. *Med Care.* 1976;14:637–641.

16. Glass R, Mulvihill MN, Smith H, et al. The 4-Score: an index for predicting a patient's non-medical hospital days. *Am J Public Health.* 1977;67:751–755.

17. Inui T, Stevenson KM, Plorde D, Murphy I. Identifying hospital patients who need early discharge planning for special disposition. *Med Care.* 1981;19:922–929.

18. Rogers J, Grower R, Supino P. Target groups for screening elderly outpatients. *Am J Prev Med.* 1988;4:27–34.

19. Wachtel TJ, Derby C, Fulton JP. Predicting the outcome of hospitalization for elderly persons: home versus nursing home. *South Med J.* 1984;77:1283–1285.

20. Winograd CH, Gerety MB, Brown E, Kolodny V. Targeting the hospitalized elderly for geriatric consultation. *J Am Geriatr Soc.* 1988;36:1113–1119.

21. Reuben DB, Wolde-Tsadik G, Pardamean BS, Hammond B, Borok GM, Rubenstein LZ, Beck JC. The use of targeting criteria in hospitalized HMO patients: results from the demonstration phase of the Hospitalized Older Persons Evaluation (HOPE) study. *J Am Geriatr Soc.* 1992;40:482–488.

22. Winograd CH, Gerety MB, Chung M, Goldstein MK, Dominguez F, Vallone R. Screening for frailty: criteria and predictors of outcomes. *J Am Geriatr Soc.* 1991;39:778–784.

23. Hogan DB, Fox RA. A prospective controlled trial of a geriatric consultation team in an acute-care hospital. *Age Ageing.* 1990;19:107–113.

24. Clark PG, Spence DL, Sheehan JL. A service/learning model for interdisciplinary teamwork in health and aging. *Gerontol Geriatr Educ.* 1986;6:3–16.

10

Geriatric Assessment in Practice

Interdisciplinary geriatric assessment programs or teams represent a high ideal, and we probably will see the development of more of these units with time. But the usefulness of the assessment instruments described in earlier chapters for the primary care physician who treats older patients cannot be overemphasized. Indeed, the primary care or generalist physician is in a fine position to be a case-finder, coordinator, and manager for older persons. In the same way, the visiting nurse can use these tools in nursing assessment to help identify the elder at risk for functional decline, hospitalization, or adverse effects from therapeutic intervention. Other health care professionals, such as social workers, will likely find brief mental status examinations and the systematic approach to eliciting values regarding treatment of tremendous assistance.

The discussion in Chapter 9 and the decision tree for long-term care in Chapter 3 illustrate how the assessment of the specific realms covered in this book facilitates the prescription of the most appropriate resources and the least restrictive environment for the older adult. After all, the provision of optimal care in the optimal setting should be the ultimate aim of systematic assessment, not the generation of scores for their own sake. To be useful, assessment should be linked to services and ongoing monitoring of the status of the patient.

The use of instruments and questionnaires for systematic clinical observation in medicine is not unprecedented. Assessment forms and instruments are widely used by clinicians who care for children. Examples include the Apgar score for assessing newborn health, the Dubowitz forms for estimation of gestational age, and the Denver Developmental Screening Examination for assessment of developmental milestones. The instruments for assessing multiple domains in the older adult, the "new technology of geriatrics,"[1] can be employed in the same way. The use of computers to record responses from patients and caregivers may someday facilitate the assessment and re-evaluation process routinely.

As Kane and Kane have stated, "More harm is done by failure to measure than by measuring with inadequate instruments."[2] Multidimensional assessment broadens the traditional medical model to include assessment of mental status and affect, functional status, social situation, economic circumstances, values, and preventive medicine strategies.

REVIEW OF THE DOMAINS OF GERIATRIC ASSESSMENT

When older patients are evaluated and treated, the effects of each medical problem on each domain of multidimensional assessment should be considered.[3] How will the treatment of a medical condition such as hypertension affect cognitive or functional status? At the same time, what are the implications of the patient's cognitive, functional, or economic status for treatment of medical conditions?

Mental Status

All health care professionals who deal with older adults should become familiar with one short mental status examination. When presented with the attitude that evaluation of cognitive function is a matter of course, the mental status examination will not be offensive to the patient or embarrassing for the examiner. At hospital admission, nursing home admission, or any time that cognitive status is an issue because of behavior, memory complaints, or functional decline, the patient's mental status should be assessed. The interpretation of the instruments described previously must be informed by the total clinical picture. It is particularly important to be aware of the cognitive effects of medications and to realize that patients with a diagnosis of Alzheimer's disease or other dementia may improve if a coexisting depression or delirium is treated.

Elderly persons have significant developmental work to do, especially in dealing with loss, and although health care professionals are unable to solve all their problems, good listening skills can be used to advantage in helping older persons come to terms with feelings like helplessness and hopelessness. Depression, a potential cause of disability, is treatable. Like most adults, older persons are not immune to the adverse effects of excessive use of alcohol or tranquilizers.

Functional Assessment

Functional assessment helps set priorities around which the medical, social, and economic resources available for problem solving can be rallied. Functional assessment also helps keep a perspective on the elder untypical of the traditional diagnosis-centered approach. Changes in function may signal a problem whose cause is best addressed, not through medical treatment, but by realignment of the social situation. Answers to questions regarding IADLs and driving habits can be used to assess outpatient ambulatory patients (cognitive impairment may be among the causes of difficulties that are reported). Older patients who are in hospitals and nursing homes should be questioned about ADLs.

Social Assessment

Most long-term care is provided by the family. Regardless of the mental, functional, and physical status of the patient, the need for nursing home placement may hinge on the availability of a willing and capable caregiver. Access to health care for the older person may depend on transportation from a caregiver. The caregiver should be considered in making recommendations for the older patient. Dementia may be associated with behavioral or psychiatric symptoms that are difficult to deal with and require support of the caregiver by the primary care physician. The domains of assessment apply to the caregiver.

Values Assessment

The treatment plan must take into account patient autonomy, informed consent, and the patient's notion of quality of life. Clinicians are in a position to help the patient and family clarify the ethical dilemmas that face them in health care decision making. The Values History (see Chapter 5) can assist the practitioner in this process. If the patient has impaired decision-making capacity, treatment issues should be discussed with the family in advance of a crisis.

Economic Assessment

The patient's economic circumstances, although not assessed in detail by the primary care practitioner, should be considered as a potential reason for lack of adherence to the therapeutic plan. Medications and supplies can be quite costly. Despite the overall improvement in the financial status of older adults in recent decades, individuals in certain groups of older persons, such as those living in rural areas, may require economic assistance.

Physical Assessment

Older persons take longer to examine than younger patients. The increased amount of time in disrobing and getting dressed, problems of hearing impairment and unstable gait, and the propensity of some older persons to be garrulous and not focused in conversation may tempt the physician to take shortcuts. Good geriatric care requires that the physician expend a greater degree of effort than with most adult patients. The presenting symptom may involve the most poorly compensated organ system, so that pneumonia or congestive heart failure, for example, may present as delirium. Problems like sexual dysfunction and urinary incontinence may not be brought directly to the physician's attention, further confusing the diagnostic picture unless addressed.

Health Maintenance and Disability Prevention

Preventive strategies may be divided into standard disease prevention and geriatric-oriented prevention; both should be considered in formulating a plan for prevention. Preventive medicine strategies have to be tailored to the individual older adult, taking into account the local conditions of practice as well as the functional and cognitive status of the patient. The medical treatment of older adults should also be informed by the recommendations of prominent expert panels, as discussed in Chapter 8. Physicians must decide which protocols are most appropriate for the older persons in their practice, since recommendations do not always take into account the special circumstances of older persons.

REMINDERS FACILITATE A SYSTEMATIC APPROACH

An outline of multidimensional assessment that can be employed in primary care geriatric practice is provided in Exhibits 10–1 to 10–4. These forms can be modified to suit the individual practitioner's practice using the instruments described in other chapters. The exhibits act as reminders of appropriate avenues of inquiry for a systematic geriatric evaluation. The multidimensional assessment forms assemble baseline data and encourage periodic review of function.

Exhibit 10–1 (page 1 of the Multidimensional Assessment Form for the Elderly) includes a place for a standard problem and medication list and a reminder to list functional difficulties and allergies. The social network diagram at the bottom of the page provides a way to illustrate the social situation.[4] Inside the box labeled "household" should be listed the names of all the persons who live with the patient. In the box above should be listed persons who live in an adjoining apartment or house who visit or help the patient (whether or not they are related to the patient). Other persons who visit or assist the patient but do not live in the same household or in the immediate vicinity should be listed either to the right if they are family members or to the left if they are friends or neighbors. The frequency and nature of any assistance provided may be noted next to the appropriate name.

Exhibit 10–2 (page 2 of the Multidimensional Assessment Form for the Elderly) serves as a reminder of the health maintenance procedures discussed in Chapter 8. When a test or procedure is performed, the date can be written in the appropriate box. Vaccinations are noted on the bottom of this form. A reminder to complete a Values History or to assess the patient for substance abuse may be a beneficial addition.

Exhibit 10–3 (page 3 of the Multidimensional Assessment Form for the Elderly) provides a reminder to assess periodically mental status (using the Short Portable Mental Status Questionnaire [SPMSQ]), activities of daily living, instrumental activities of daily living, and feelings. During stressful periods, such as following the loss of a spouse or posthospitalization, frequent assessment of cognitive status, emotional status, and functioning would be desirable. If the SPMSQ is used, the evaluation may be supplemented with the written parts of the mental status examination outlined in Chapter 2 (writing and construction ability). The rationale for using the SPMSQ is that the SPMSQ is entirely oral and can be supplemented with a single blank piece of paper on which the patient performs the written parts of the mental status examination (writing his or her signature, writing a sentence, and making a clock drawing). Alternatively, the Folstein Mini-Mental State Examination could be substituted for the SPMSQ, and Exhibit 10–3 could be modified to include a complete depression scale, such as the Geriatric Depression Scale. The questions in Exhibit 10–3 that deal with feelings were selected because somatic complaints that are included in most of the depression assessment instruments discussed in Chapter 2 would presumably be addressed in the medical-oriented care of the patient. Exhibit 10–4 (page 4 of the Multidimensional Assessment Form for the Elderly) contains another flowchart that combines laboratory values and health promotion activities, including vaccinations.

Exhibit 10–1 Multidimensional Assessment Form for the Elderly (page 1)

Patient Name: _____

PROBLEM LIST (Show start and stop dates)

Medical Problems	Medications
_____	_____
_____	_____
_____	_____
_____	_____
_____	_____
_____	_____
_____	_____
_____	_____
_____	_____
_____	_____
_____	_____
_____	_____
_____	_____
_____	_____
_____	_____
_____	_____

Functional Problems	Allergies
_____	_____
_____	_____

SOCIAL ASSESSMENT

Social Network Diagram

Friends and Neighbors	Date of Assessment: _____
	Family Members
_____	_____

Persons living close by

_____

Household

For the social network diagram, indicate who visits the patient and how often.

Source: The social network diagram is adapted with permission from *British Medical Journal* (1976; 1:144), Copyright © 1976, British Medical Association.

Exhibit 10–2 Multidimensional Assessment Form for the Elderly (page 2)

Patient Name: _____

	61	62	63	64	65	66	67	68	69	70
BP										
PAP SMEAR										
PELVIC EX										
BREAST EX										
MAMMOGRAP										
STOOL OB										
RECTAL EX										
SIGMOID'Y										
VISION EX										
HEARING										
HEIGHT										
THYROID										

	71	72	73	74	75	76	77	78	79	80
BP										
PAP SMEAR										
PELVIC EX										
BREAST EX										
MAMMOGRAP										
STOOL OB										
RECTAL EX										
SIGMOID'Y										
VISION EX										
HEARING										
HEIGHT										
THYROID										

	81	82	83	84	85	86	87	88	89	90
BP										
PAP SMEAR										
PELVIC EX										
BREAST EX										
MAMMOGRAP										
STOOL OB										
RECTAL EX										
SIGMOID'Y										
VISION EX										
HEARING										
HEIGHT										
THYROID										

Vaccinations:
Date:

TETANUS										
INFLUENZA										
PNEUMOCOCCAL		(Given one time only)								

Exhibit 10–3 Multidimensional Assessment Form for the Elderly (page 3)

Patient Name: _____

SPMSQ[1]	Date of Assessment							
1. Today's date?								
2. Day of week?								
3. What place is this?								
4. Phone number?								
5. How old are you?								
6. Date of birth?								
7. Who is the president?								
8. Prior president?								
9. Mother's maiden name?								
10. 20 − 3? (down to 2)								

ADL Index[2]	Date of Assessment							
1. Uses the toilet?								
2. Feeds self?								
3. Dresses self?								
4. Grooms self?								
5. Ambulates alone?								
6. Bathes alone?								
Informant:								

IADL Index[3]	Date of Assessment							
1. Uses the phone?								
2. Able to shop?								
3. Prepares meals?								
4. Does housework?								
5. Does laundry?								
6. Travels alone?								
7. Takes own meds?								
8. Handles own money?								
Informant:								

Feelings	Date of Assessment							
1. Difficult sleep?								
2. Awaken fresh?								
3. Good appetite?								
4. Feel blue often?								
5. Crying spells?								
6. Feel tired a lot?								
7. Hopeful?								
8. Feel useful?								
9. Enjoy things?								

Sources: [1]*Journal of American Geriatrics Society* (1975;23:433–441), Copyright © 1975, American Geriatrics Society; [2]*Journal of American Medical Association* (1963;185:914–919), Copyright © 1963, American Medical Association; [3]*Multidimensional Functional Assessment Questionnaire,* ed 2 (pp 169–170) by Duke University Center for the Study of Aging and Human Development, 1978.

Exhibit 10–4 Multidimensional Assessment Form for the Elderly (page 4) (Alternate Form)

Patient Name: _____

Lab Flow Chart   Date of Assessment

GLUCOSE										
POTASSIUM										
SODIUM										
BUN										
CREAT										
HCT										
HB										
MCV										
WBC										
CHOLEST										
TRIGLYC										

Health Maintenance Record

BP										
PAP SMEAR										
PELVIC EX										
BREAST EX										
MAMMOGRAP										
STOOL OB										
RECTAL EX										
SIGMOID'Y										
VISION EX										
HEARING										
HEIGHT										
THYROID										

Vaccinations
Date:

TETANUS										
INFLUENZA										

PNEUMOCOCCAL   [   ] (Given one time only)

ALLERGIES: _____

MAJOR HEALTH PROBLEMS:

_____   _____
_____   _____
_____   _____
_____   _____
_____   _____

ESTABLISHING THE GERIATRIC ASSESSMENT PROGRAM

The principal theme of this book is that the use of assessment instruments in evaluating various domains is an essential part of the care of elderly persons. It is hoped that the use of such instruments in systematic assessment will help practitioners gain a more complete view of the needs of patients. Chapter 9 describes a model for geriatric assessment, the Deaconess ElderCare program at the New England Deaconess Hospital in Boston. Essential principles of the program include (1) targeting geriatric assessment toward appropriate patients, (2) employing an interdisciplinary approach, (3) developing an extended team of professionals, (4) maintaining a patient-centered focus, (5) implementating diagnostic and care plans through empowerment of primary care providers, and (6) actively participating in the management and coordination of treatment and services along a continuum of care over time and across settings.

One of the first questions to be answered in establishing a geriatric assessment team is the composition of the core team. In part the make-up depends on the primary function of the team. If the objective is rehabilitation, for example, occupational therapists and physical therapists may form part of the core team, taking a more active role than as "extended team members" (see Chapter 9). If diagnosis is the major goal, the team may be set up differently. Each institution must decide what resources are available and what it can offer. A geriatric assessment program might ideally want to use a team consisting of a physician, nurse, and social worker and always want to include a home visit, but it may have to vary its standard protocol. Sometimes the assessment will be carried out by the physician as well as a nurse or social worker, and sometimes only one of the professional staff will perform the home visit (or in certain instances the home visit will be skipped). An institution may flexibly vary its protocol, within the limits of certain minimal and maximal standards, based on the resources that are available. It also may take into account variations in staffing (e.g., due to staff vacations).

A hospital, managed health care plan, or medical center may consider using assistants trained to perform portions of the geriatric assessment, and the authors have seen proposals for medical assistants or retired volunteers, such as a retired clergy, to carry out the multidimensional assessment after training. The main worry is that the field of geriatric assessment is new, and even health professionals, such as physicians, nurses, and social workers, still have much to learn about the appropriate use and benefit of the methods and skills. Geriatric assessment should probably remain the province of trained health professionals, who can continue to advance our understanding of how best to care for the elderly.

As mentioned in Chapter 9, referral to geriatric assessment programs may be made by families concerned about elderly family members, seeking advice on such issues as alternatives to institutional care, decisions about placement in a nursing home, or polypharmacy. In many cases, families are seeking a second opinion. The staff person assigned to handle the first phone contact will discover that not all families are actually seeking a geriatric assessment; some are really searching for a primary care physician to take charge of the elderly family member's care. The geriatric assessment program should work hand in hand with some other type of primary care resource. A geriatric assessment program might fit with a family health center, an outpatient medical clinic, a geriatric clinic, or selected family physicians or internists.

When the patient has a primary care physician, it is imperative to refer the patient back to the referring physician in order to maintain good relations with community physicians. Many patients are referred for evaluation by social agencies, so early contact and familiarization with the professionals and services available to the community are important. Some patients do not have a regular physician, and then it is possible to follow them in a geriatric or primary care setting, that is, working in collaboration with the geriatric assessment program.

Geriatric assessment programs have been established throughout the United States in university medical centers, community hospitals, county health departments, and other settings. Some are experiencing significant difficulties in obtaining payment. Directors of geriatric assessment programs have informally communicated to the authors that the geriatric assessment program is often a "loss leader." The value of such a program to the hospital or institution is believed to compensate for the financial loss.

Some institutions bill separately for components of the geriatric assessment (e.g., the comprehensive history and physical examination, the nursing examination, the physical therapy assessment, and the nutritional assessment). Physicians and institutions will have to follow carefully the results of billing for prolonged evaluation and management services. For example, although the Current Procedure Terminology (CPT) 1994 codes contain Modifier-21 (the highest level in a given category of service), whether Medicare and the changing health care system will reimburse for extended services remains to be seen.

An exciting aspect of a geriatric assessment program is that the program can serve as the hub of an entire range of services devoted to geriatrics and long-term care. The geriatric assessment team is a good initial focus for development of what might be called an "umbrella" for programs on aging, such as a center on aging or an interdisciplinary program on aging. An institution might develop many services around the centerpiece of a geriatric assessment program (Table 10–1).

All the services listed in Table 10–1 can be strategically planned or catalyzed by a hospital employing the geriatric assessment program as a focal point. The geriatric assessment program can be the initial demonstration of institutional commitment in this area. The institution can then create services that the patients need while working closely with the agencies or persons already providing relevant services in the community. A small, tightly knit team is flexible enough to offer individualized attention, such as home visits. When a personal physician is available,

Table 10–1 Services That Can Be Developed Around a Geriatric Assessment Program

1. Respite care
2. Homemaker services
3. Caretaker support group
4. Caretaker educational program
5. Information or information and referral hotline
6. Elderly transportation services
7. Geriatric day care
8. Widow or widower support group
9. Geriatric assessment team (inpatient)
10. Geriatric assessment inpatient unit
11. Osteoporosis clinic
12. Retirement counseling or insurance counseling
13. Legal and financial services for the elderly
14. Educational programs and lectures for the elderly
15. Alzheimer's disease assessment and treatment program
16. Intermediate care facilities
17. Skilled nursing facilities
18. Alzheimer's disease day care
19. Case management program
20. Upgraded rehabilitation, including inpatient rehabilitation
21. Newsletter to the elderly
22. Hospice
23. Retirement center or life care facilities
24. Satellite geriatric primary care clinics
25. Geriatric psychiatric unit
26 Travel services for the elderly
27. Senior or golden years membership plan (providing a number of benefits or enhancements for seniors who join the hospital's membership plan)

the patient should be referred back, and the team should provide the information and recommendations that are the result of the assessment.

INTEGRATING GERIATRIC ASSESSMENT INTO PRIMARY CARE

In the future, we can hope that reimbursement for geriatric assessment in primary care practice will include new fee codes that will be granted for clinical effort that exceeds traditional office or clinic care. Geriatric assessment is already mandated in long-term care settings.[5] In the meantime, components of the assessment can be carried out over a period of outpatient visits scheduled one or two weeks apart. Using the assessment instruments described in this book may ensure completeness. When a problem is detected by geriatric assessment, it can be explored in greater detail.

Used as an adjunct to the clinical examination, geriatric assessment tools have the potential to improve the quality of the evaluation of the older patient. In a classic study of the unmet needs of older persons, Williamson and colleagues[6] found many important but unrecognized problems and impairments. Barber and Wallis[7] employed multidimensional assessment forms to enable general practitioners to screen elderly patients for social, functional, and economic difficulties. The result was that many previously unknown conditions were uncovered. Pinholt and colleagues[8] showed how using instruments such as the ones discussed in this book improved the evaluation process for older patients. In that study, 79 elderly persons were assessed using simple measures of cognitive functioning (Cognitive Capacity Screening Examination), nutritional state (history, physical examination, and serum albumin), visual acuity (reading the newspaper), gait (observation), and function in activities of daily living. The assessments were compared with unassisted evaluations. Assuming the assessment instruments to be correct, the study physicians and nurses had low rates of detection: mental impairment, 32%; vision impairment, 33%; nutritional deficiency, 58%; and incontinence, 65%. Miller and coworkers[9] examined 183 medical outpatients aged 70 and older. While over half of the patients had at least one meaningful impairment in cognitive function (Folstein Mini-Mental State Examination), affect (Geriatric Depression Scale), gait (Tinetti Test of Gait and Balance), or nutritional status (serum albumin), few abnormalities had been recognized and addressed by the medical care team.

Standard use of such instruments would facilitate the development of a common language of assessment, leading to improved communication among professionals caring for the elderly. Description of a patient by functional ability complements the medical problem list. When a patient is reported to have a certain score on a mental status examination, everyone would understand how to interpret it. Questions prompting consultation might be more clearly defined, enhancing communication between generalists and specialists.

Making observations with standard instruments could lead to a better understanding of the relationships among the mental, affective, functional, social, economic, and physical spheres. Multidimensional assessment can be a tool for achieving the type of holistic view so often espoused but so frequently ignored in actual practice. For example, evaluation instruments might be introduced into residency and medical school education as learning tools to teach a multidimensional approach.[10]

To emphasize a point made in the previous chapter, for geriatric assessment to have an impact on care, the assessment results must be applied in the primary care setting. Studies that demonstrate the utility of geriatric assessment consultation in inpatient settings have involved practitioners who have followed through on recommendations.[11] Practitioners can develop working relationships with geriatric assessment teams (where available) so that the continuity of care in the community can be maintained. Even when a geriatric assessment service is not available, primary care professionals caring for older adults in the hospital and in other settings can apply the principles of geriatric assessment on their own.

CONCLUSION

Multidimensional assessment of older adults is a challenging clinical task. Geriatric medicine melds the "art" and "science" of medicine inasmuch as ethical issues frequently arise in conjunction with treatment issues. There are times that the "principle of minimal interference"[12] is appropriate and wise. In other situations, care providers should "go all out" regardless of the patient's age. Considerable wisdom and clinical experience are needed to weigh the multidimensional factors that go into treatment decisions. Practitioners who can assess the physical, mental, functional, social, economic, and ethical factors that determine the health status of elderly persons can be more effective, more realistic, and, it is hoped, wiser in managing their care.

REFERENCES

1. Epstein AM, Hall JA, Besdine R, et al. The emergence of geriatric assessment units: the "new technology of geriatrics." *Ann Intern Med.* 1987;106:299–303.

2. Kane RA, Kane RL. *Assessing the Elderly: A Practical Guide to Measurement.* Lexington, Mass: Lexington Books, 1981.

3. Gallo JJ, Stanley L, Zack N, Reichel W. Multidimensional assessment of the older patient. In: Reichel W, ed. *Clinical Aspects of Aging.* 4th ed. Baltimore, Md: Williams & Wilkins, 1995:15–30.

4. Capildeo R, Court C, Rose FC. Social network diagram. *Br Med J.* 1976;1:143–144.

5. Levenson SA, ed. *Medical Direction in Long-Term Care.* 2nd ed. Durham, NC: Carolina Academic Press, 1993.

6. Williamson J, Stokoe IH, Gray S, et al. Old people at home: their unreported needs. *Lancet.* 1964;1:1117–1120.

7. Barber JH, Wallis JB. Assessment of the elderly in general practice. *J R Coll Gen Pract.* 1976;26:106–114.

8. Pinholt EM, Kroenke K, Hanley JF, et al. Functional assessment of the elderly: a comparison of standard instruments with clinical judgment. *Arch Intern Med.* 1987;147:484–488.

9. Miller DK, Morley JE, Rubenstein LZ, Pietruszka FM, Strome LS. Formal geriatric assessment instruments and the care of older general medical outpatients. *J Am Geriatr Soc.* 1990;38:645–651.

10. Besdine RW. The educational utility of comprehensive functional assessment in the elderly. *J Am Geriatr Soc.* 1983;31:651–656.

11. Rubenstein LZ, Stuck AE, Siu AL, Wieland D. Impacts of geriatric evaluation and management programs on defined outcomes: overview of the evidence. *J Am Geriatr Soc.* 1991;39(9, pt 2):8–16.

12. Seegal D. The principle of minimal interference in the management of the elderly patient. *J Chronic Dis.* 1964;17:299–300.

Index